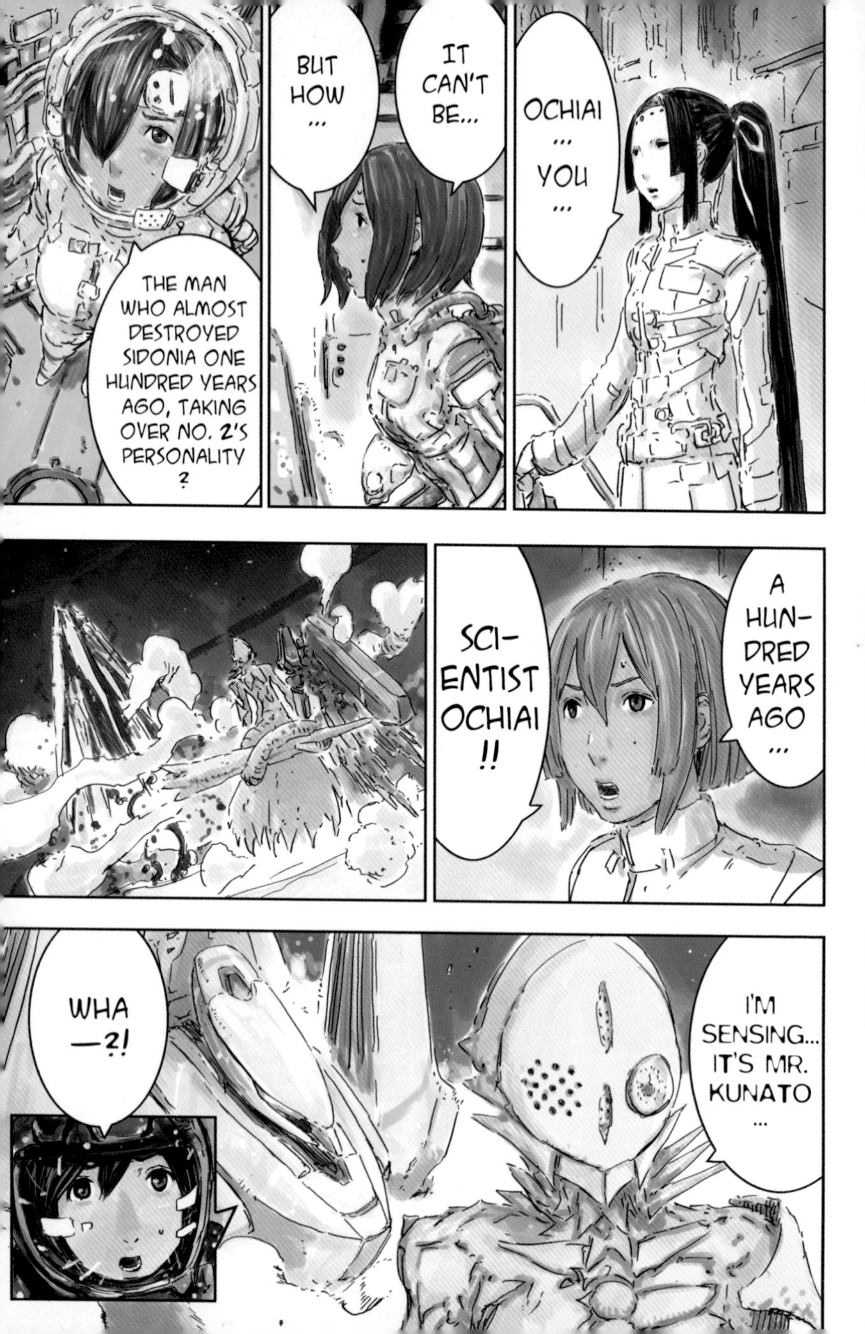
OCHIAI ... YOU ...
IT CAN'T BE...
BUT HOW ...
THE MAN WHO ALMOST DESTROYED SIDONIA ONE HUNDRED YEARS AGO, TAKING OVER NO. 2'S PERSONALITY ?
A HUN-DRED YEARS AGO ...
SCI-ENTIST OCHIAI !!
I'M SENSING... IT'S MR. KUNATO ...
WHA —?!

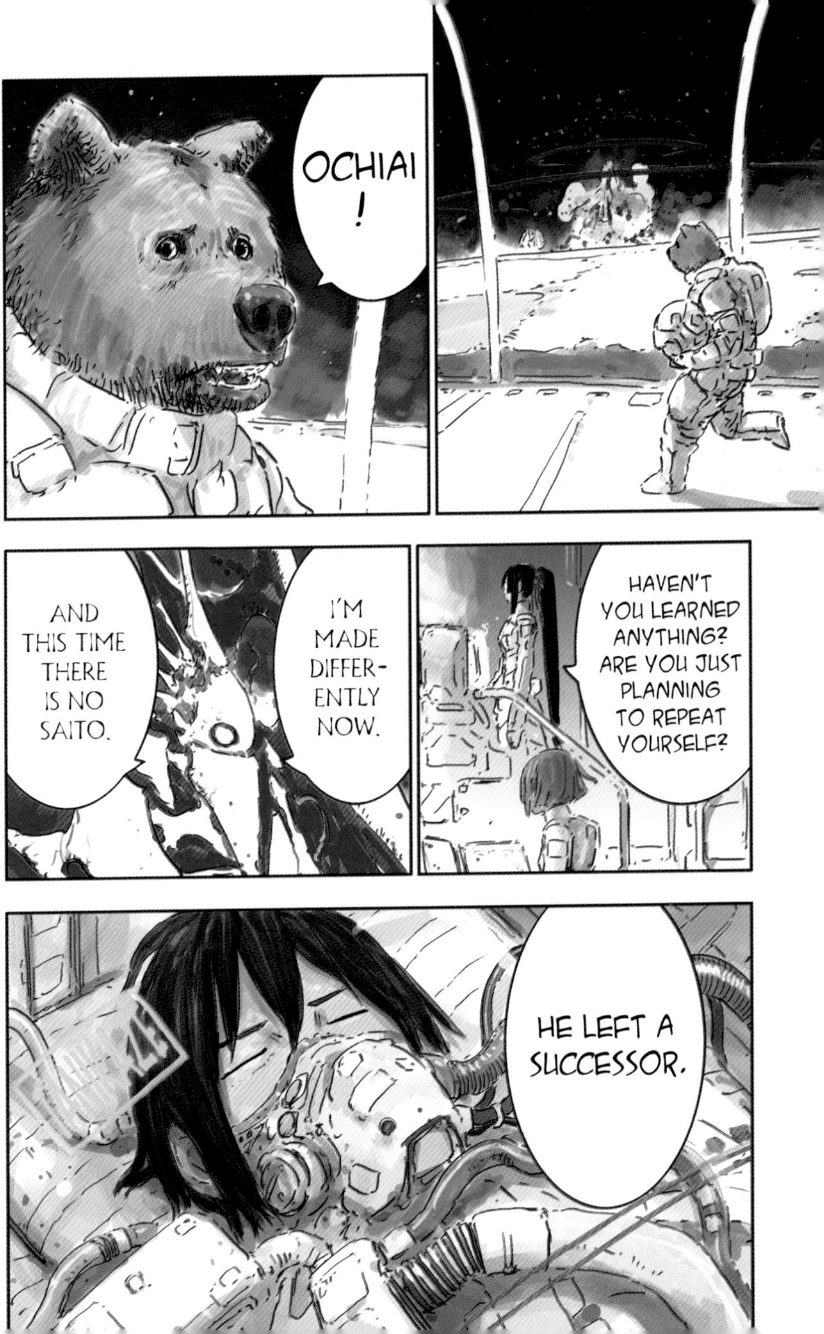
OCHIAI !
HAVEN'T YOU LEARNED ANYTHING? ARE YOU JUST PLANNING TO REPEAT YOURSELF?
I'M MADE DIFFER-ENTLY NOW.
AND THIS TIME THERE IS NO SAITO.
HE LEFT A SUCCESSOR.

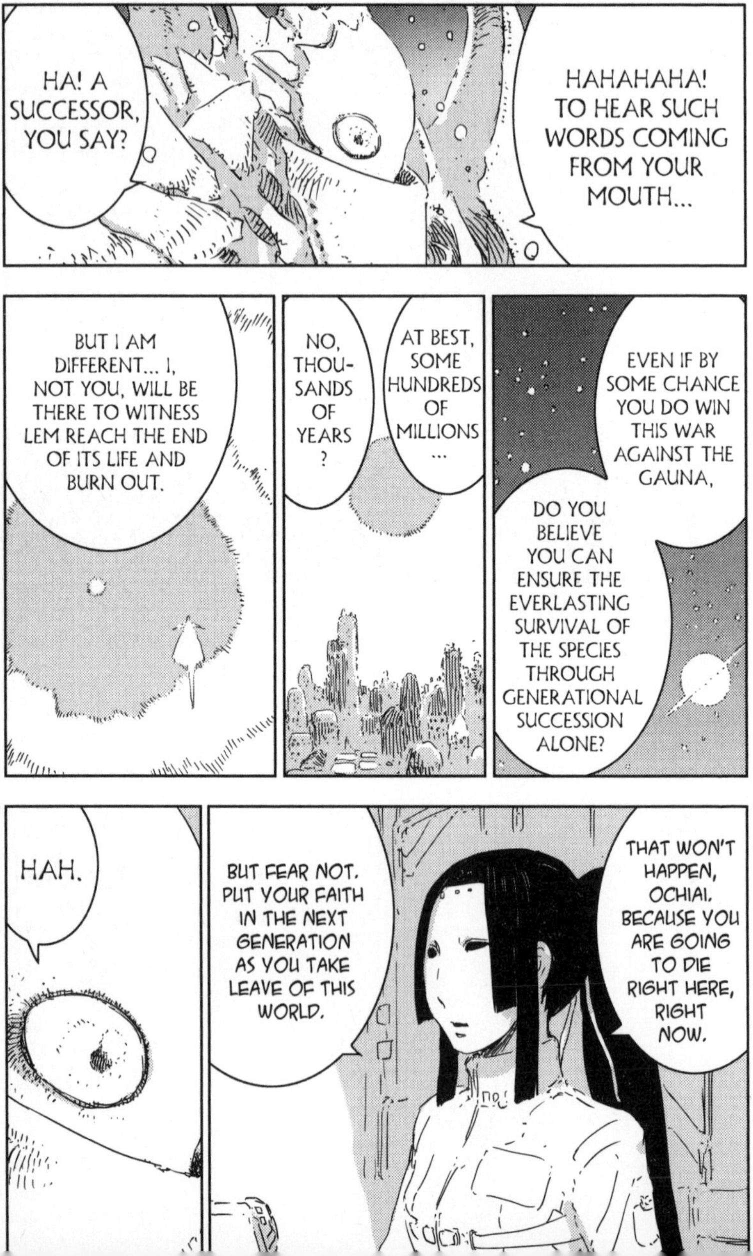
HAHAHAHA! TO HEAR SUCH WORDS COMING FROM YOUR MOUTH...
HA! A SUCCESSOR, YOU SAY?
EVEN IF BY SOME CHANCE YOU DO WIN THIS WAR AGAINST THE GAUNA,
DO YOU BELIEVE YOU CAN ENSURE THE EVERLASTING SURVIVAL OF THE SPECIES THROUGH GENERATIONAL SUCCESSION ALONE?
AT BEST, SOME HUNDREDS OF MILLIONS...
NO, THOUSANDS OF YEARS?
BUT I AM DIFFERENT... I, NOT YOU, WILL BE THERE TO WITNESS LEM REACH THE END OF ITS LIFE AND BURN OUT.
THAT WON'T HAPPEN, OCHIAI. BECAUSE YOU ARE GOING TO DIE RIGHT HERE, RIGHT NOW.
BUT FEAR NOT. PUT YOUR FAITH IN THE NEXT GENERATION AS YOU TAKE LEAVE OF THIS WORLD.
HAH.

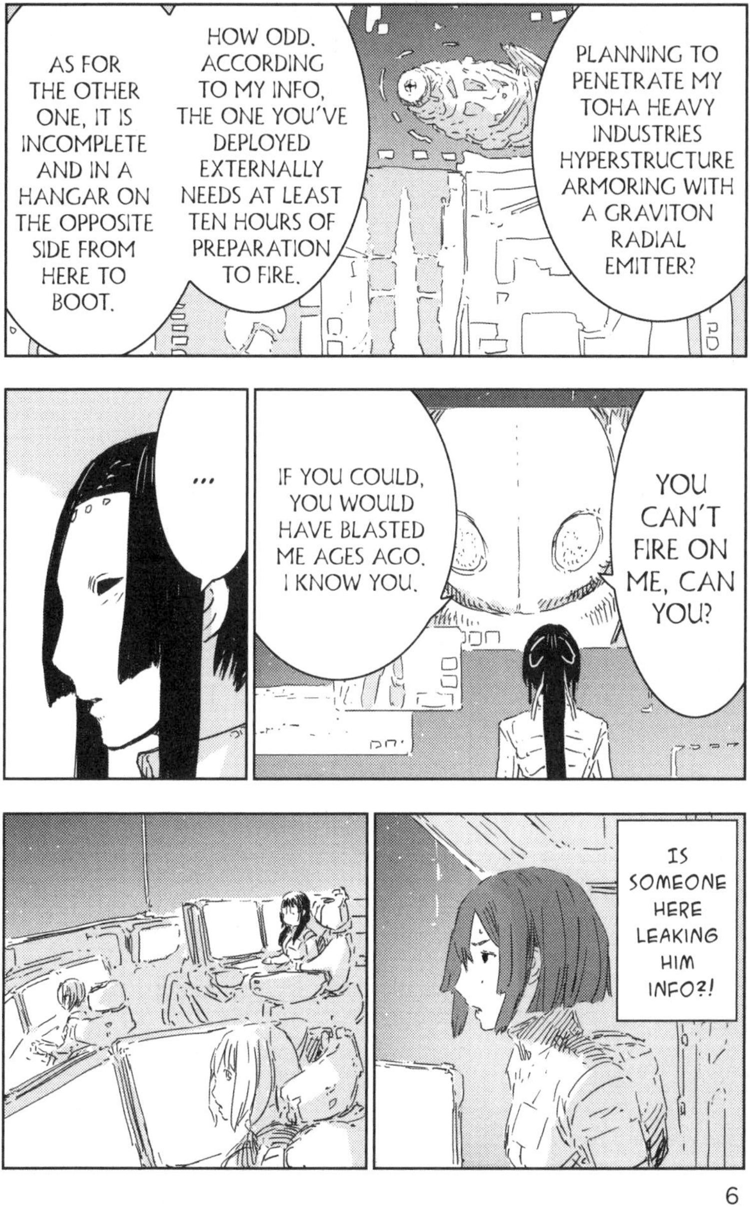
PLANNING TO PENETRATE MY TOHA HEAVY INDUSTRIES HYPERSTRUCTURE ARMORING WITH A GRAVITON RADIAL EMITTER?
HOW ODD. ACCORDING TO MY INFO, THE ONE YOU'VE DEPLOYED EXTERNALLY NEEDS AT LEAST TEN HOURS OF PREPARATION TO FIRE.
AS FOR THE OTHER ONE, IT IS INCOMPLETE AND IN A HANGAR ON THE OPPOSITE SIDE FROM HERE TO BOOT.
YOU CAN'T FIRE ON ME, CAN YOU?
IF YOU COULD, YOU WOULD HAVE BLASTED ME AGES AGO. I KNOW YOU.
...
IS SOMEONE HERE LEAKING HIM INFO?!

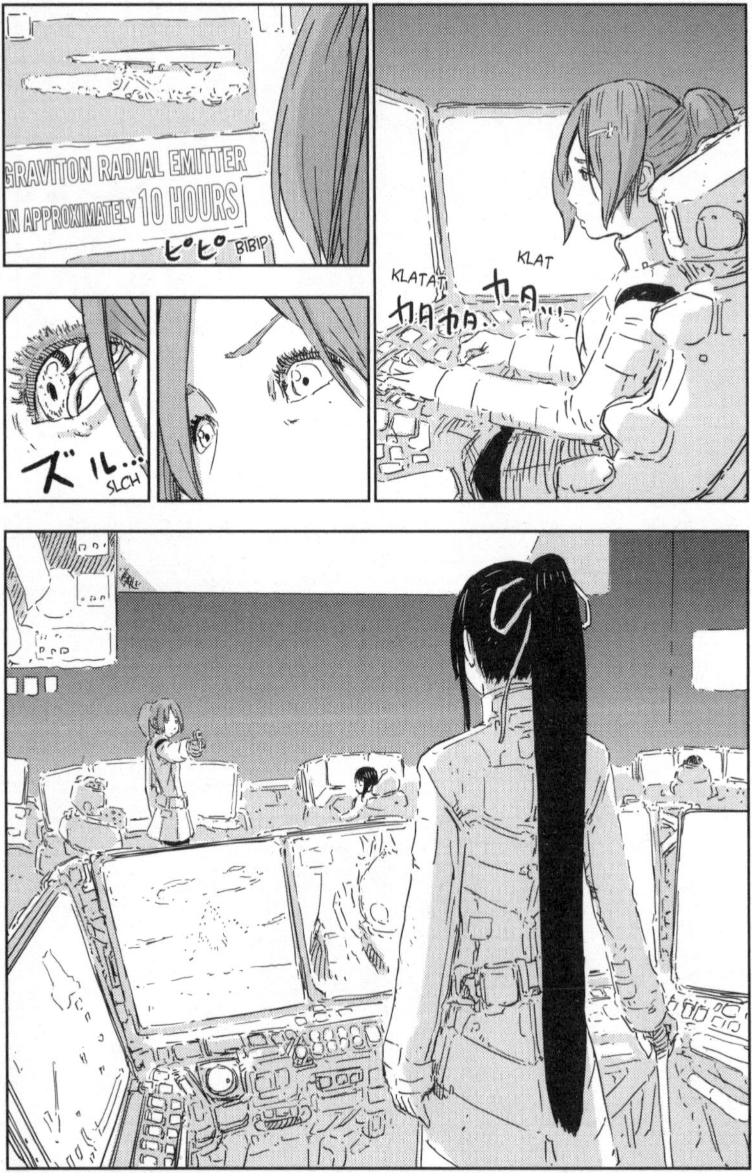
カタカタ‥
KLATAT
カタッ!
KLAT
GRAVITON RADIAL EMITTER
IN APPROXIMATELY 10 HOURS
ピピ
BIBIP
ズル…
SLCH

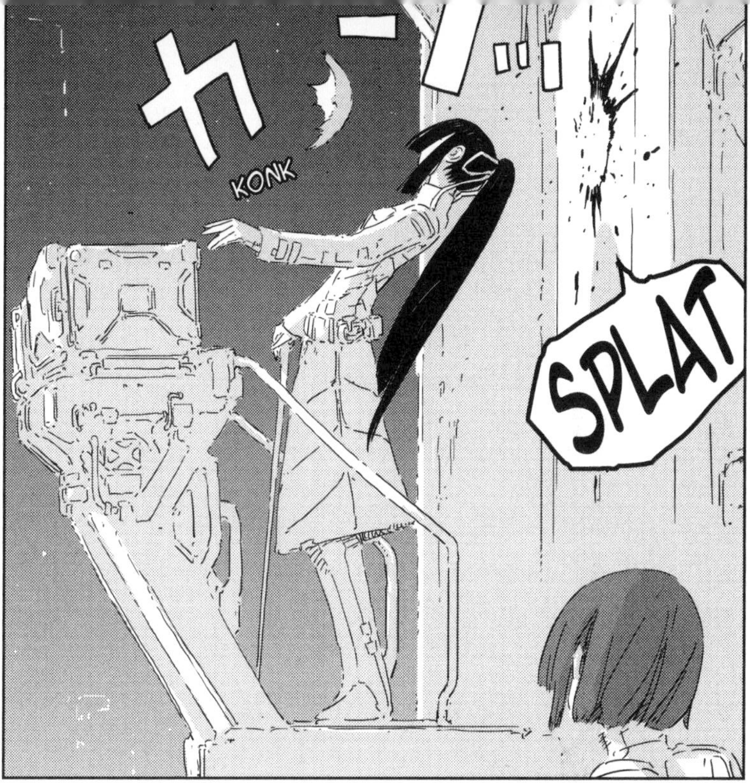
カン
KONK
SPLAT
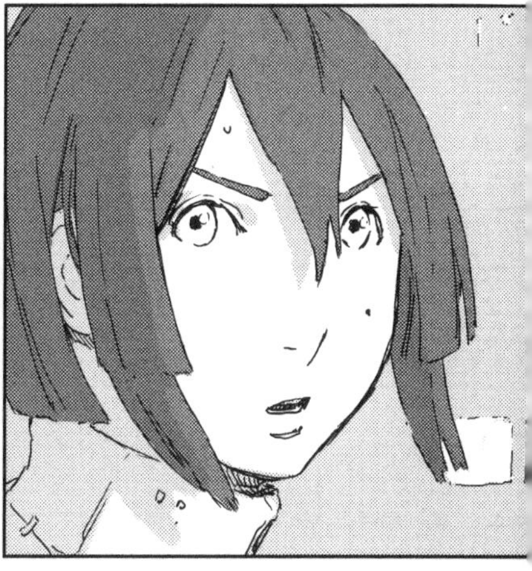
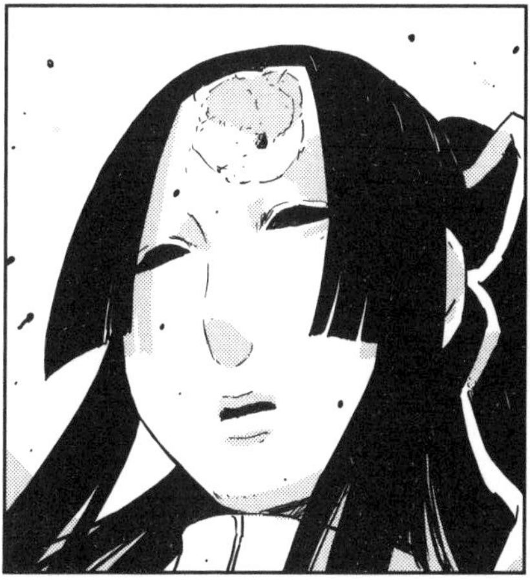

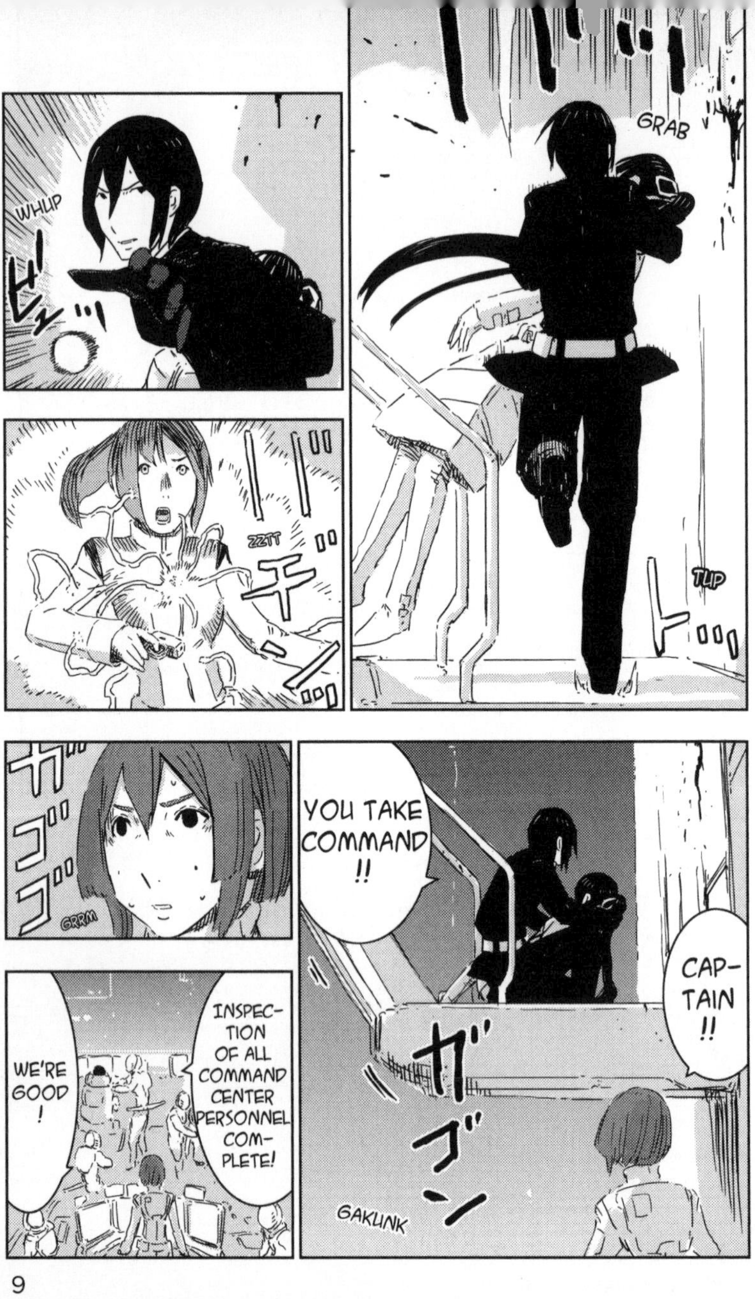
GRAB
TLIP
WHUP
ZZTT
YOU TAKE COMMAND !!
CAP-TAIN !!
GAKUNK
GRRM
INSPECTION OF ALL COMMAND CENTER PERSONNEL COMPLETE!
WE'RE GOOD !

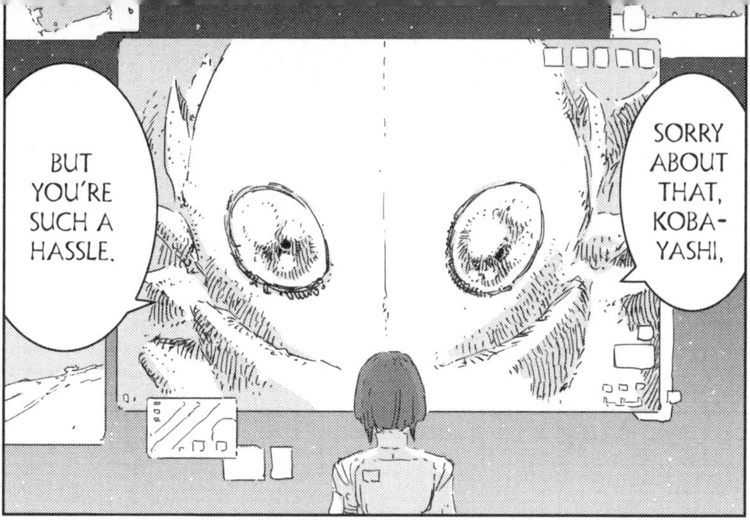
SORRY ABOUT THAT, KOBA-YASHI,
BUT YOU'RE SUCH A HASSLE.
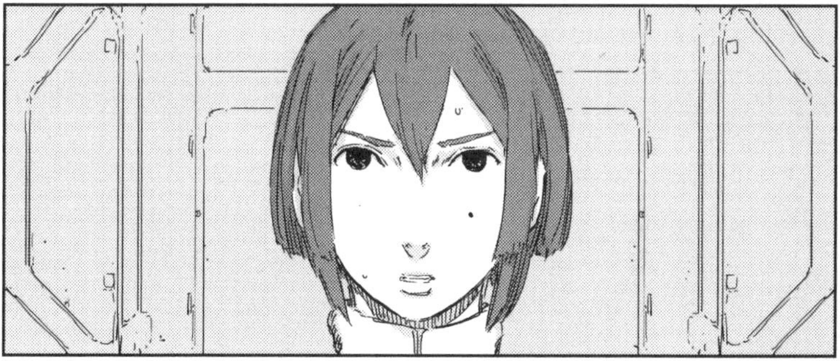
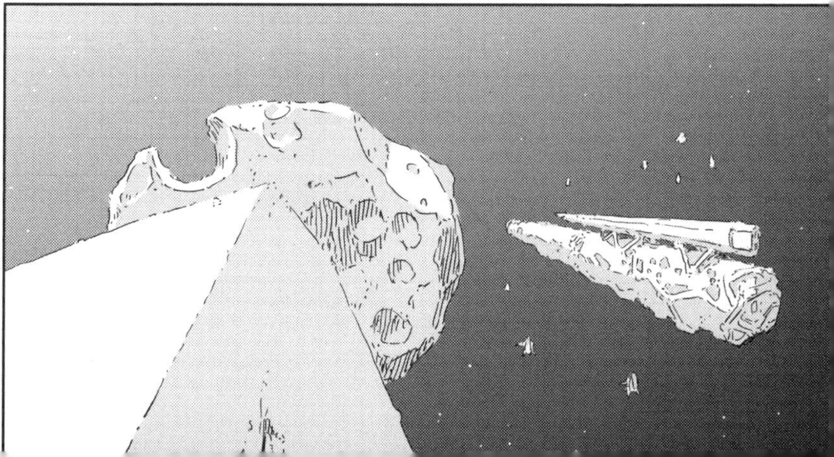

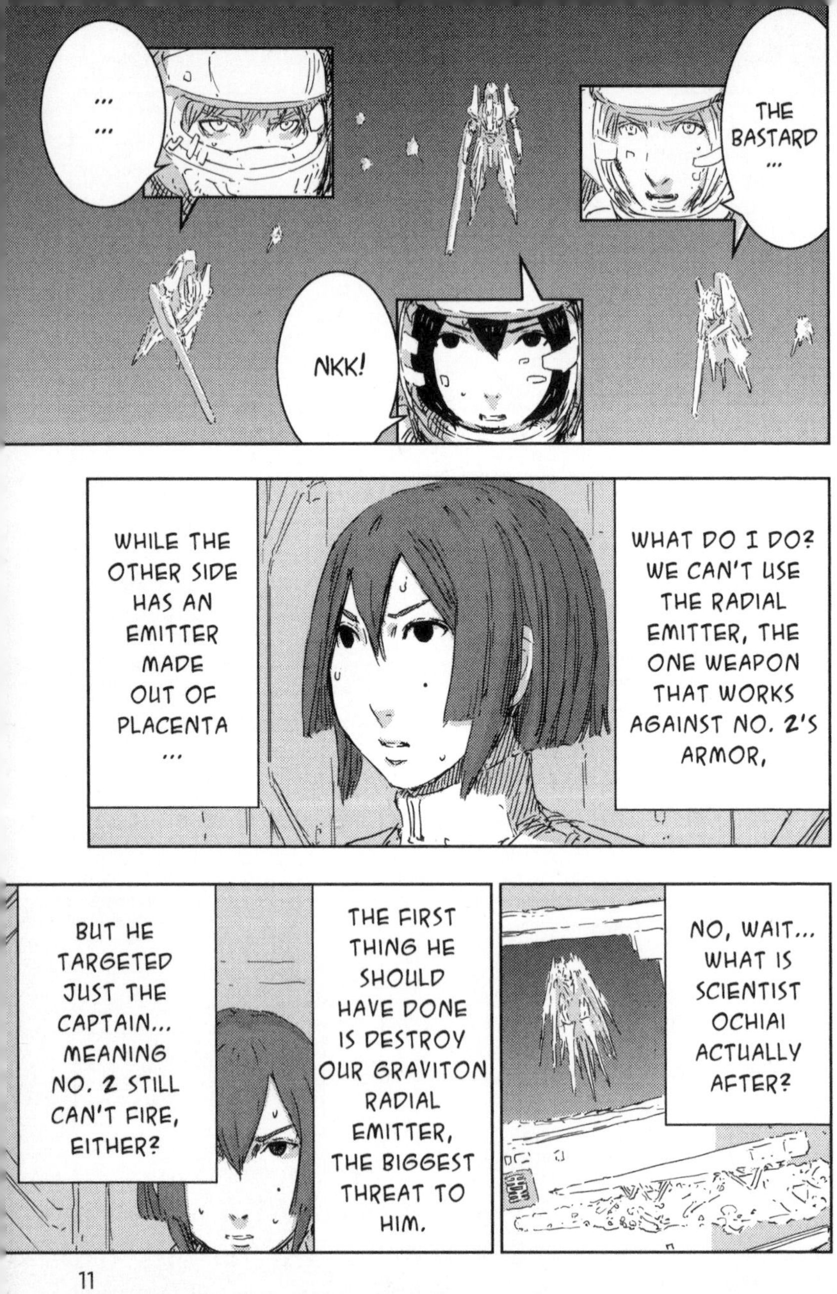
THE BASTARD ...
... ...
NKK!
WHAT DO I DO? WE CAN'T USE THE RADIAL EMITTER, THE ONE WEAPON THAT WORKS AGAINST NO. 2'S ARMOR,
WHILE THE OTHER SIDE HAS AN EMITTER MADE OUT OF PLACENTA ...
NO, WAIT... WHAT IS SCIENTIST OCHIAI ACTUALLY AFTER?
THE FIRST THING HE SHOULD HAVE DONE IS DESTROY OUR GRAVITON RADIAL EMITTER, THE BIGGEST THREAT TO HIM.
BUT HE TARGETED JUST THE CAPTAIN... MEANING NO. 2 STILL CAN'T FIRE, EITHER?

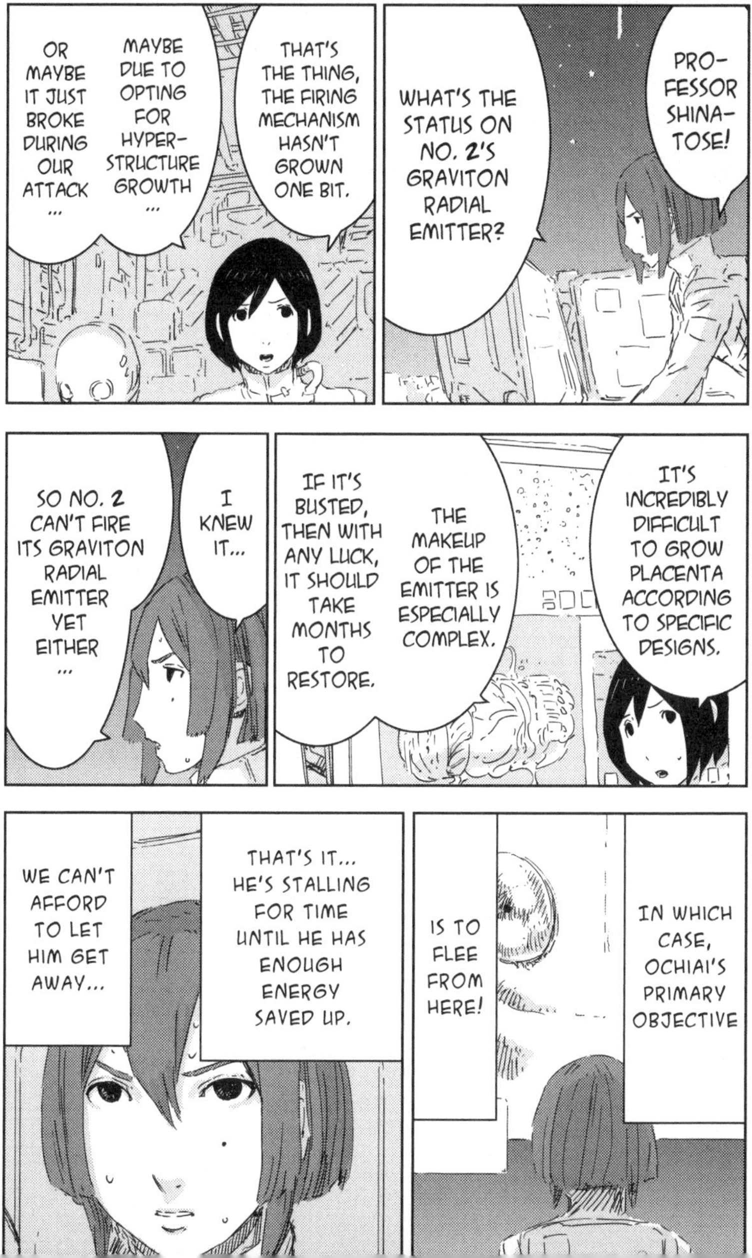
PRO-FESSOR SHINA-TOSE!
WHAT'S THE STATUS ON NO. 2'S GRAVITON RADIAL EMITTER?
THAT'S THE THING, THE FIRING MECHANISM HASN'T GROWN ONE BIT.
MAYBE DUE TO OPTING FOR HYPER-STRUCTURE GROWTH...
OR MAYBE IT JUST BROKE DURING OUR ATTACK...
IT'S INCREDIBLY DIFFICULT TO GROW PLACENTA ACCORDING TO SPECIFIC DESIGNS.
THE MAKEUP OF THE EMITTER IS ESPECIALLY COMPLEX.
IF IT'S BUSTED, THEN WITH ANY LUCK, IT SHOULD TAKE MONTHS TO RESTORE.
I KNEW IT...
SO NO. 2 CAN'T FIRE ITS GRAVITON RADIAL EMITTER YET EITHER...
IN WHICH CASE, OCHIAI'S PRIMARY OBJECTIVE
IS TO FLEE FROM HERE!
THAT'S IT... HE'S STALLING FOR TIME UNTIL HE HAS ENOUGH ENERGY SAVED UP.
WE CAN'T AFFORD TO LET HIM GET AWAY...

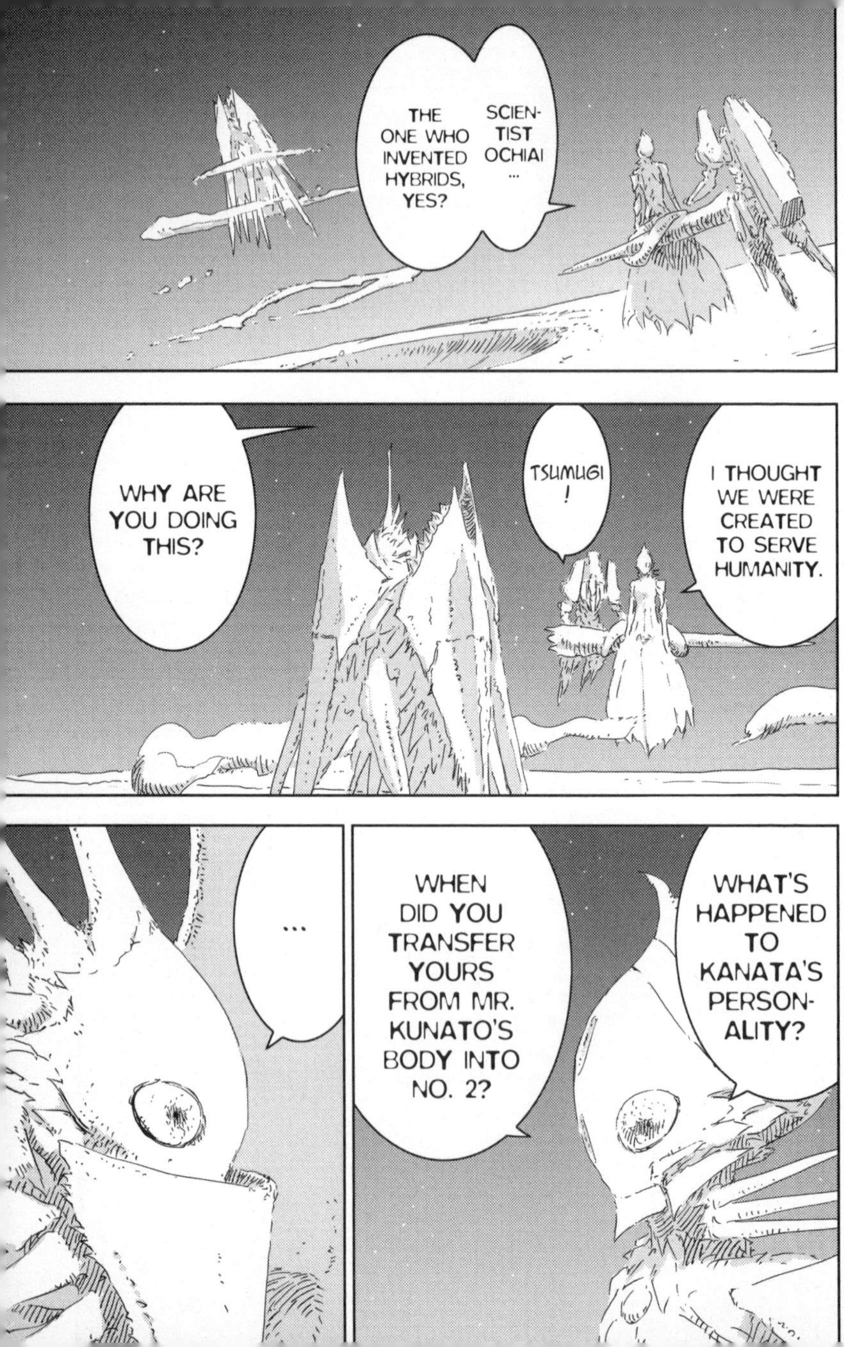
SCIENTIST OCHIAI ...
THE ONE WHO INVENTED HYBRIDS, YES?
I THOUGHT WE WERE CREATED TO SERVE HUMANITY.
TSUMUGI!
WHY ARE YOU DOING THIS?
WHAT'S HAPPENED TO KANATA'S PERSONALITY?
WHEN DID YOU TRANSFER YOURS FROM MR. KUNATO'S BODY INTO NO. 2?
...

TSUMUGI, SHINATOSE UNIT— YOU CAN'T TAKE ON NO. 2 BY YOURSELVES!
GET BACK!
THEY RECALLED THEIR TROOPS... IS THAT ASSISTANT UP TO SOMETHING?
NO... THEY HAVE NO MEANS OF HARMING ME OTHER THAN THE RADIAL EMITTER...
VOOF
STILL, I'D BEST EXERCISE CAUTION. I OUGHT TO DESTROY THEIRS, AT LEAST.
I'D HOPED TO WIPE OUT THE SIDONIA ALONG WITH THEM, BUT IF IT CAN'T BE HELPED...

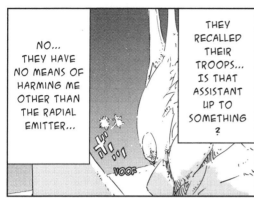

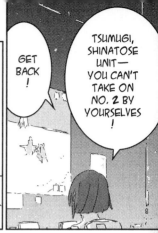

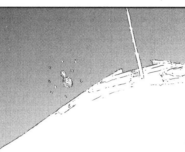

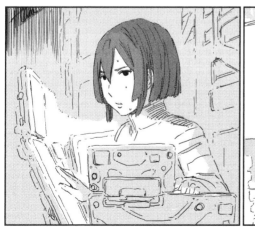

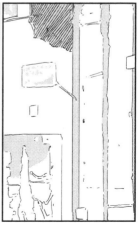

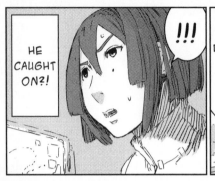

HE CAUGHT ON?!

!!!

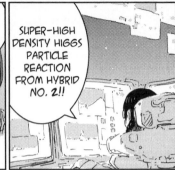

SUPER-HIGH DENSITY HIGGS PARTICLE REACTION FROM HYBRID NO. 2!!

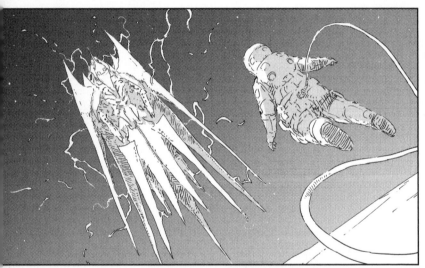

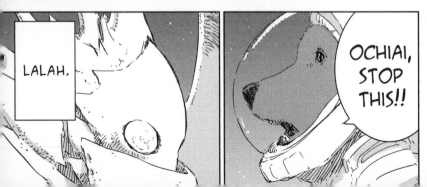

LALAH.

OCHIAI, STOP THIS!!

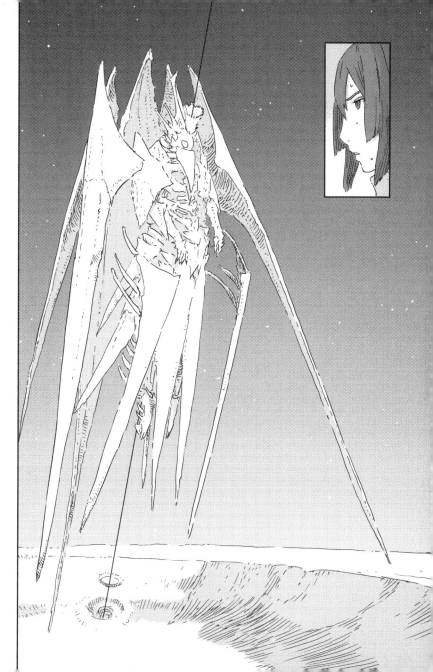

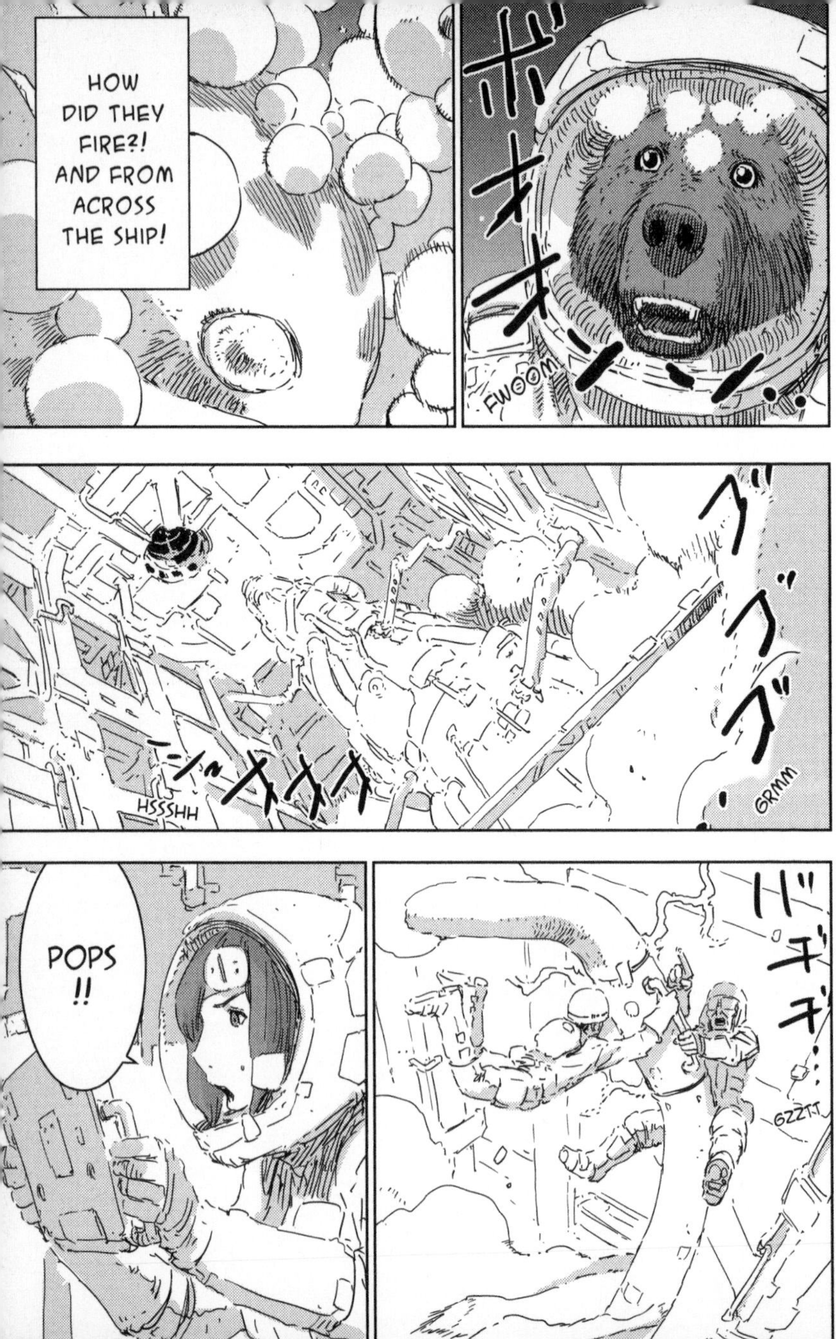
ボォォン……
FWOOM
HOW DID THEY FIRE?! AND FROM ACROSS THE SHIP!
ヴヴヴ…
GRMM
シュハァァァ
HSSSHH
ドギギ…
GZZTT
POPS !!

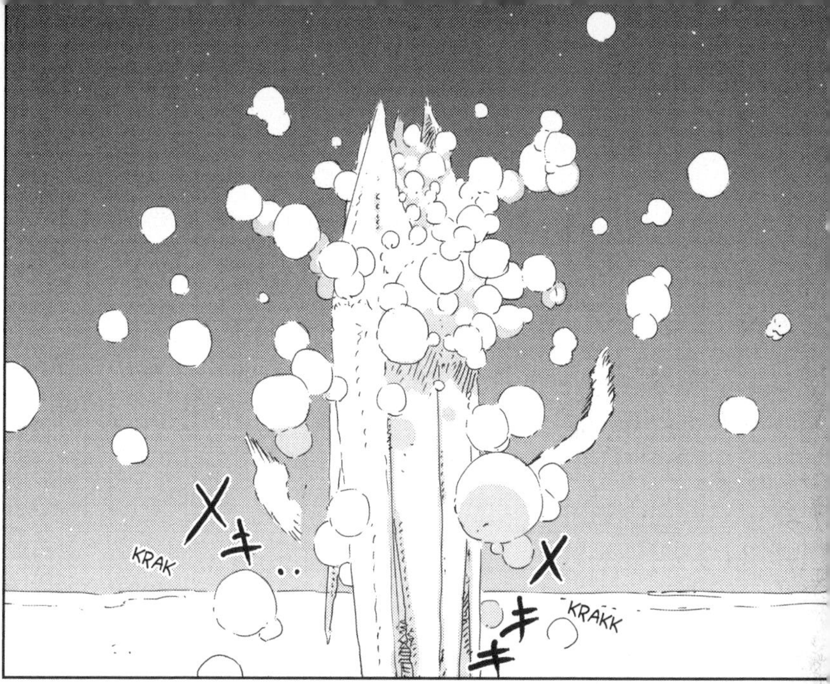
メキ..
KRAK
メキキ
KRAKK
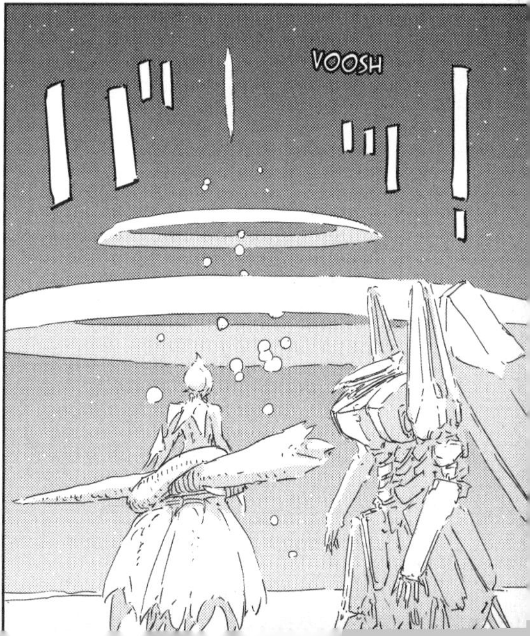
VOOSH
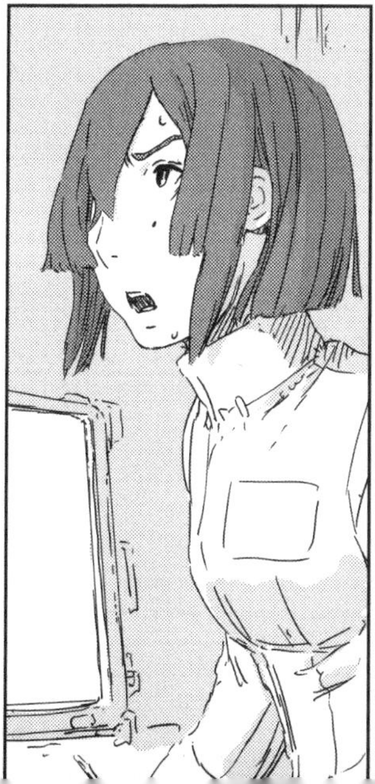

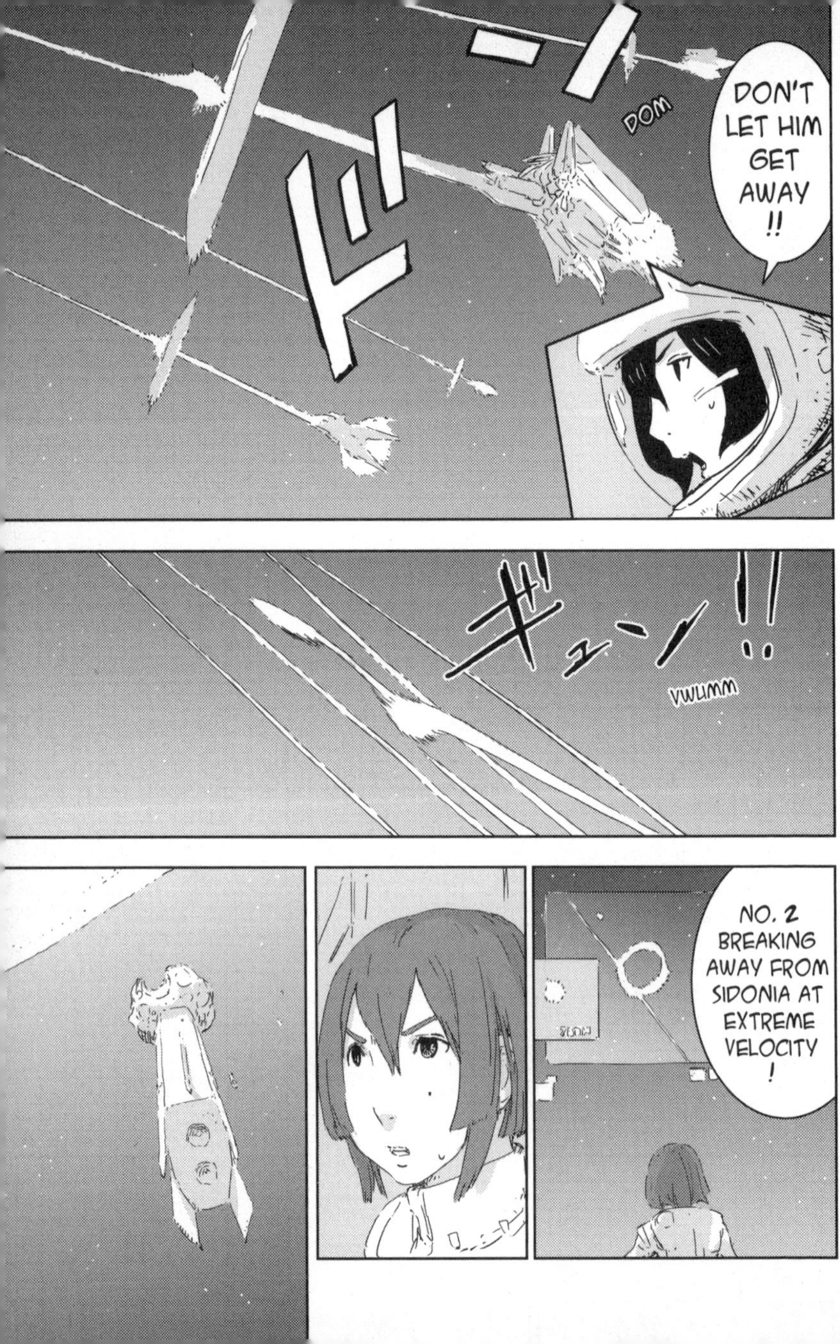
DON'T LET HIM GET AWAY !!
DOM
ギューン!!
VWUMM
NO. 2 BREAKING AWAY FROM SIDONIA AT EXTREME VELOCITY !

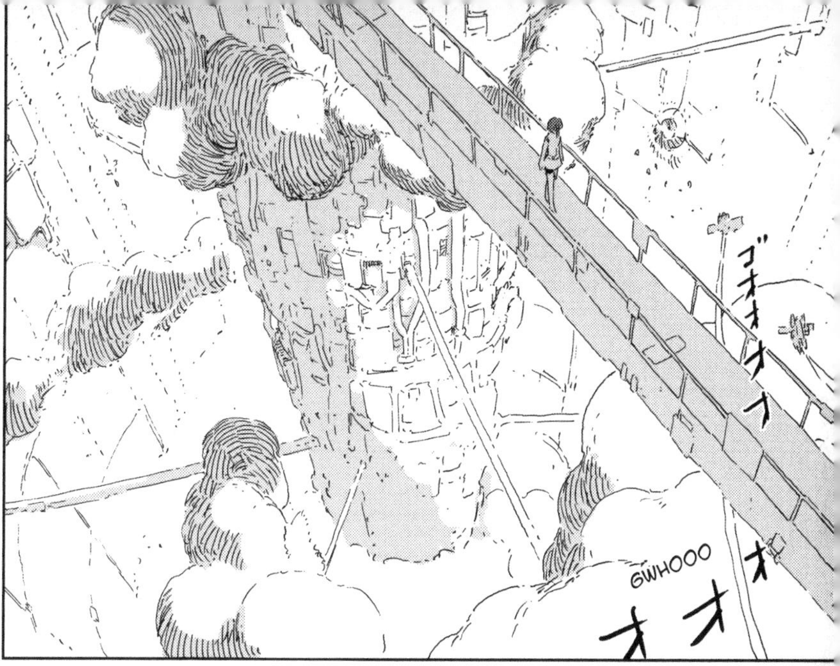
ゴオオオオ
GWHOOO
オオオ
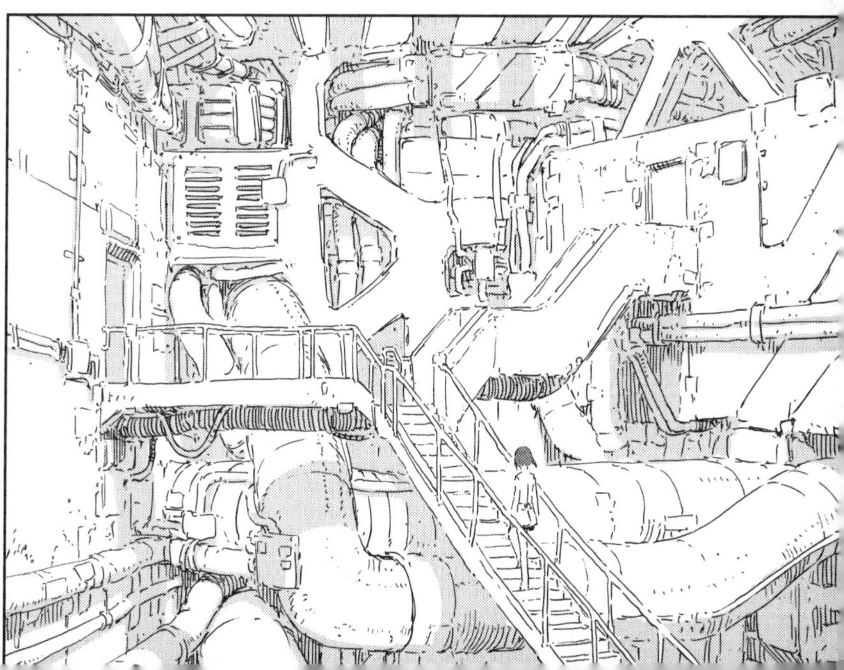

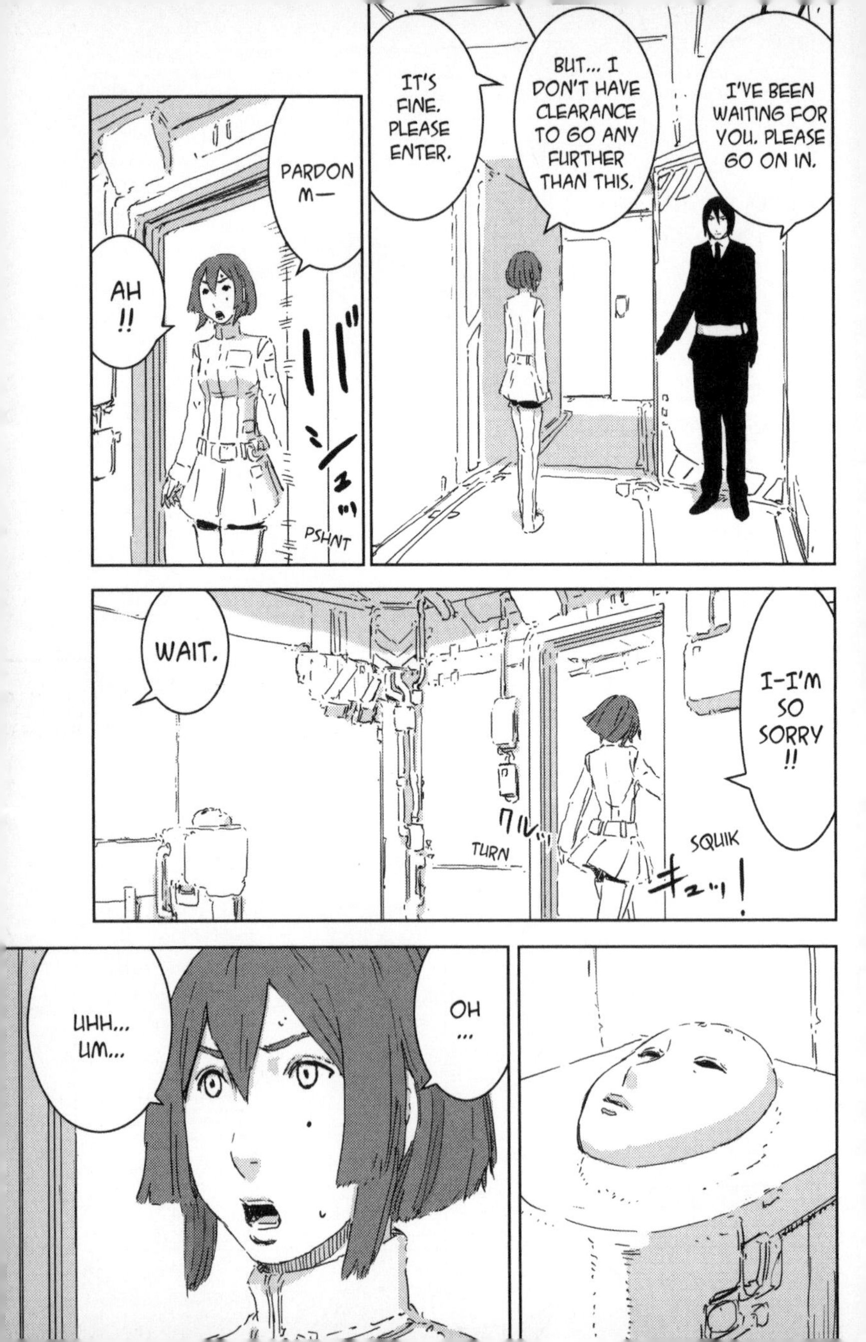
I'VE BEEN WAITING FOR YOU. PLEASE GO ON IN.
BUT... I DON'T HAVE CLEARANCE TO GO ANY FURTHER THAN THIS.
IT'S FINE. PLEASE ENTER.
PSHNT
PARDON M—
AH !!
I-I'M SO SORRY !!
SQUIK
TURN
WAIT.
OH ...
UHH... UM...

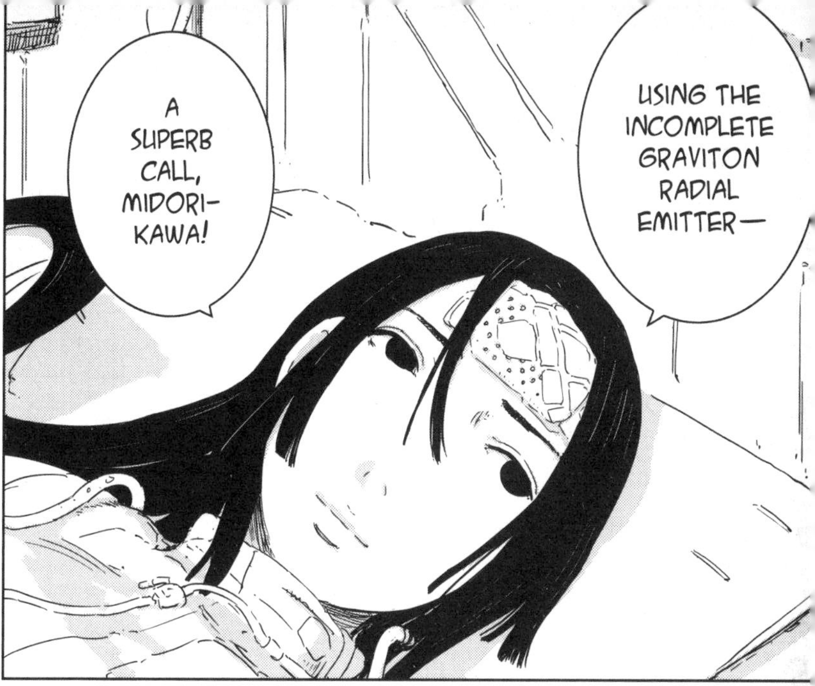
USING THE INCOMPLETE GRAVITON RADIAL EMITTER—
A SUPERB CALL, MIDORI-KAWA!

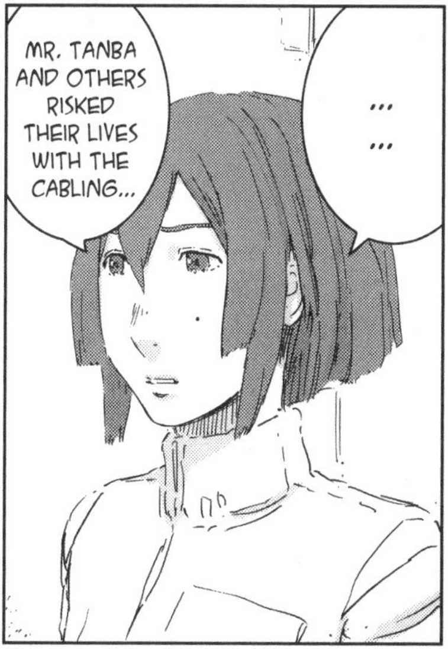
... ...
MR. TANBA AND OTHERS RISKED THEIR LIVES WITH THE CABLING...

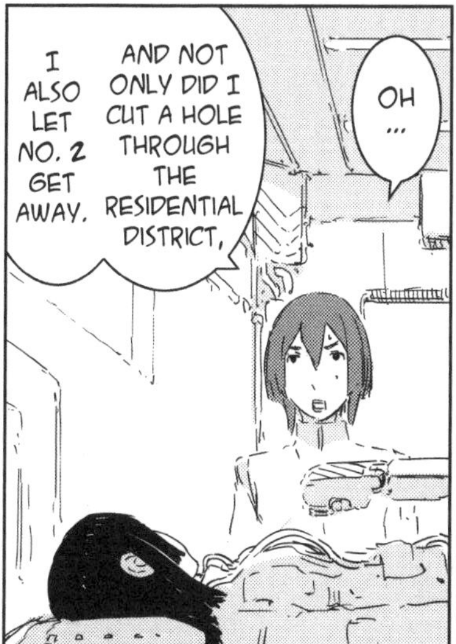
OH ...
AND NOT ONLY DID I CUT A HOLE THROUGH THE RESIDENTIAL DISTRICT,
I ALSO LET NO. 2 GET AWAY.

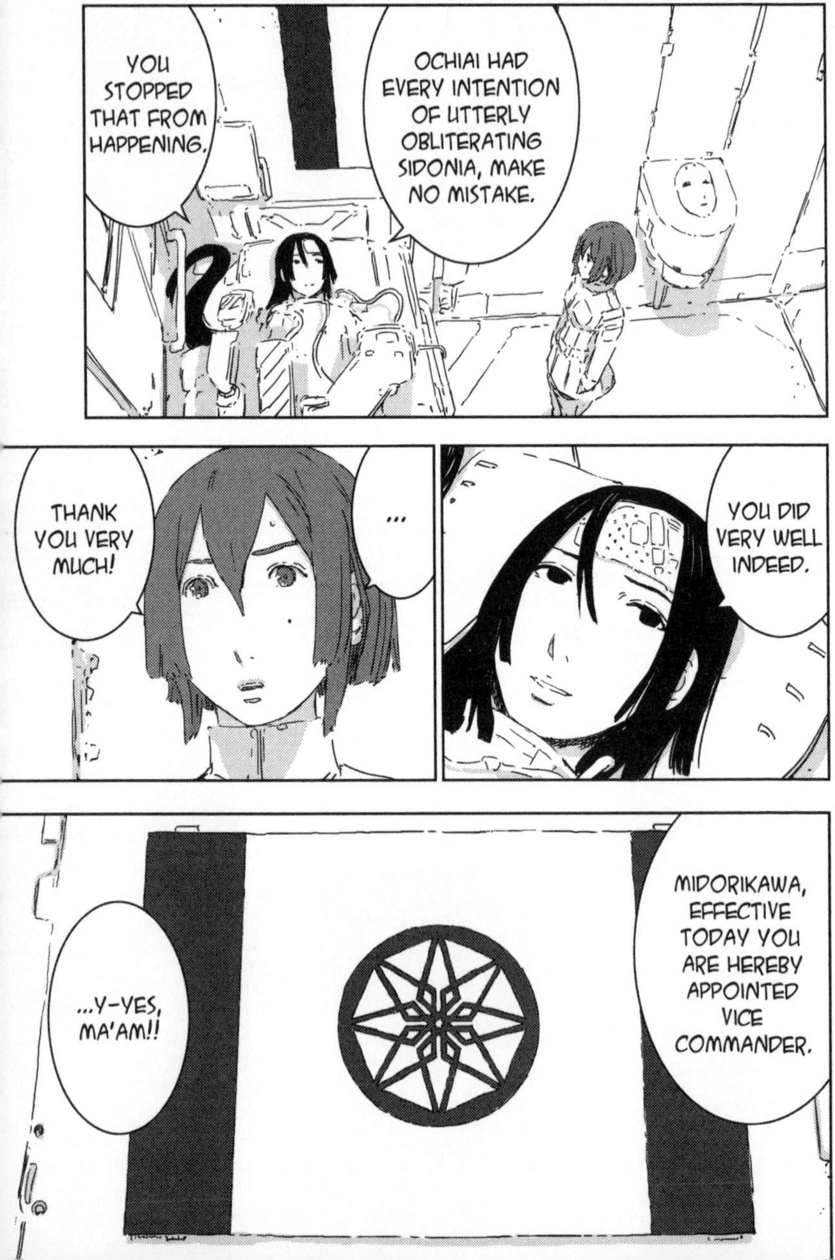
OCHIAI HAD EVERY INTENTION OF UTTERLY OBLITERATING SIDONIA, MAKE NO MISTAKE.
YOU STOPPED THAT FROM HAPPENING.
YOU DID VERY WELL INDEED.
...
THANK YOU VERY MUCH!
MIDORIKAWA, EFFECTIVE TODAY YOU ARE HEREBY APPOINTED VICE COMMANDER.
...Y-YES, MA'AM!!

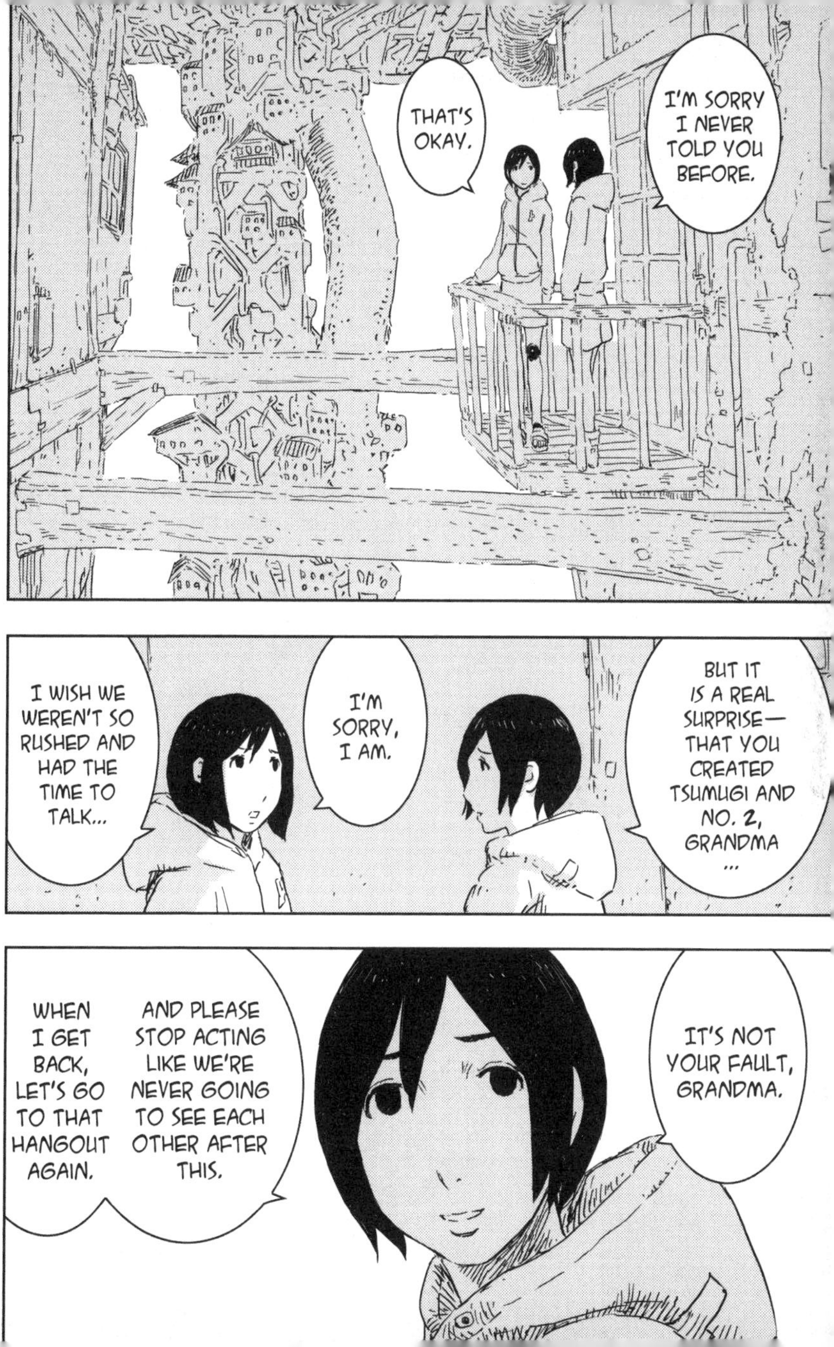
I'M SORRY I NEVER TOLD YOU BEFORE.
THAT'S OKAY.
BUT IT IS A REAL SURPRISE— THAT YOU CREATED TSUMUGI AND NO. 2, GRANDMA ...
I'M SORRY, I AM.
I WISH WE WEREN'T SO RUSHED AND HAD THE TIME TO TALK...
IT'S NOT YOUR FAULT, GRANDMA.
AND PLEASE STOP ACTING LIKE WE'RE NEVER GOING TO SEE EACH OTHER AFTER THIS.
WHEN I GET BACK, LET'S GO TO THAT HANGOUT AGAIN.

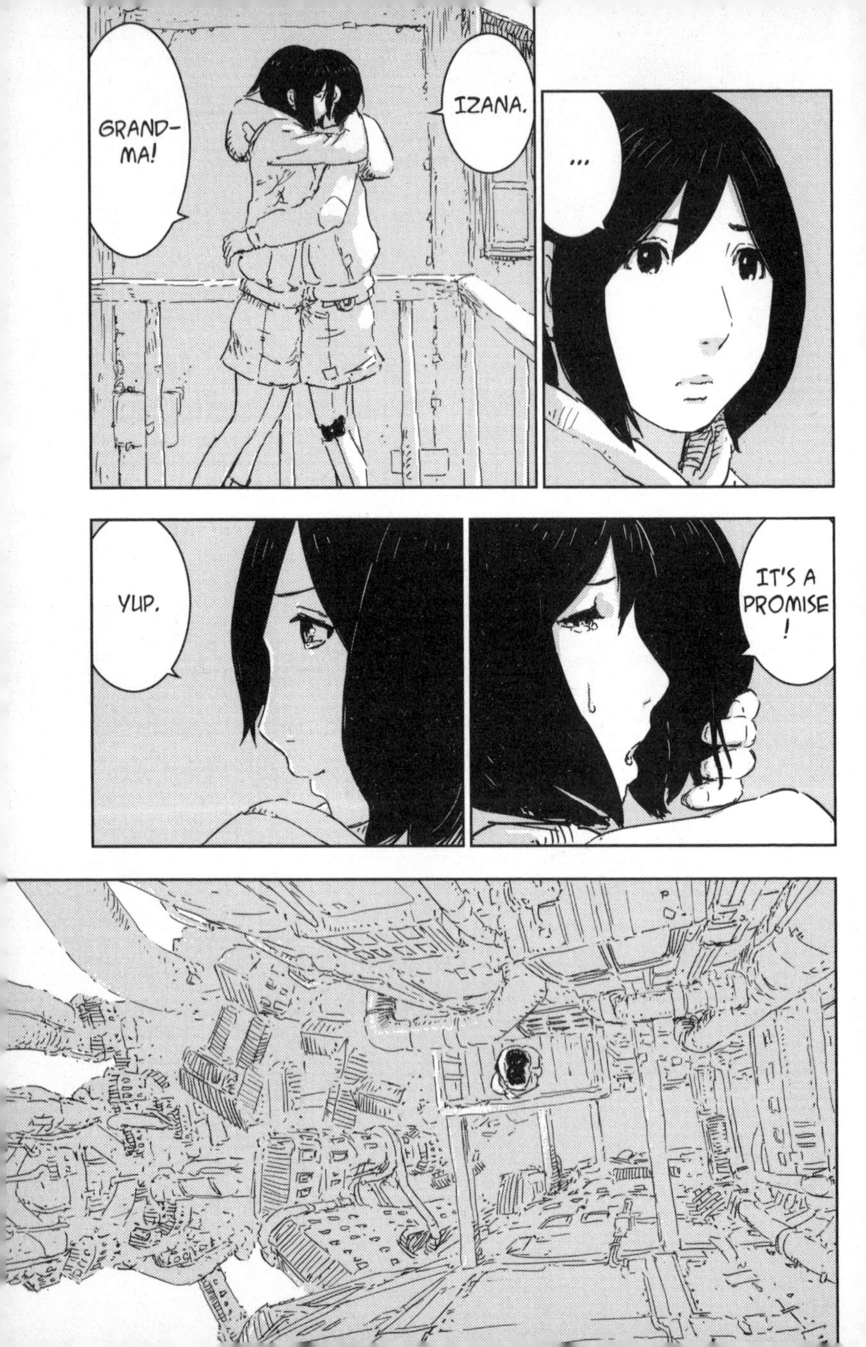
...
IZANA.
GRAND-MA!
IT'S A PROMISE!
YUP.

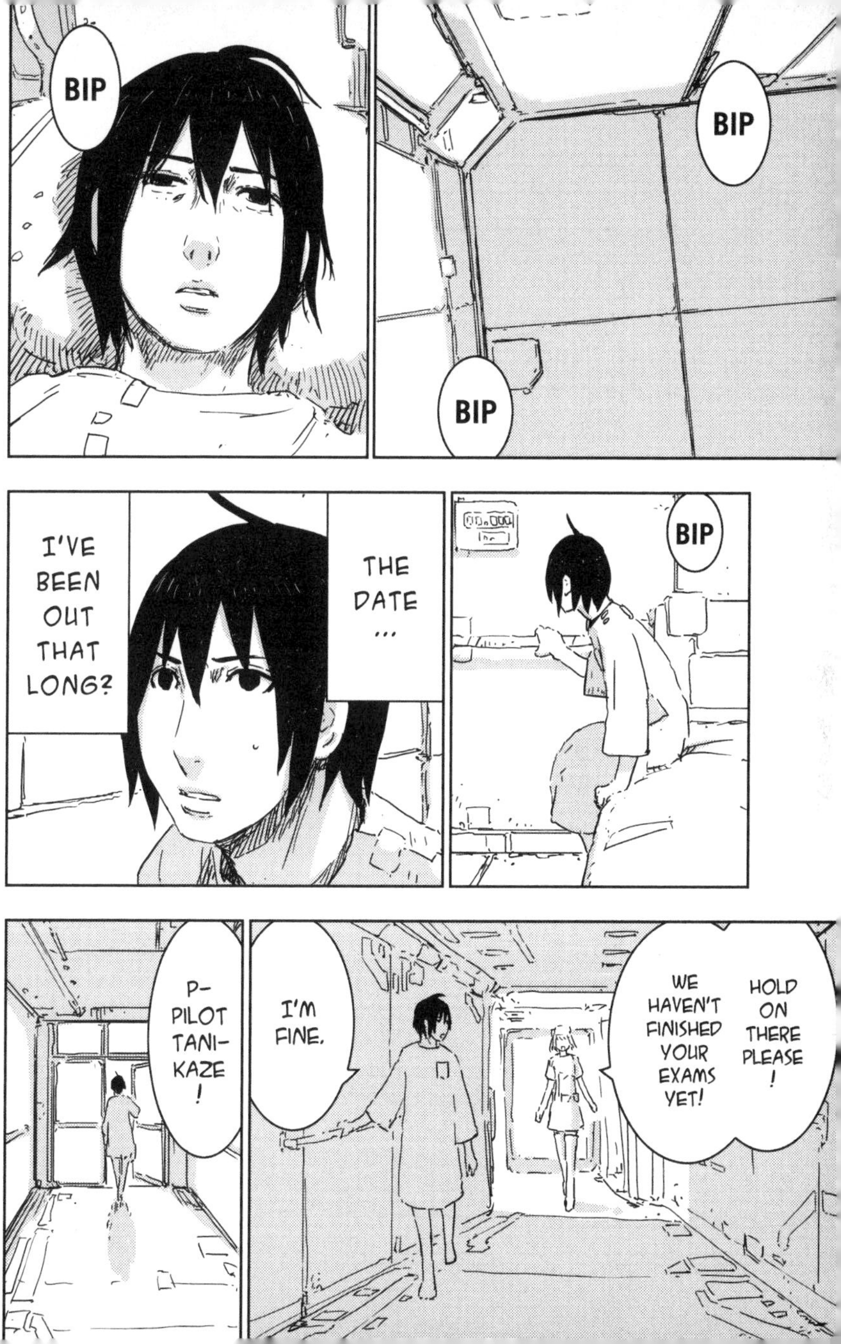
BIP
BIP
BIP
BIP
THE DATE …
I'VE BEEN OUT THAT LONG?
HOLD ON THERE PLEASE!
WE HAVEN'T FINISHED YOUR EXAMS YET!
I'M FINE.
P-PILOT TANI-KAZE!

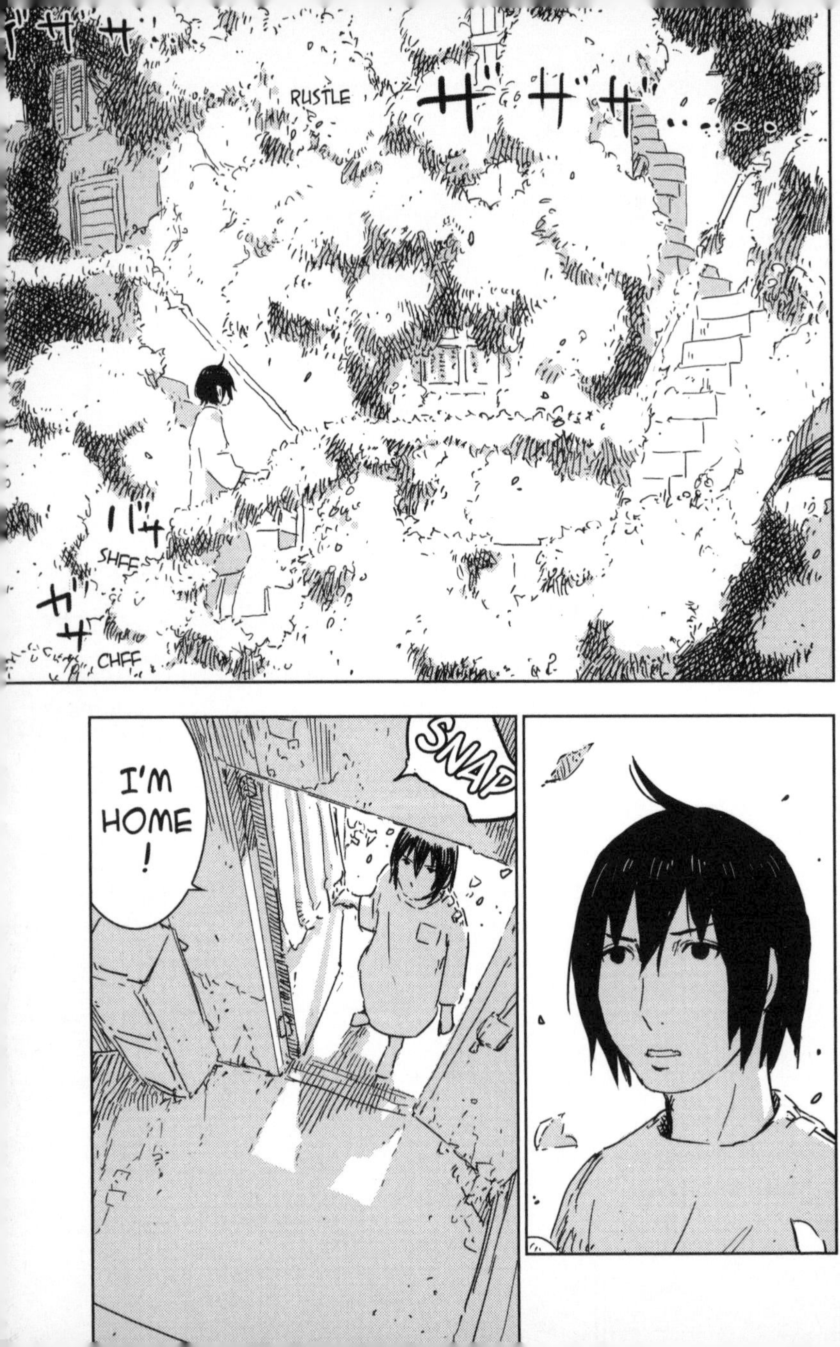
RUSTLE
SHFF
CHFF
SNAP
I'M HOME!

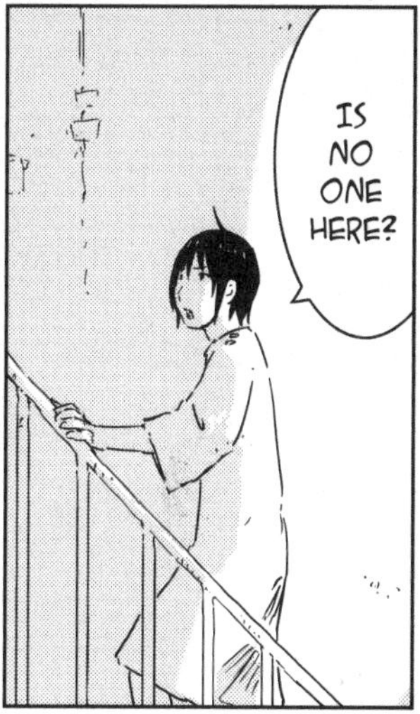
IS NO ONE HERE?
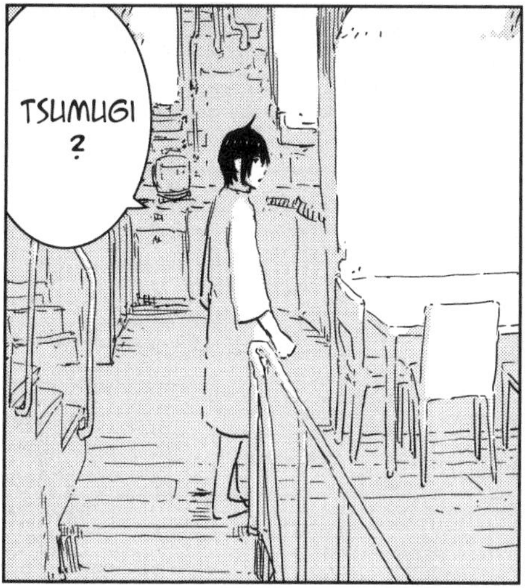
TSUMUGI?
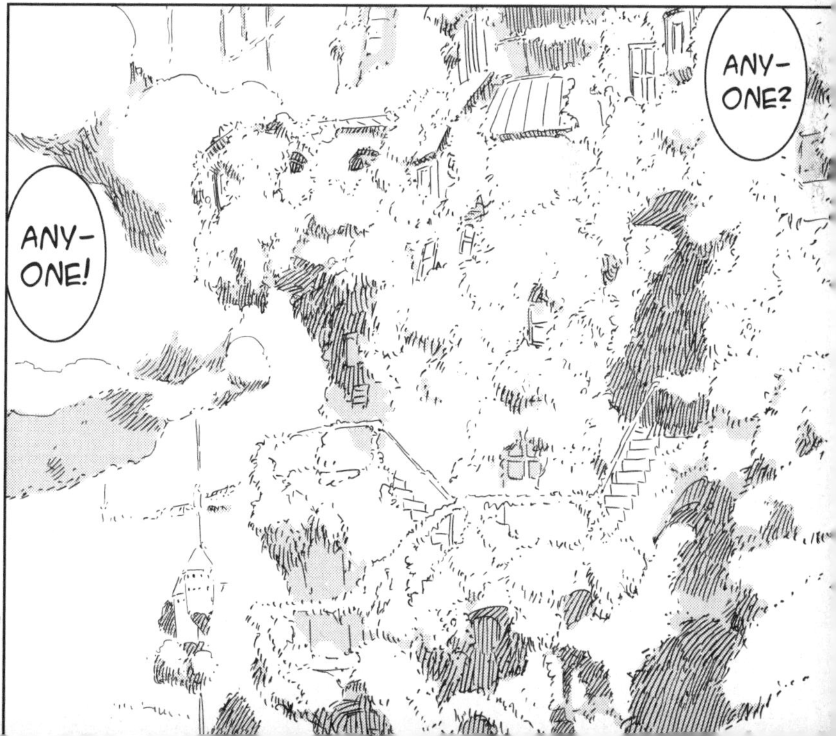
ANY-ONE?
ANY-ONE!

Chapter 65: END

シドニアの騎士
KNIGHTS OF SIDONIA

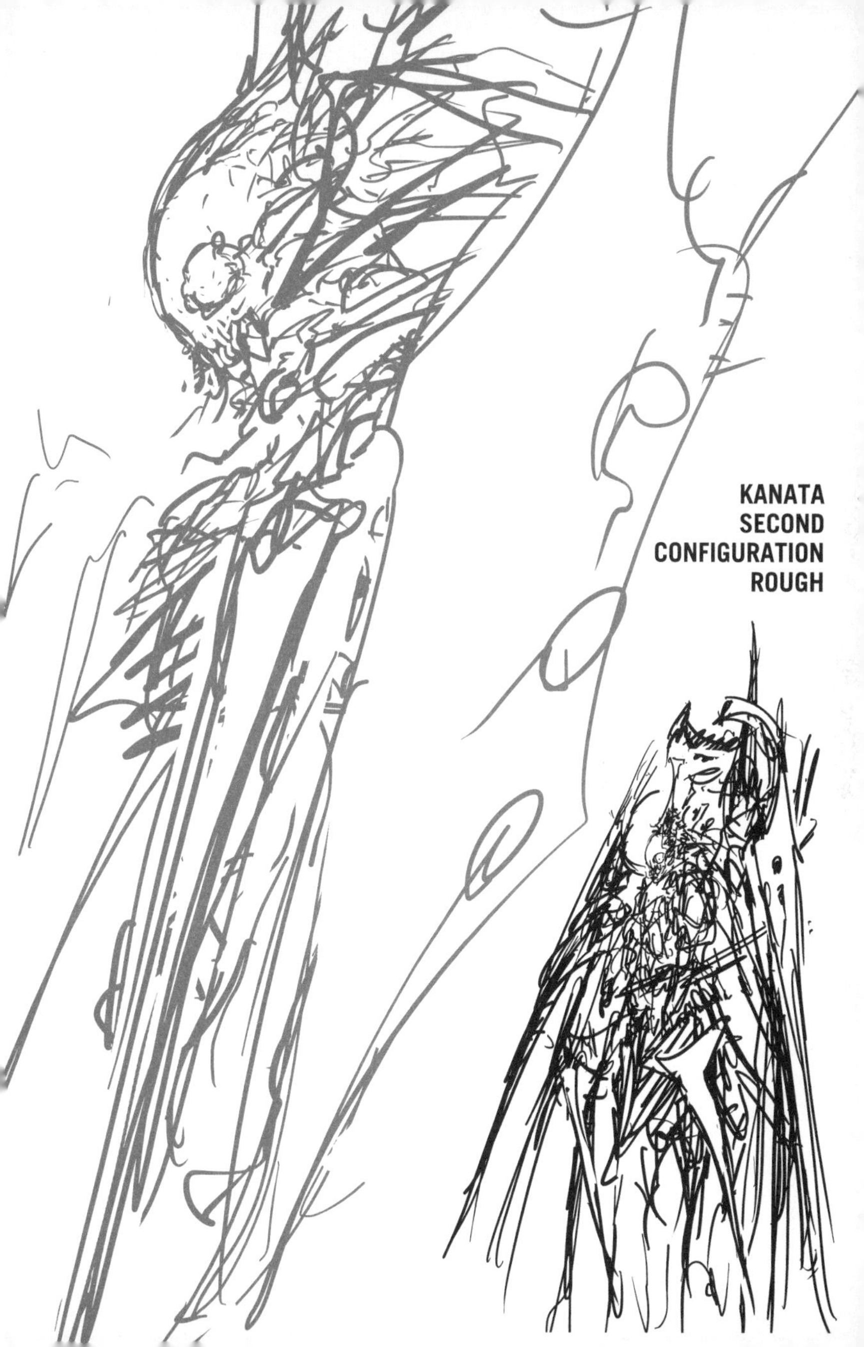

KANATA SECOND CONFIGURATION ROUGH

Chapter 66: Captain Kobayashi's Lingering Attachment

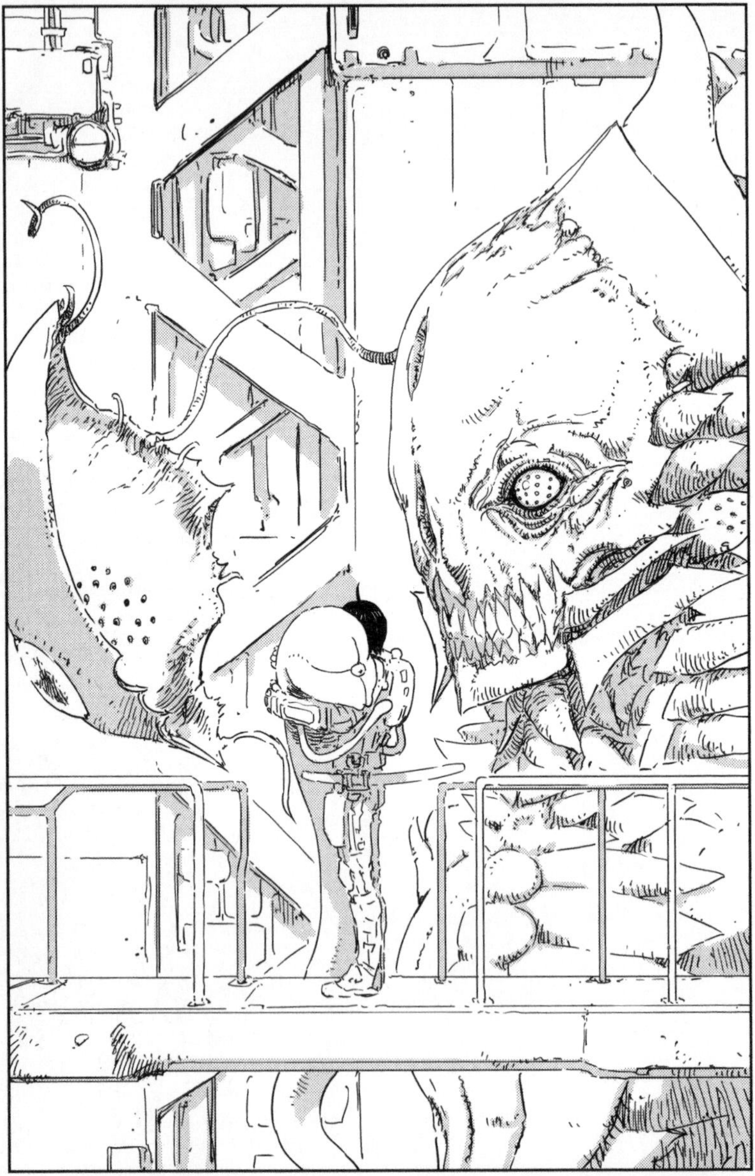

One Hundred Sights of Sidonia Part Fifty: Hybrid No. 1 Hangar

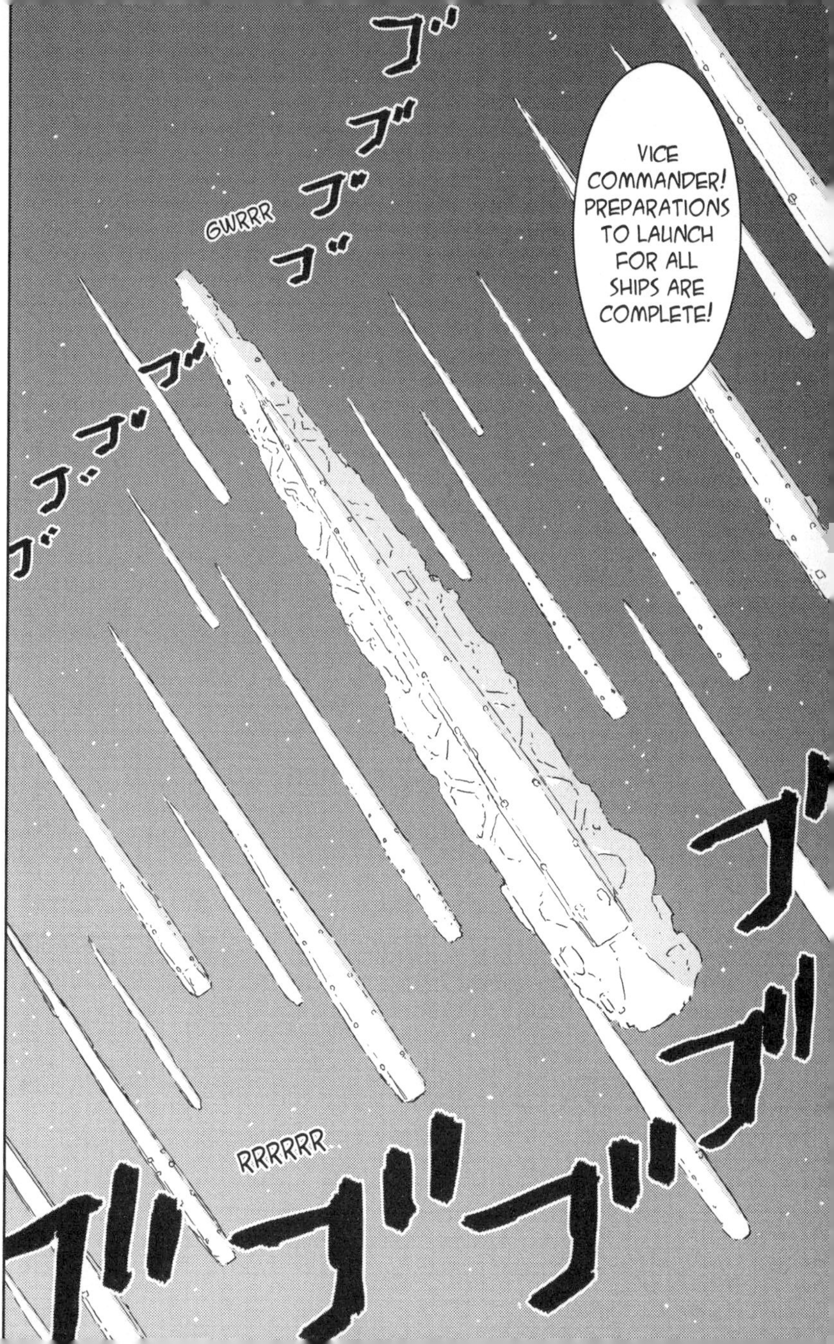
VICE COMMANDER! PREPARATIONS TO LAUNCH FOR ALL SHIPS ARE COMPLETE!
GWRRR
RRRRRR

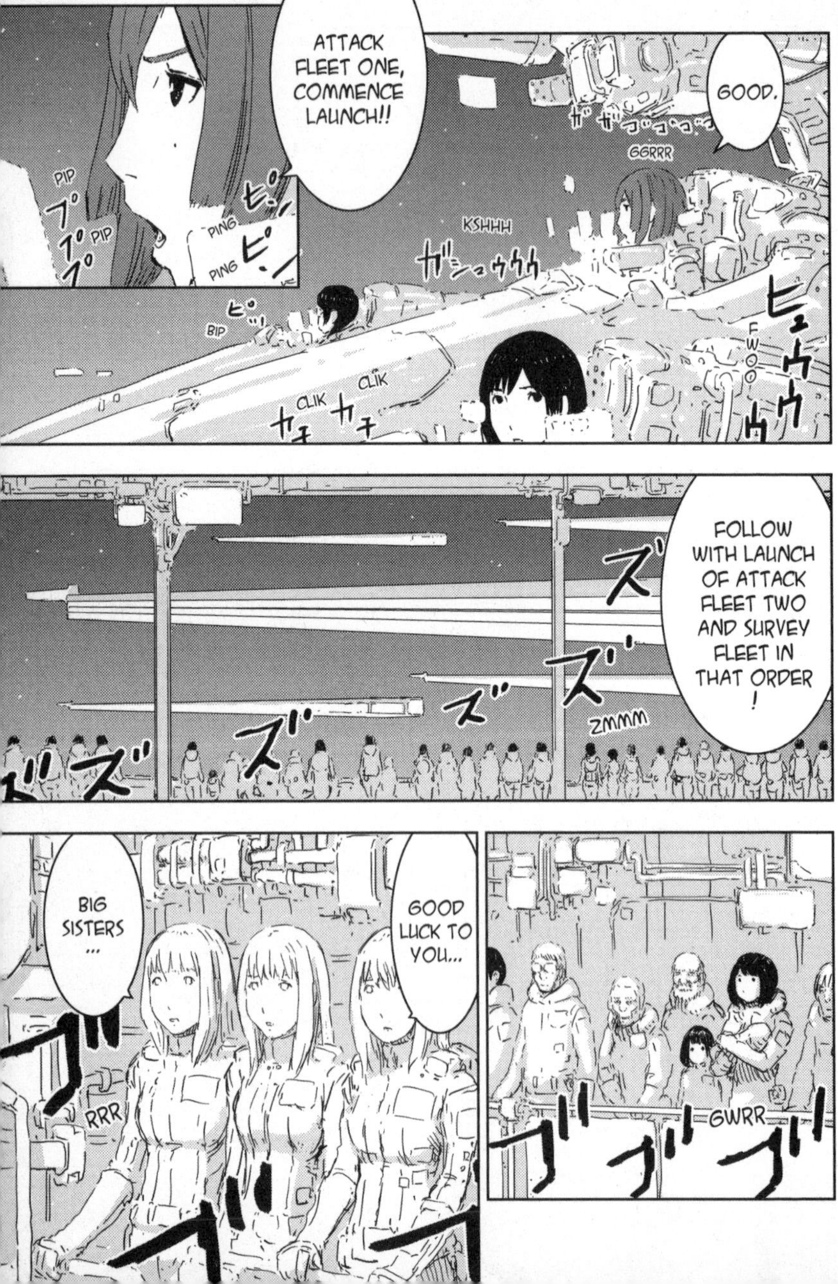
ATTACK FLEET ONE, COMMENCE LAUNCH!!
PIP PIP
PING PING
GOOD.
GGRRR
KSHHH
BIP
CLIK CLIK
FWOOO
FOLLOW WITH LAUNCH OF ATTACK FLEET TWO AND SURVEY FLEET IN THAT ORDER!
ZMMM
GWRR
GOOD LUCK TO YOU...
BIG SISTERS...
RRR

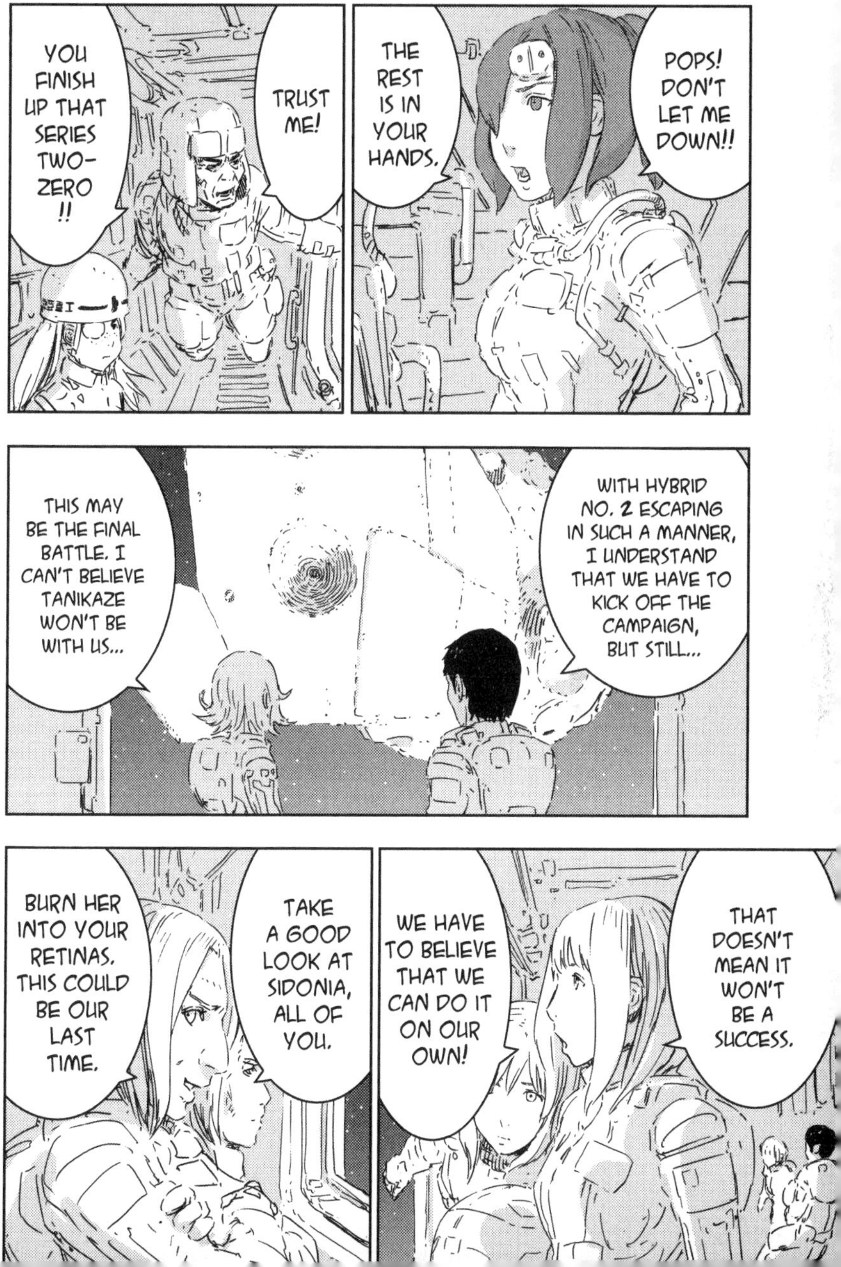
POPS! DON'T LET ME DOWN!!
THE REST IS IN YOUR HANDS.
TRUST ME!
YOU FINISH UP THAT SERIES TWO-ZERO!!
WITH HYBRID NO. 2 ESCAPING IN SUCH A MANNER, I UNDERSTAND THAT WE HAVE TO KICK OFF THE CAMPAIGN, BUT STILL...
THIS MAY BE THE FINAL BATTLE. I CAN'T BELIEVE TANIKAZE WON'T BE WITH US...
THAT DOESN'T MEAN IT WON'T BE A SUCCESS.
WE HAVE TO BELIEVE THAT WE CAN DO IT ON OUR OWN!
TAKE A GOOD LOOK AT SIDONIA, ALL OF YOU.
BURN HER INTO YOUR RETINAS. THIS COULD BE OUR LAST TIME.

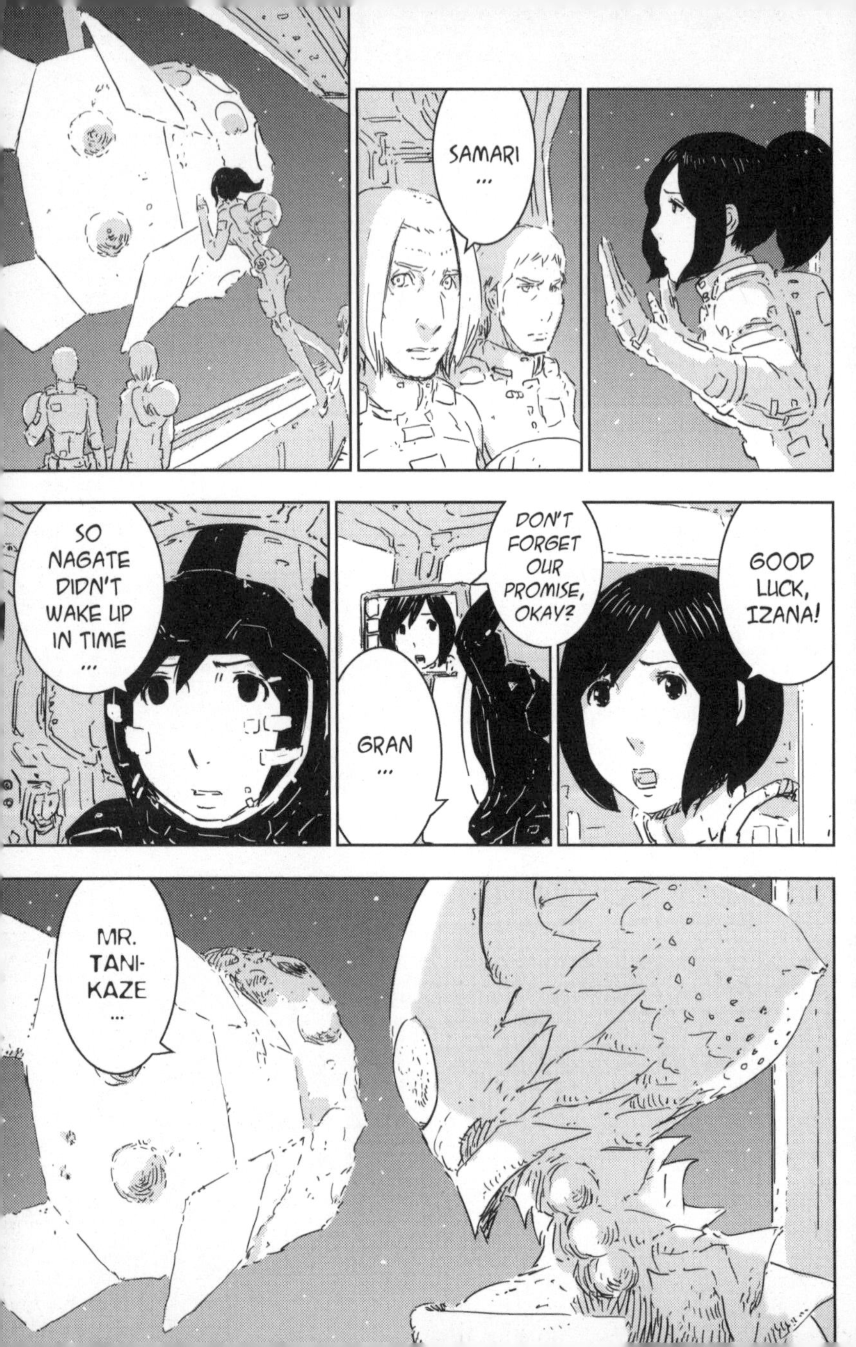
SAMARI ...
GOOD LUCK, IZANA!
DON'T FORGET OUR PROMISE, OKAY?
GRAN ...
SO NAGATE DIDN'T WAKE UP IN TIME ...
MR. TANI-KAZE ...

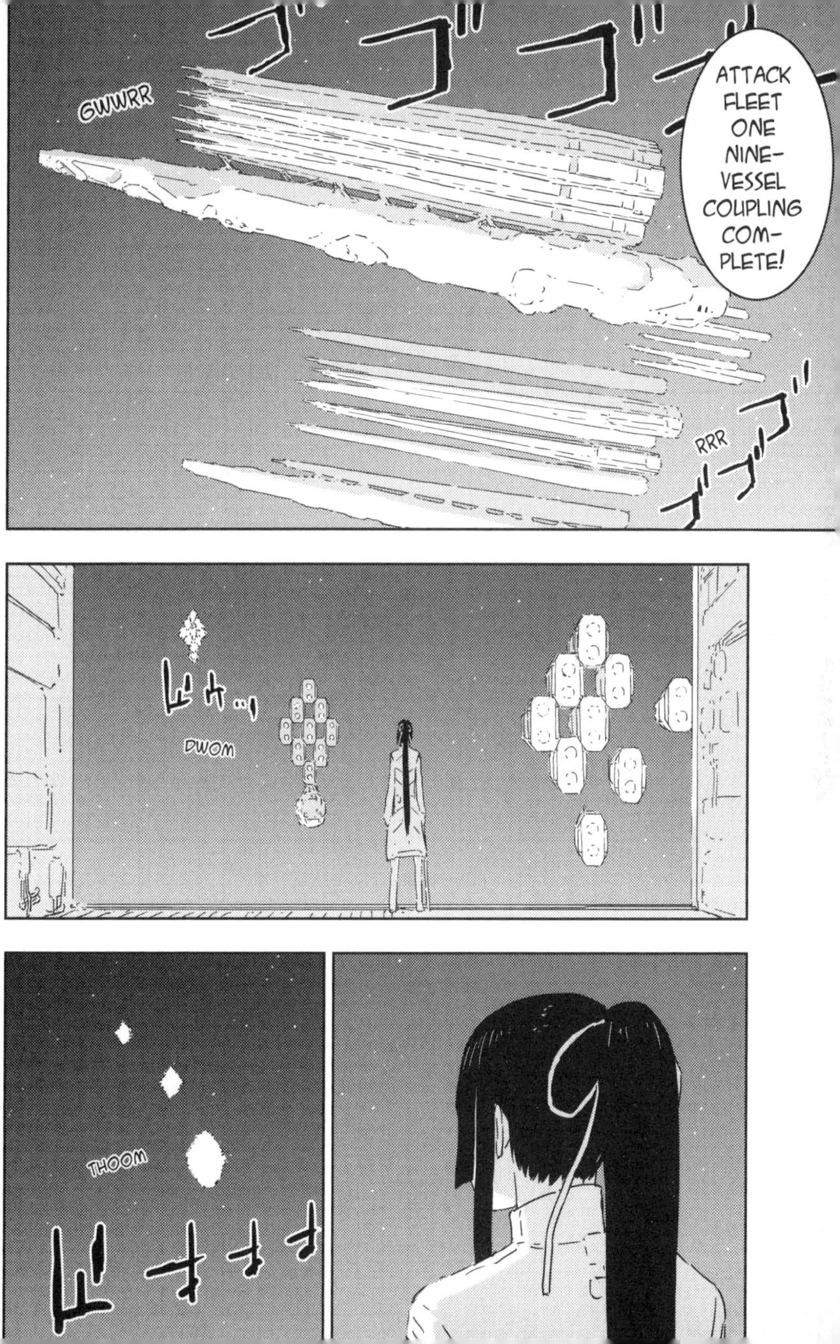
GWWRR
ATTACK FLEET ONE NINE-VESSEL COUPLING COM-PLETE!
RRR
DWOM
THOOM

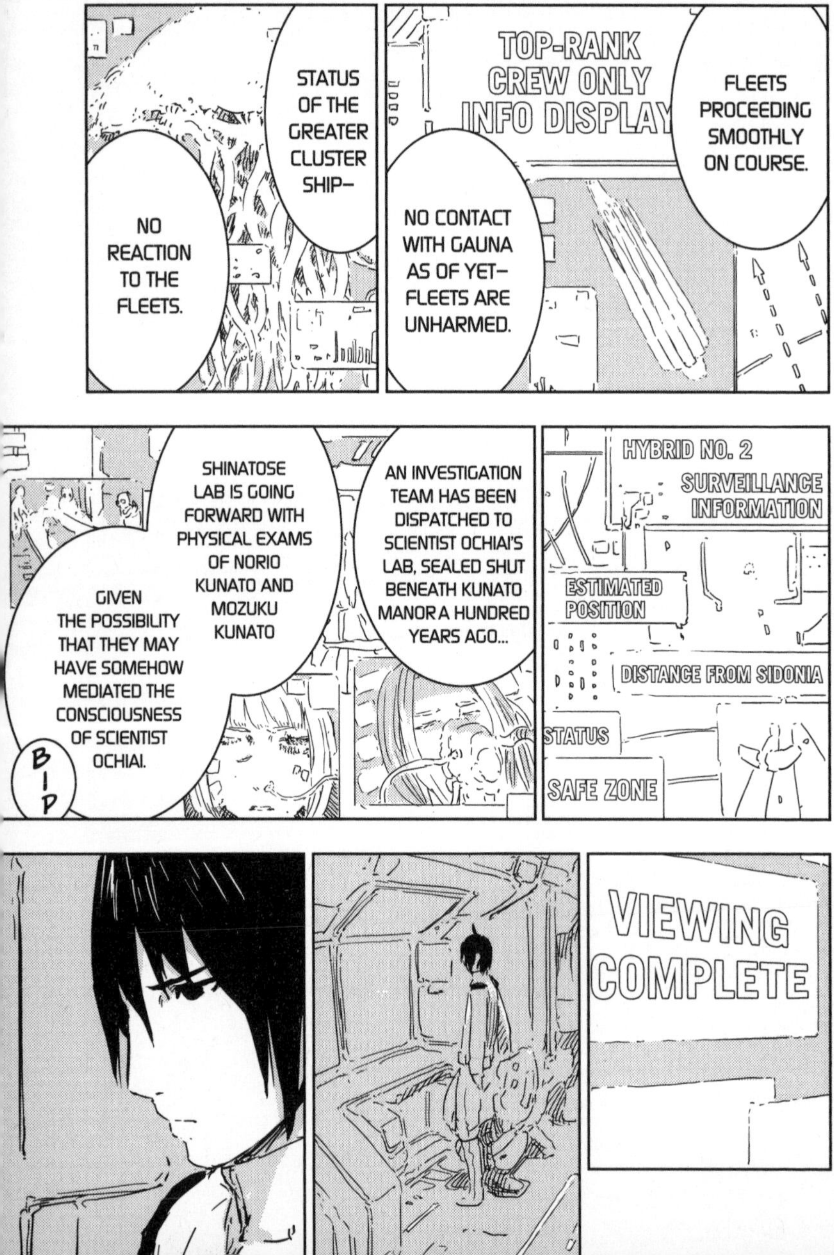
TOP-RANK CREW ONLY INFO DISPLAY
FLEETS PROCEEDING SMOOTHLY ON COURSE.
NO CONTACT WITH GAUNA AS OF YET— FLEETS ARE UNHARMED.
STATUS OF THE GREATER CLUSTER SHIP—
NO REACTION TO THE FLEETS.
HYBRID NO. 2
SURVEILLANCE INFORMATION
ESTIMATED POSITION
DISTANCE FROM SIDONIA
STATUS
SAFE ZONE
AN INVESTIGATION TEAM HAS BEEN DISPATCHED TO SCIENTIST OCHIAI'S LAB, SEALED SHUT BENEATH KUNATO MANOR A HUNDRED YEARS AGO...
SHINATOSE LAB IS GOING FORWARD WITH PHYSICAL EXAMS OF NORIO KUNATO AND MOZUKU KUNATO
GIVEN THE POSSIBILITY THAT THEY MAY HAVE SOMEHOW MEDIATED THE CONSCIOUSNESS OF SCIENTIST OCHIAI.
BIP
VIEWING COMPLETE

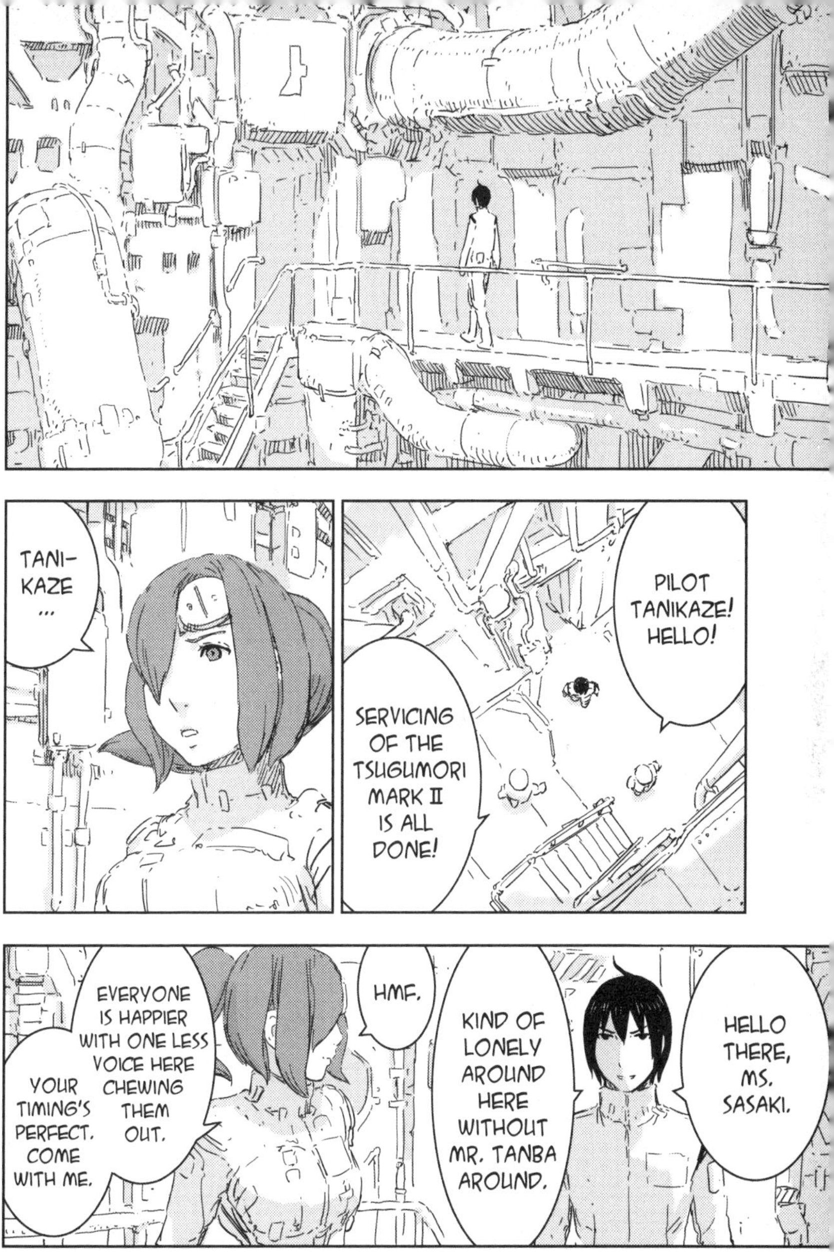
PILOT TANIKAZE! HELLO!
SERVICING OF THE TSUGUMORI MARK II IS ALL DONE!
TANI-KAZE ...
HELLO THERE, MS. SASAKI.
KIND OF LONELY AROUND HERE WITHOUT MR. TANBA AROUND.
HMF.
EVERYONE IS HAPPIER WITH ONE LESS VOICE HERE CHEWING THEM OUT.
YOUR TIMING'S PERFECT. COME WITH ME.

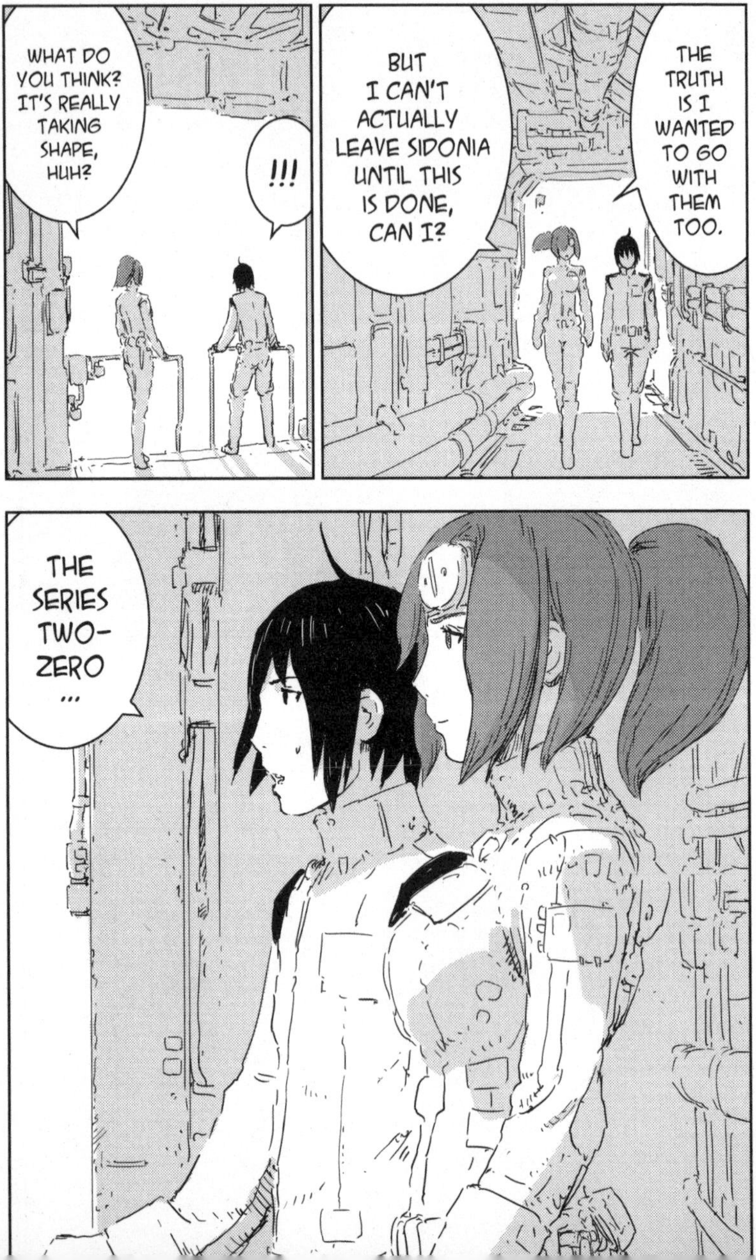
THE TRUTH IS I WANTED TO GO WITH THEM TOO.
BUT I CAN'T ACTUALLY LEAVE SIDONIA UNTIL THIS IS DONE, CAN I?
WHAT DO YOU THINK? IT'S REALLY TAKING SHAPE, HUH?
!!!
THE SERIES TWO-ZERO ...

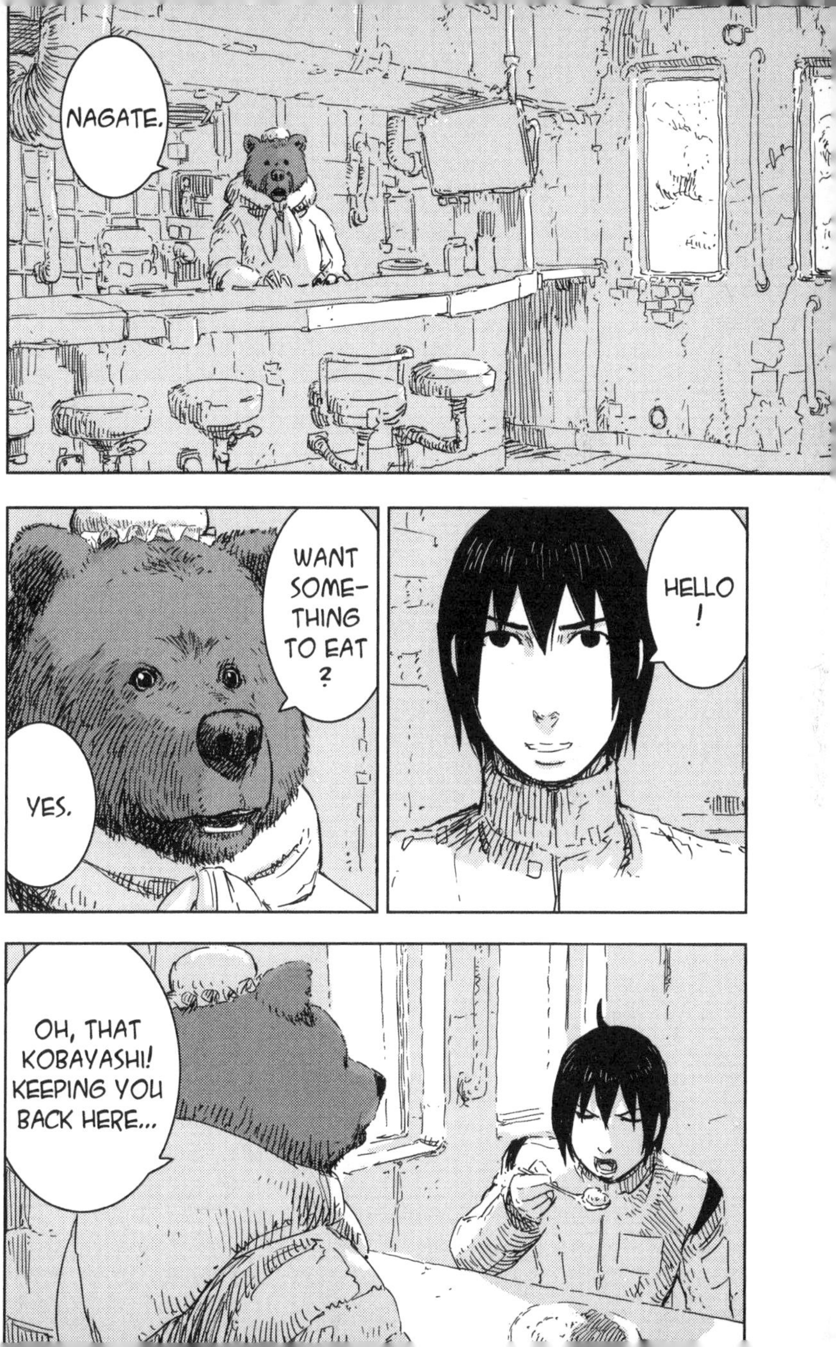
NAGATE.
HELLO!
WANT SOME-THING TO EAT?
YES.
OH, THAT KOBAYASHI! KEEPING YOU BACK HERE...

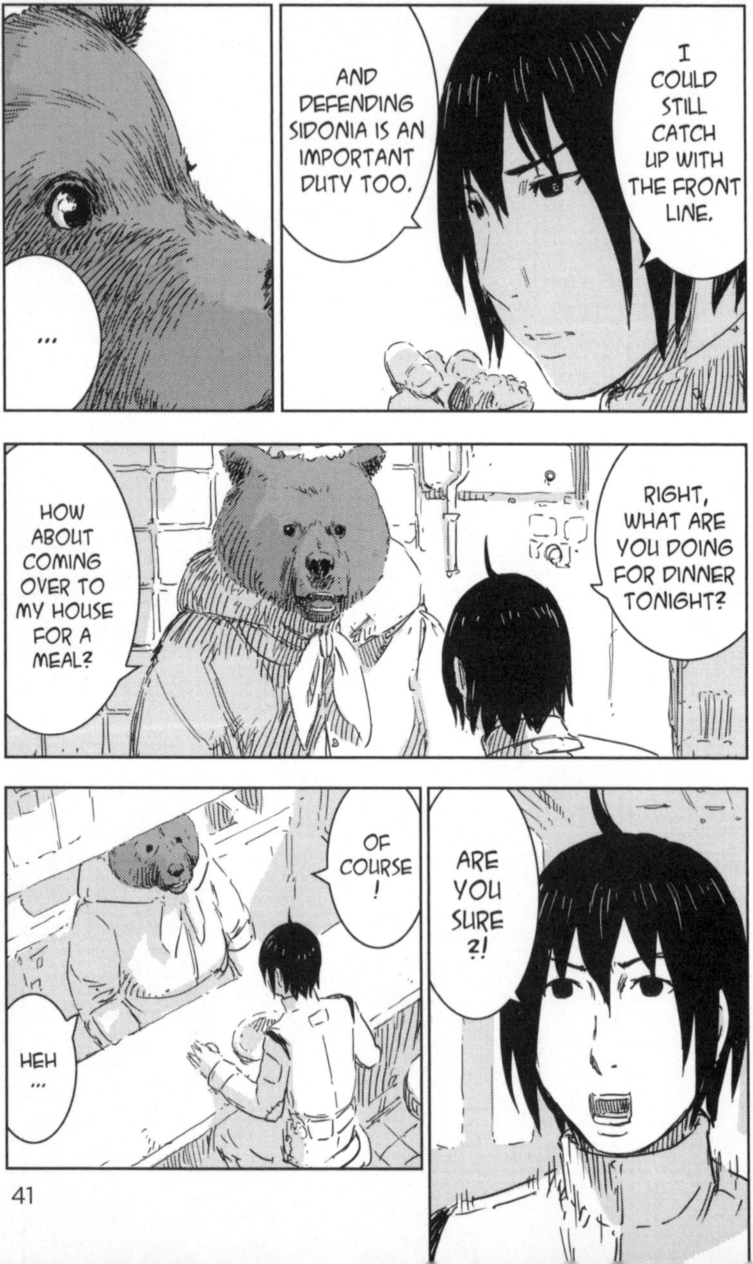
I COULD STILL CATCH UP WITH THE FRONT LINE.
AND DEFENDING SIDONIA IS AN IMPORTANT DUTY TOO.
...
RIGHT, WHAT ARE YOU DOING FOR DINNER TONIGHT?
HOW ABOUT COMING OVER TO MY HOUSE FOR A MEAL?
ARE YOU SURE?!
OF COURSE!
HEH...

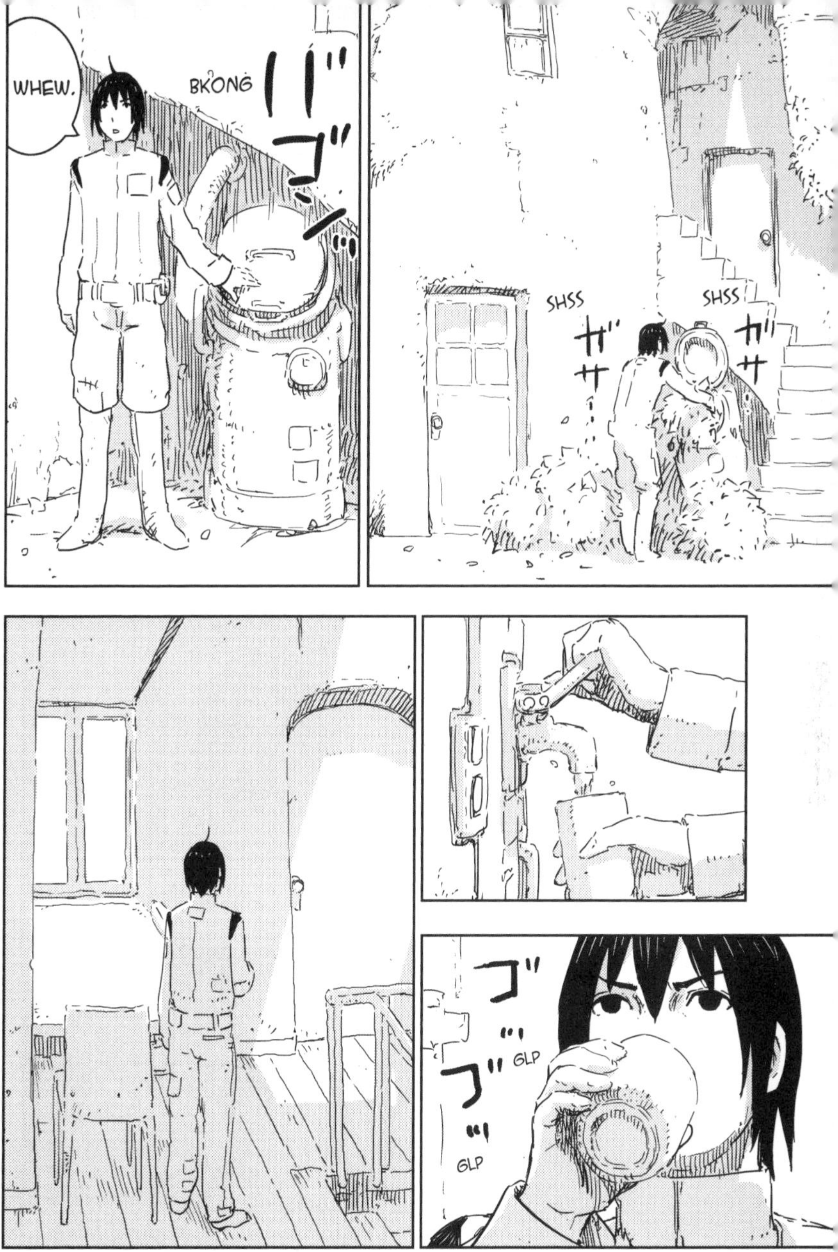
SHSS
ガサ
SHSS
ガサ
WHEW.
BKONG
GLP
GLP

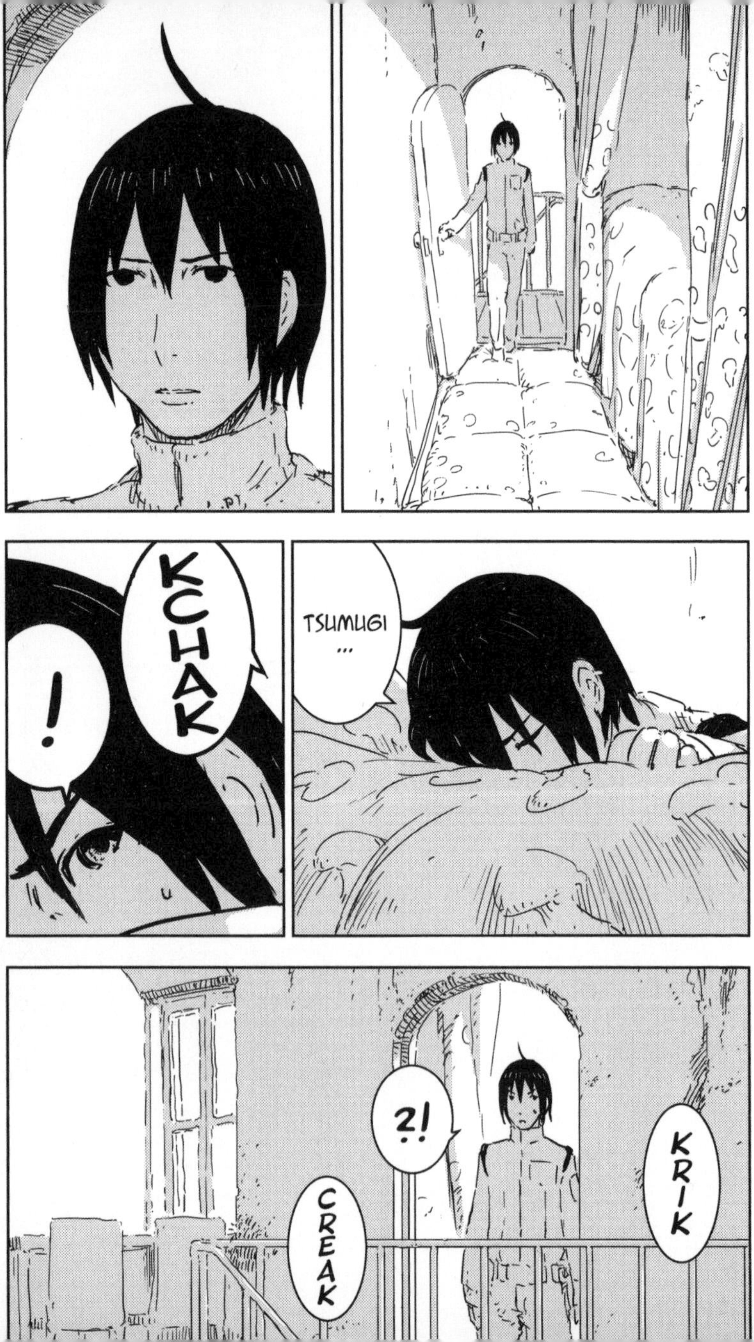
TSUMUGI ...
KCHAK
!
KRIK
?!
CREAK

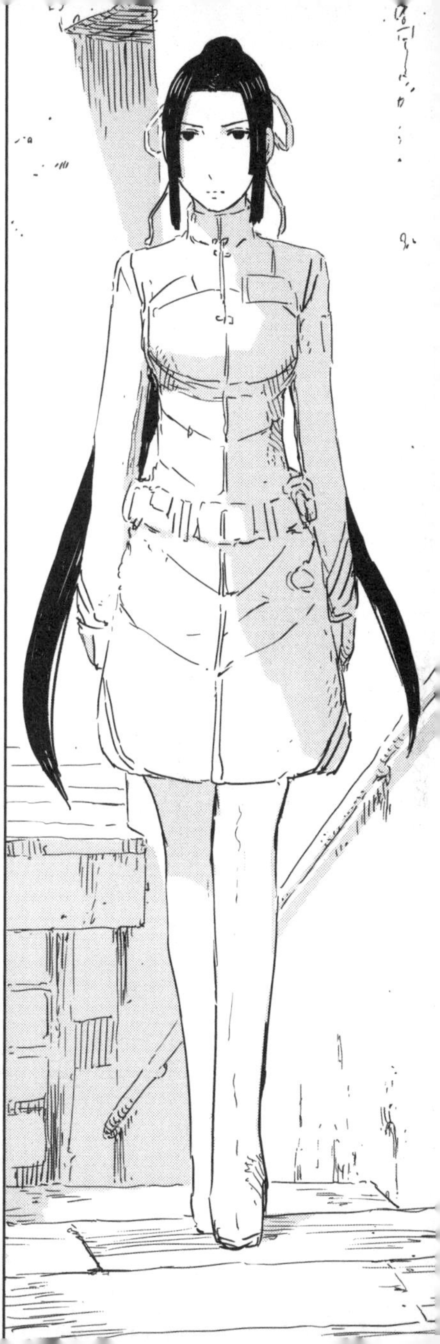
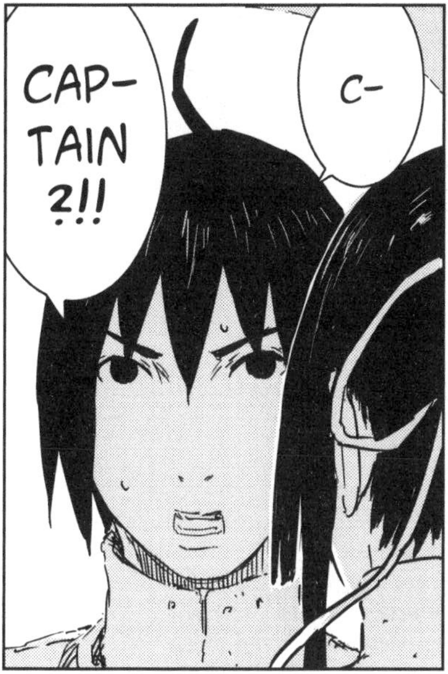
C-
CAP-TAIN?!!
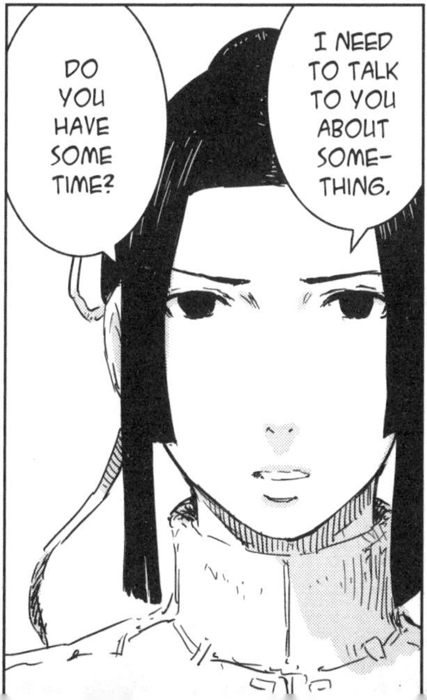
I NEED TO TALK TO YOU ABOUT SOME-THING.
DO YOU HAVE SOME TIME?

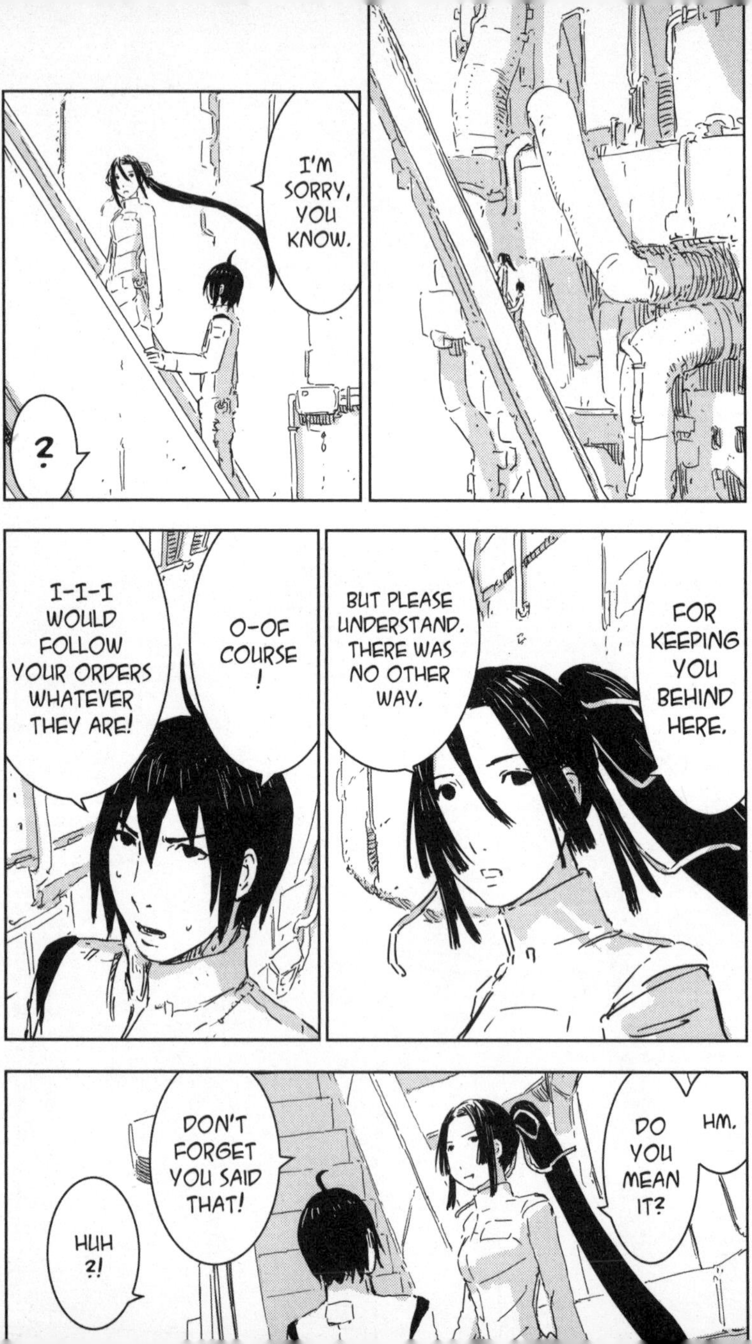
I'M SORRY, YOU KNOW.
?
FOR KEEPING YOU BEHIND HERE.
BUT PLEASE UNDERSTAND. THERE WAS NO OTHER WAY.
O-OF COURSE!
I-I-I WOULD FOLLOW YOUR ORDERS WHATEVER THEY ARE!
HM.
DO YOU MEAN IT?
DON'T FORGET YOU SAID THAT!
HUH?!

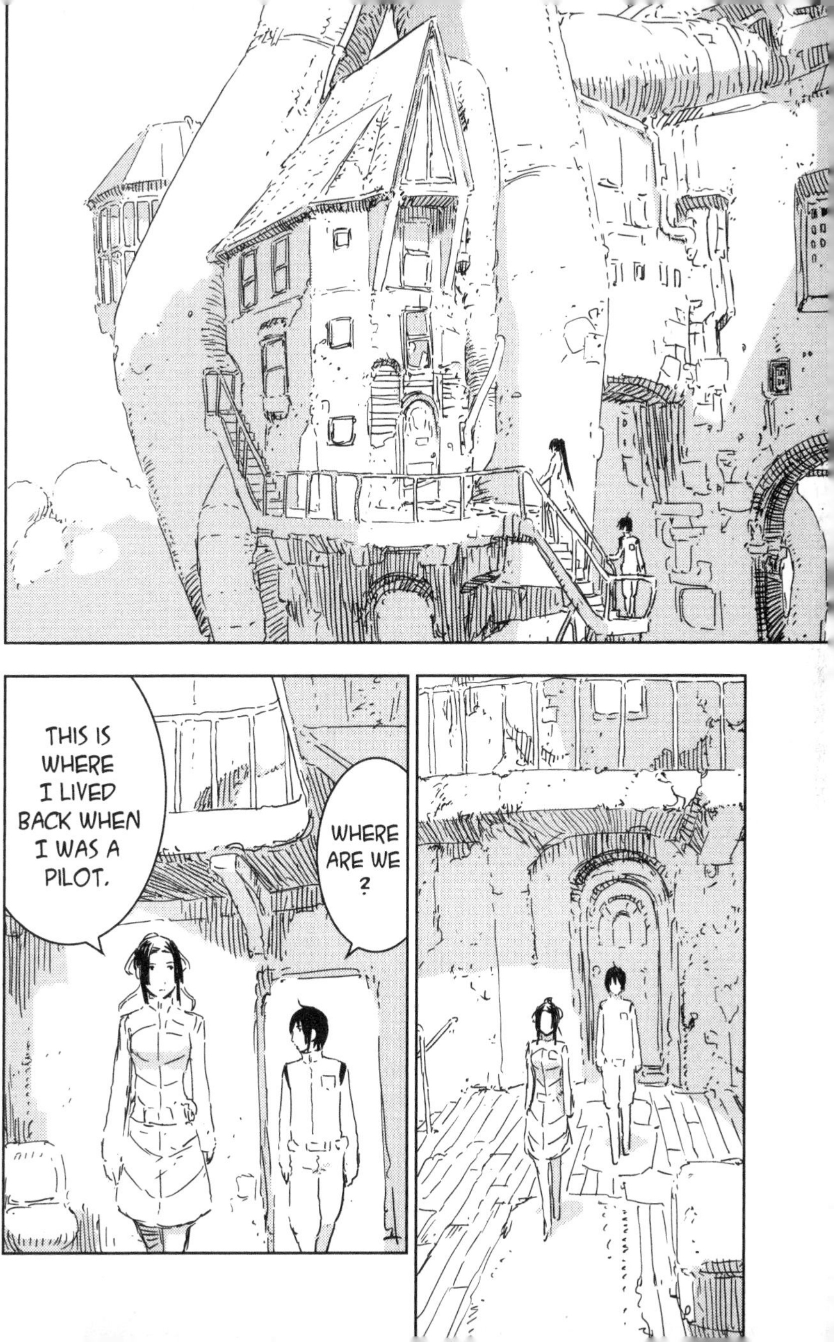
WHERE ARE WE ?
THIS IS WHERE I LIVED BACK WHEN I WAS A PILOT.

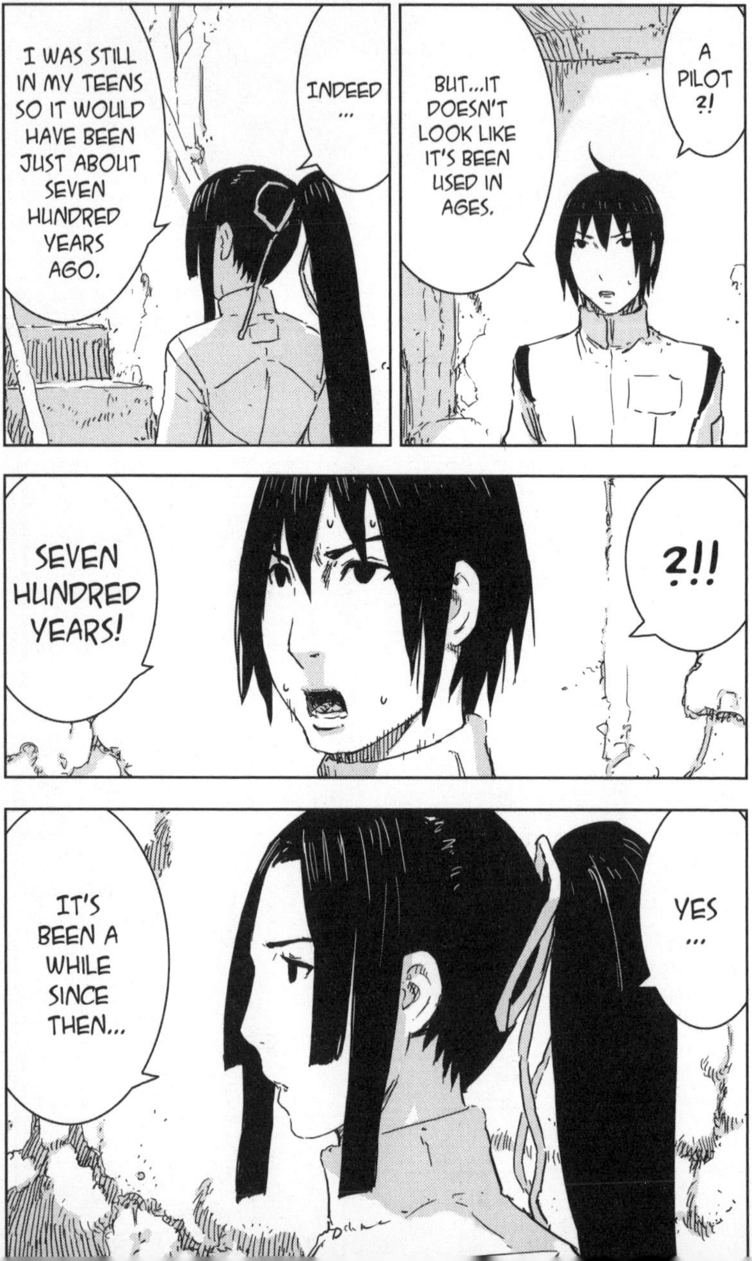
A PILOT ?!
BUT...IT DOESN'T LOOK LIKE IT'S BEEN USED IN AGES.
INDEED ...
I WAS STILL IN MY TEENS SO IT WOULD HAVE BEEN JUST ABOUT SEVEN HUNDRED YEARS AGO.
?!!
SEVEN HUNDRED YEARS!
YES ...
IT'S BEEN A WHILE SINCE THEN...

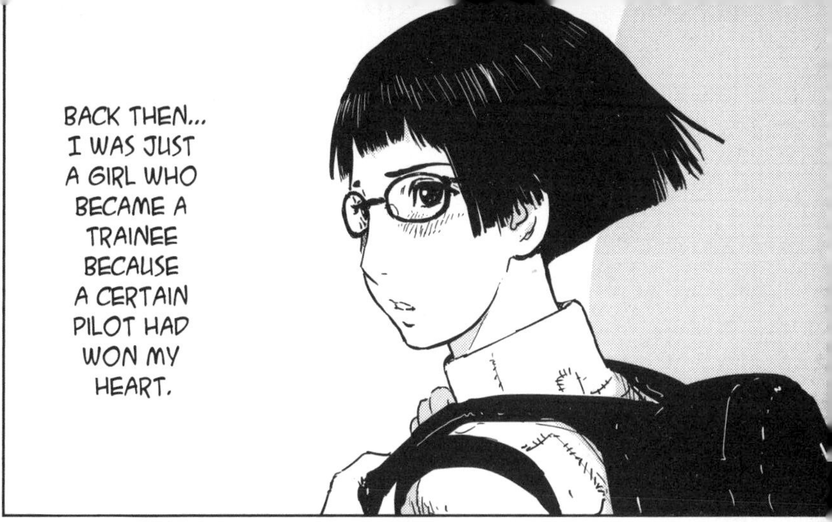
BACK THEN... I WAS JUST A GIRL WHO BECAME A TRAINEE BECAUSE A CERTAIN PILOT HAD WON MY HEART.
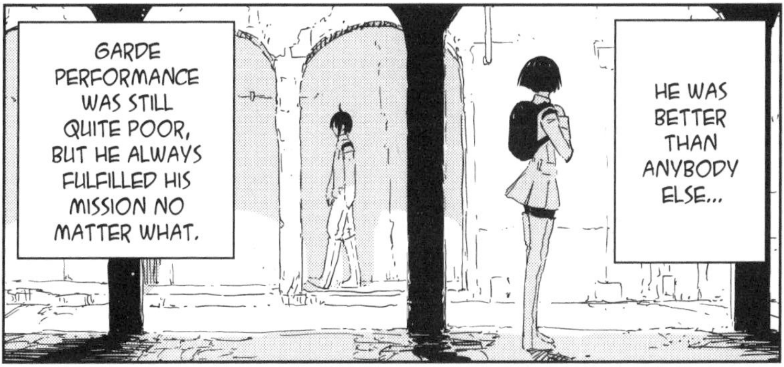
HE WAS BETTER THAN ANYBODY ELSE...
GARDE PERFORMANCE WAS STILL QUITE POOR, BUT HE ALWAYS FULFILLED HIS MISSION NO MATTER WHAT.
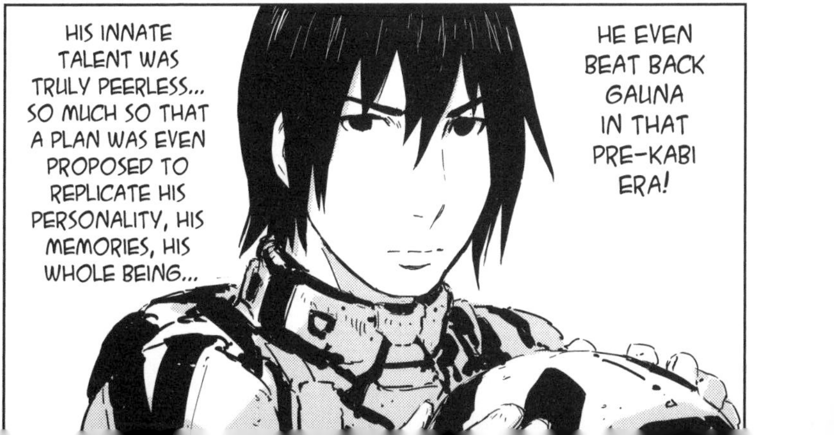
HE EVEN BEAT BACK GAUNA IN THAT PRE-KABI ERA!
HIS INNATE TALENT WAS TRULY PEERLESS... SO MUCH SO THAT A PLAN WAS EVEN PROPOSED TO REPLICATE HIS PERSONALITY, HIS MEMORIES, HIS WHOLE BEING...

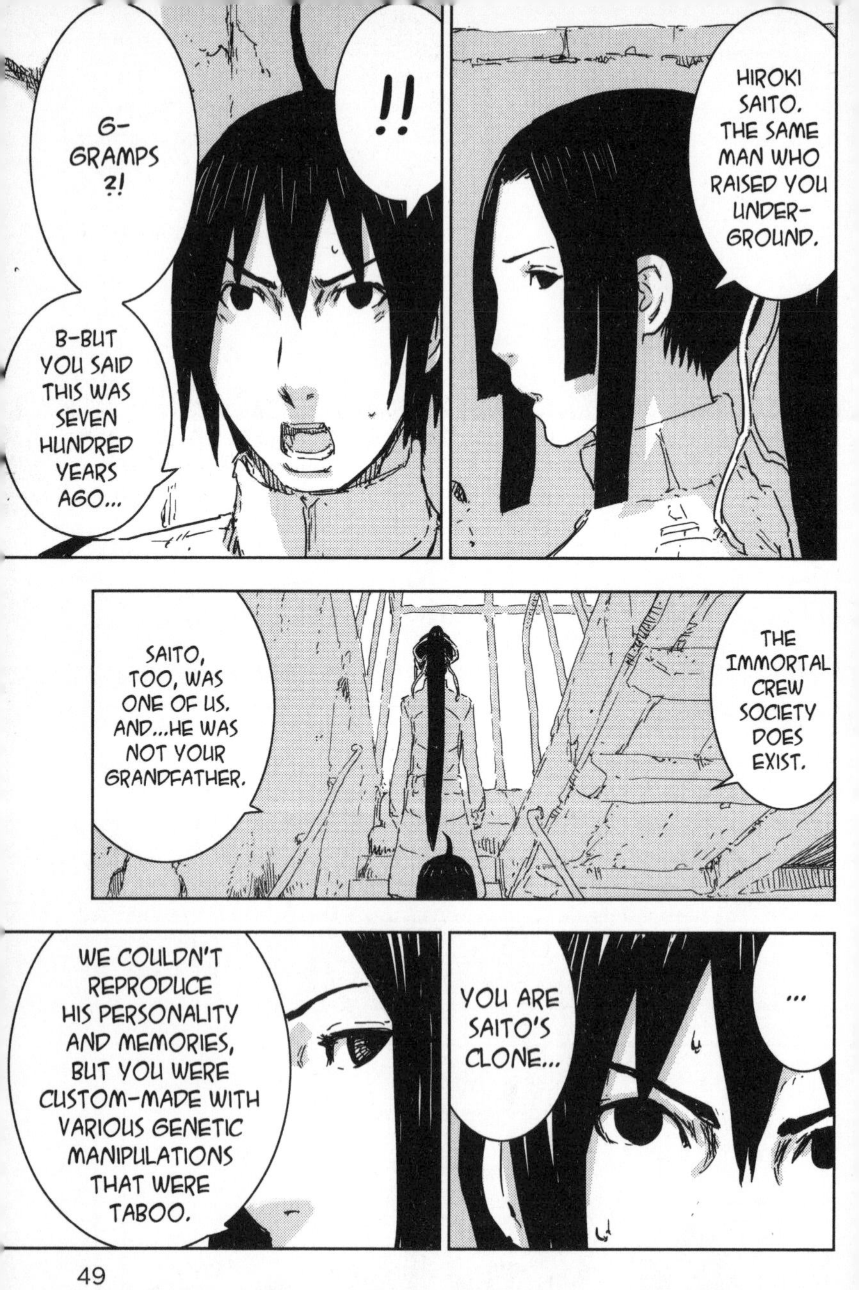
HIROKI SAITO. THE SAME MAN WHO RAISED YOU UNDER-GROUND.
!!
G-GRAMPS ?!
B-BUT YOU SAID THIS WAS SEVEN HUNDRED YEARS AGO...
THE IMMORTAL CREW SOCIETY DOES EXIST.
SAITO, TOO, WAS ONE OF US. AND...HE WAS NOT YOUR GRANDFATHER.
...
YOU ARE SAITO'S CLONE...
WE COULDN'T REPRODUCE HIS PERSONALITY AND MEMORIES, BUT YOU WERE CUSTOM-MADE WITH VARIOUS GENETIC MANIPULATIONS THAT WERE TABOO.

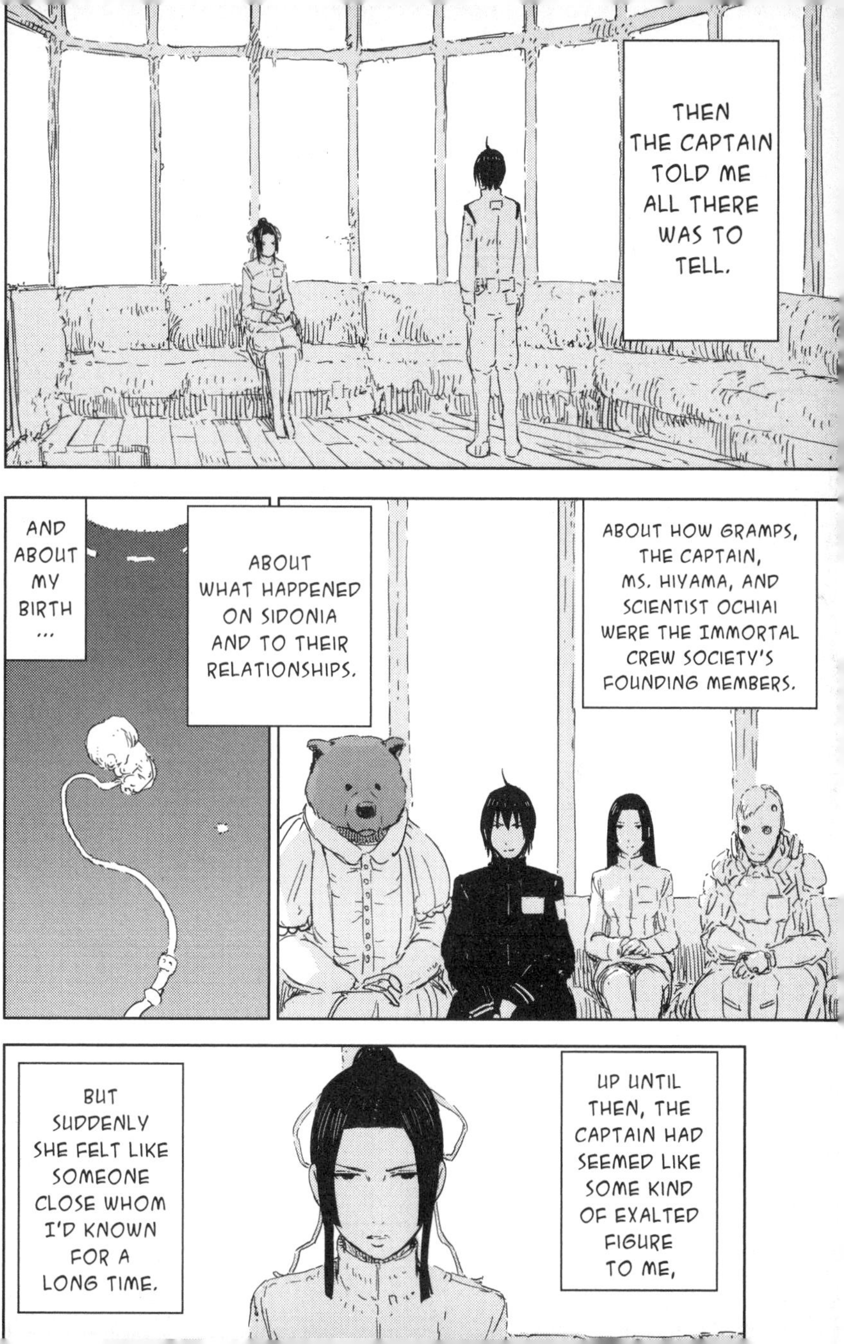
THEN THE CAPTAIN TOLD ME ALL THERE WAS TO TELL.
ABOUT HOW GRAMPS, THE CAPTAIN, MS. HIYAMA, AND SCIENTIST OCHIAI WERE THE IMMORTAL CREW SOCIETY'S FOUNDING MEMBERS.
ABOUT WHAT HAPPENED ON SIDONIA AND TO THEIR RELATIONSHIPS.
AND ABOUT MY BIRTH ...
UP UNTIL THEN, THE CAPTAIN HAD SEEMED LIKE SOME KIND OF EXALTED FIGURE TO ME,
BUT SUDDENLY SHE FELT LIKE SOMEONE CLOSE WHOM I'D KNOWN FOR A LONG TIME.

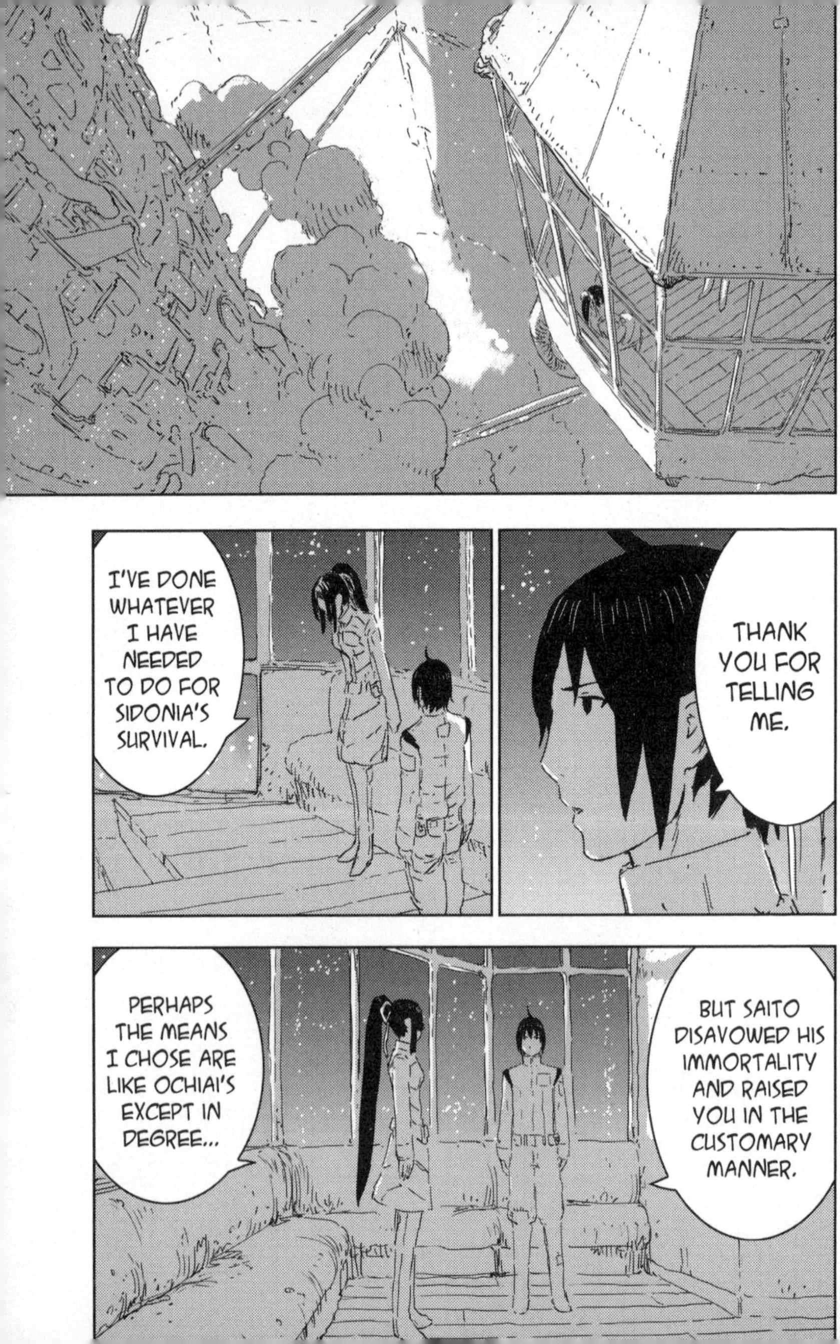
THANK YOU FOR TELLING ME.
I'VE DONE WHATEVER I HAVE NEEDED TO DO FOR SIDONIA'S SURVIVAL.
BUT SAITO DISAVOWED HIS IMMORTALITY AND RAISED YOU IN THE CUSTOMARY MANNER.
PERHAPS THE MEANS I CHOSE ARE LIKE OCHIAI'S EXCEPT IN DEGREE...

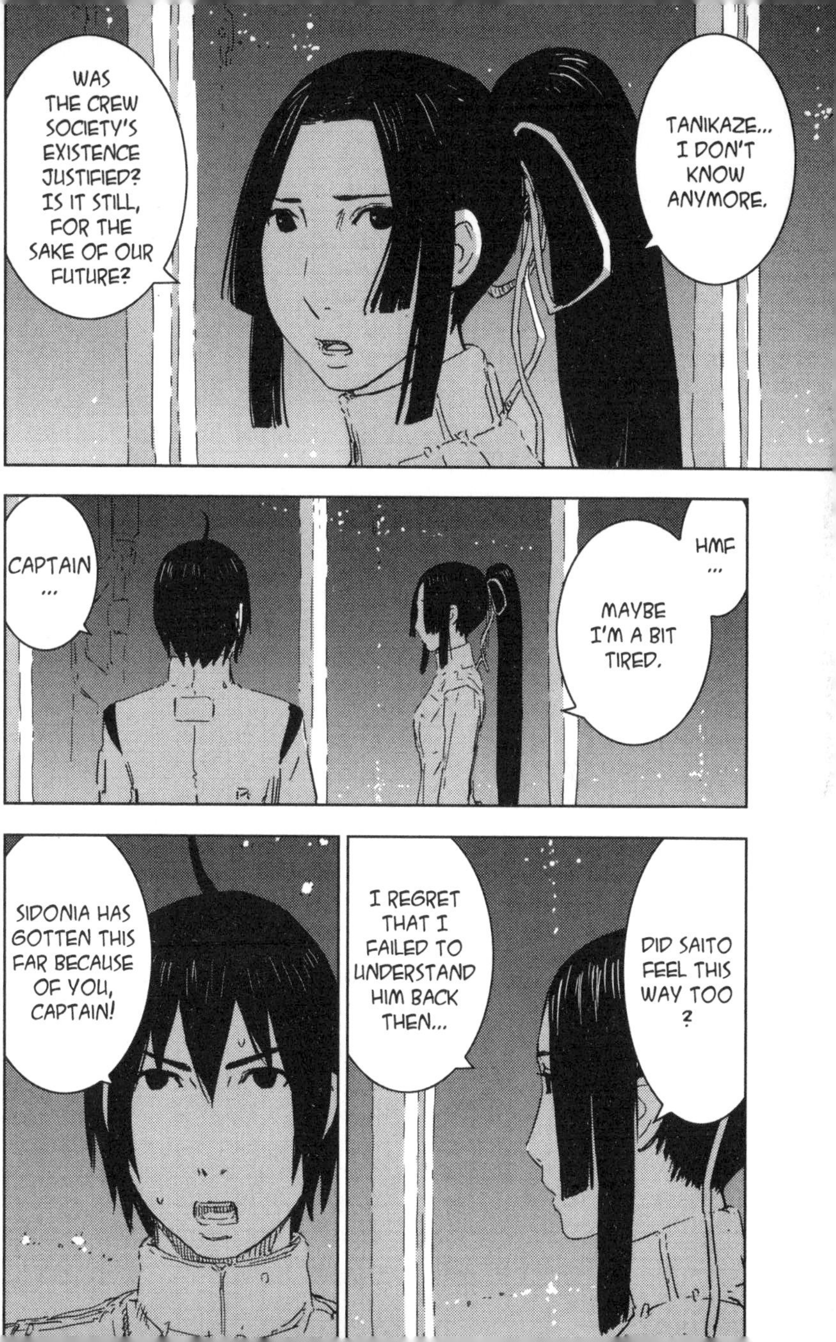
TANIKAZE... I DON'T KNOW ANYMORE.
WAS THE CREW SOCIETY'S EXISTENCE JUSTIFIED? IS IT STILL, FOR THE SAKE OF OUR FUTURE?
HMF... MAYBE I'M A BIT TIRED.
CAPTAIN...
DID SAITO FEEL THIS WAY TOO?
I REGRET THAT I FAILED TO UNDERSTAND HIM BACK THEN...
SIDONIA HAS GOTTEN THIS FAR BECAUSE OF YOU, CAPTAIN!

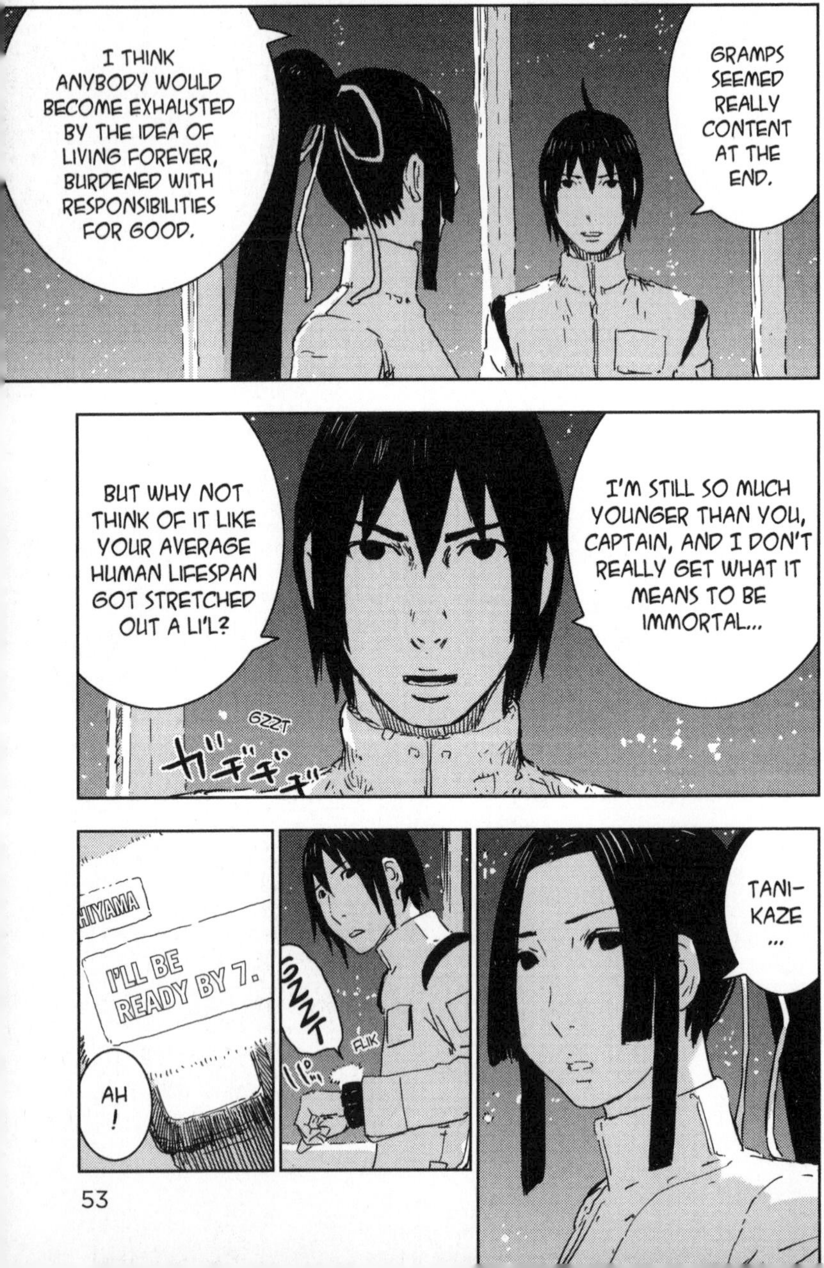
GRAMPS SEEMED REALLY CONTENT AT THE END.
I THINK ANYBODY WOULD BECOME EXHAUSTED BY THE IDEA OF LIVING FOREVER, BURDENED WITH RESPONSIBILITIES FOR GOOD.
I'M STILL SO MUCH YOUNGER THAN YOU, CAPTAIN, AND I DON'T REALLY GET WHAT IT MEANS TO BE IMMORTAL...
BUT WHY NOT THINK OF IT LIKE YOUR AVERAGE HUMAN LIFESPAN GOT STRETCHED OUT A LI'L?
GZZT
TANI-KAZE ...
FLIK
HIYAMA
I'LL BE READY BY 7.
AH !

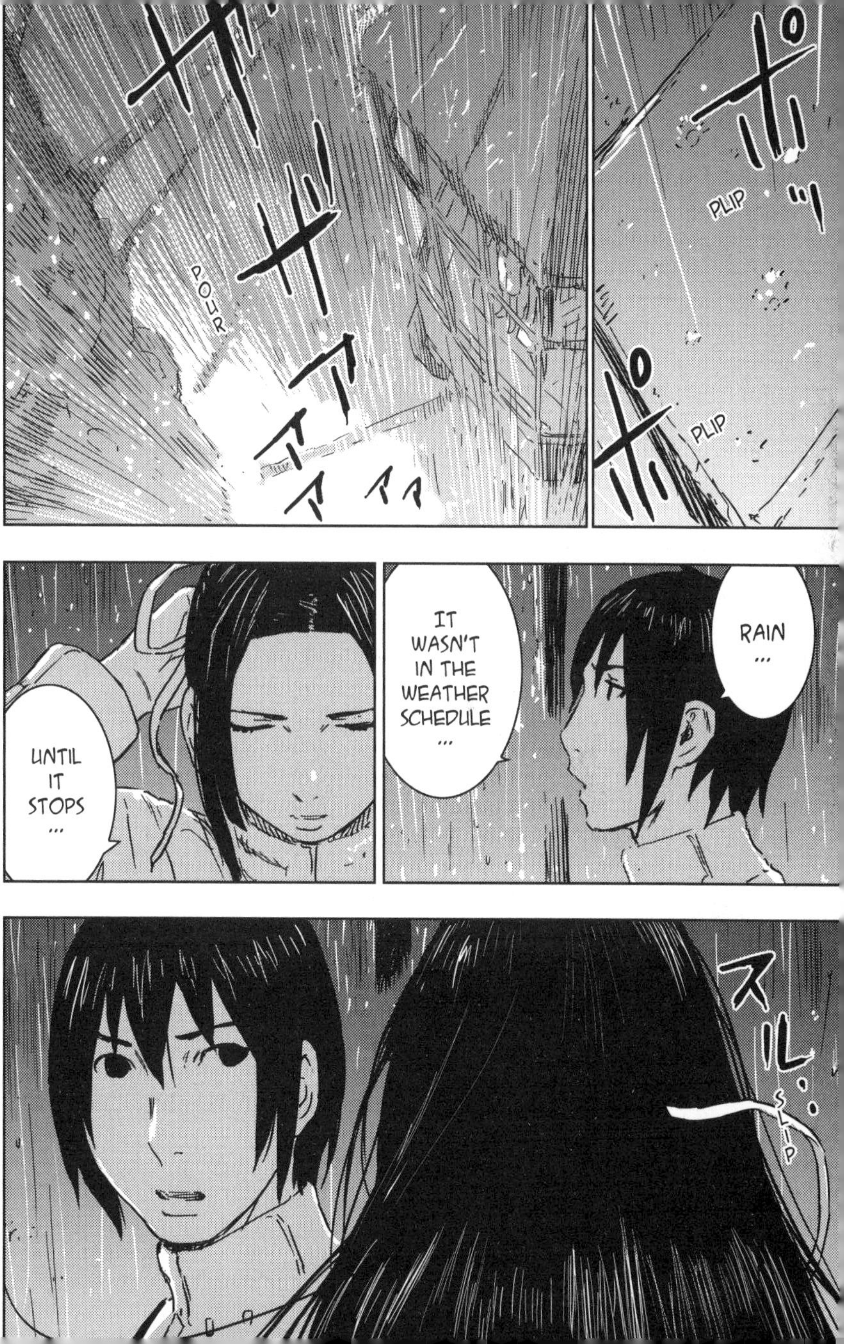
PLIP
PLIP
POUR
RAIN ...
IT WASN'T IN THE WEATHER SCHEDULE ...
UNTIL IT STOPS ...
SLIP

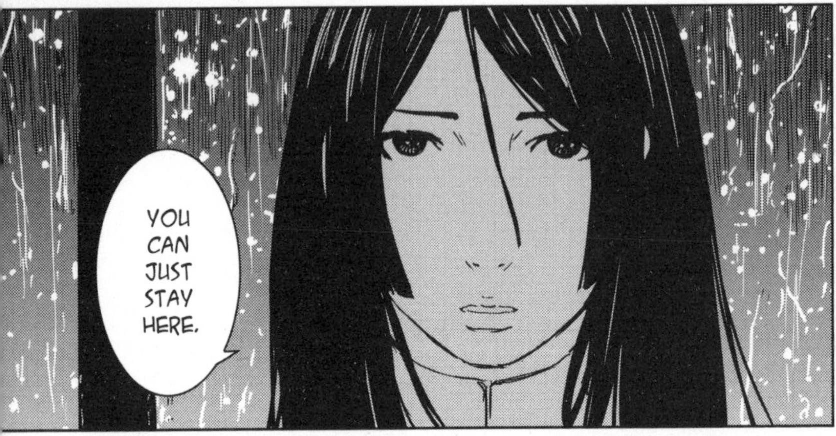
YOU CAN JUST STAY HERE.
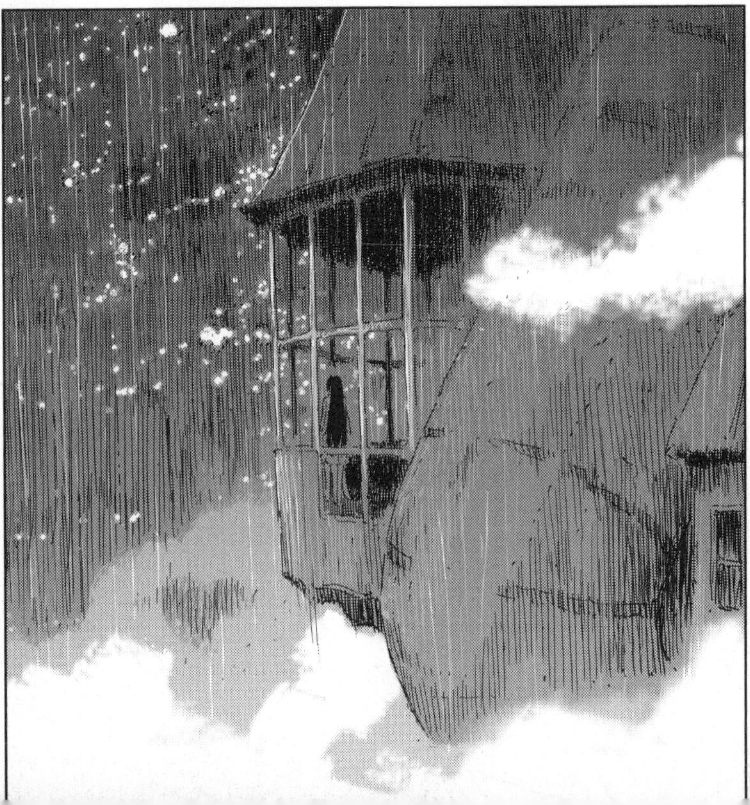

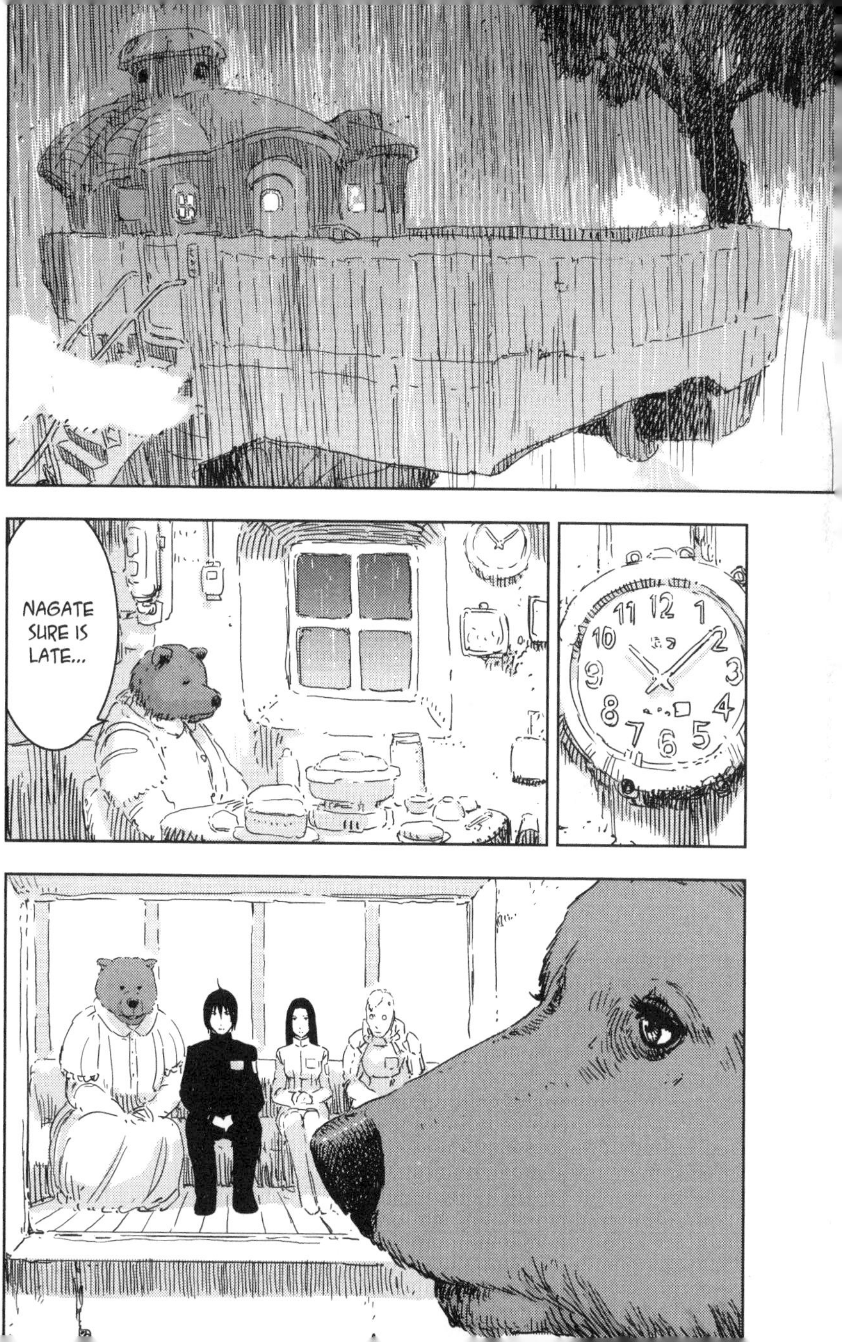
NAGATE SURE IS LATE...

Chapter 67: The Attack Fleets' Pinch

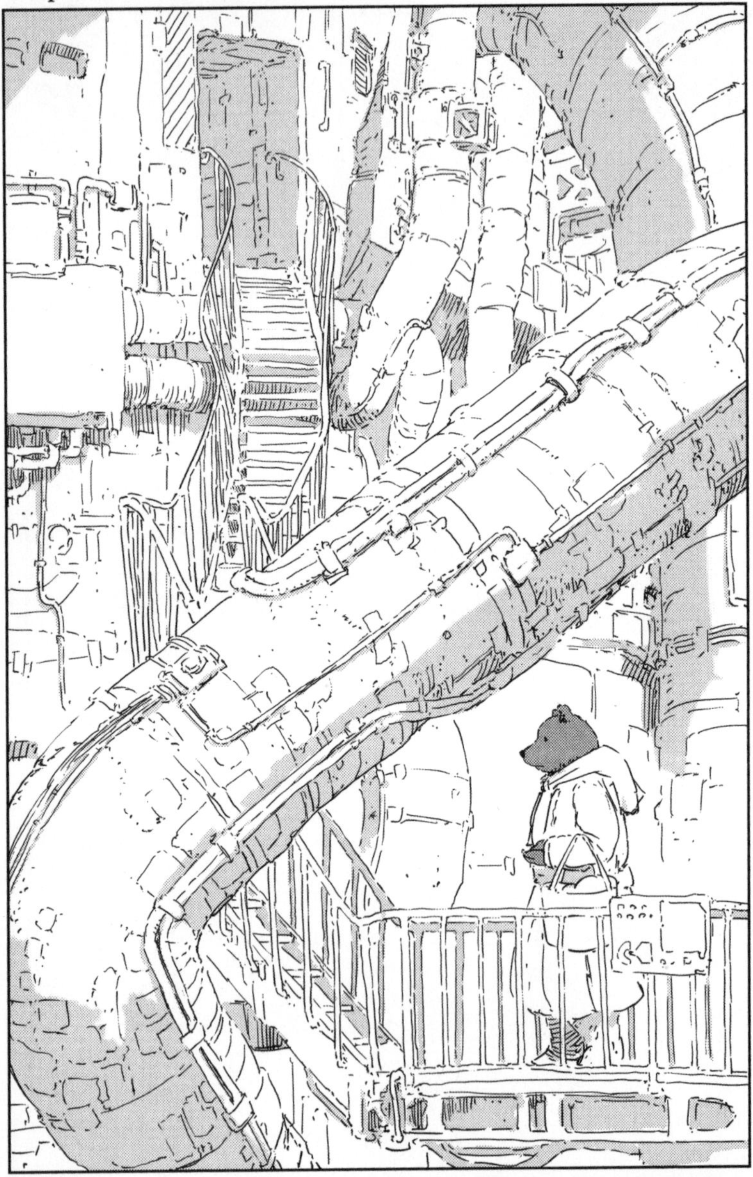

One Hundred Sights of Sidonia Part Fifty-One:
Uppermost Stratum Area Marketplace

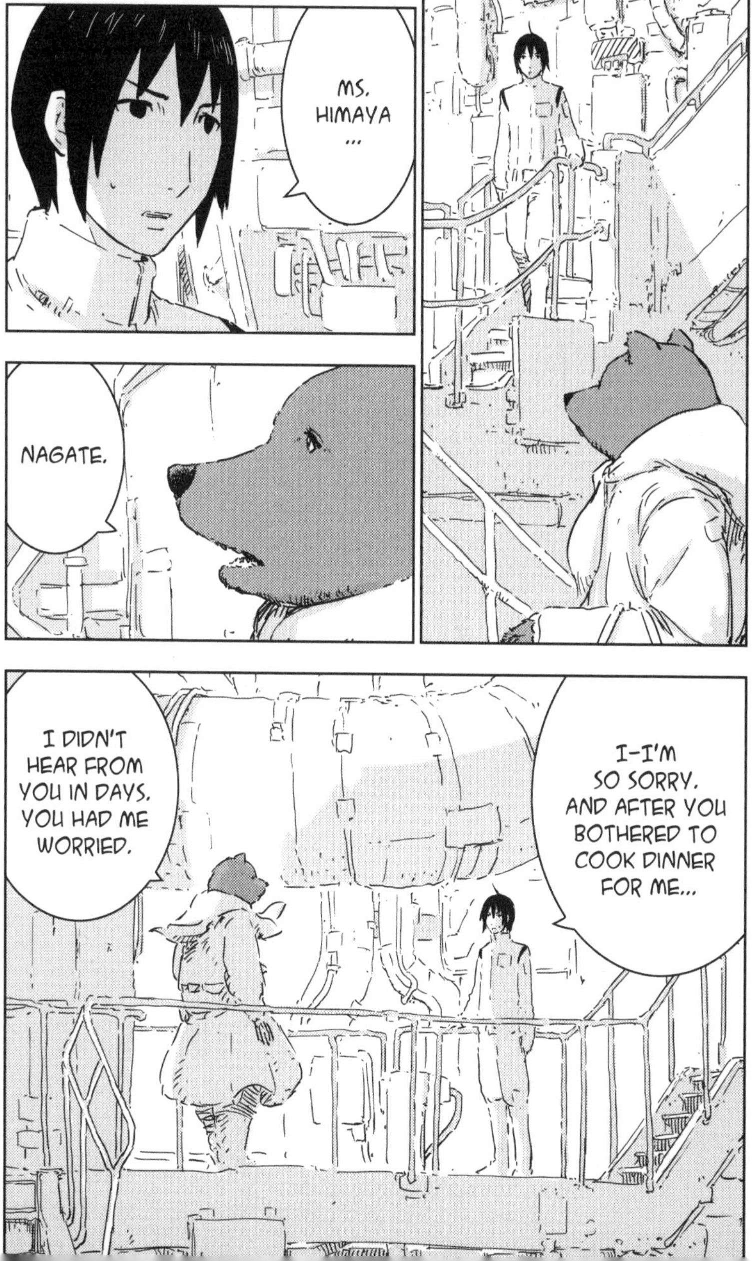
MS. HIMAYA ...
NAGATE.
I DIDN'T HEAR FROM YOU IN DAYS. YOU HAD ME WORRIED.
I-I'M SO SORRY. AND AFTER YOU BOTHERED TO COOK DINNER FOR ME...

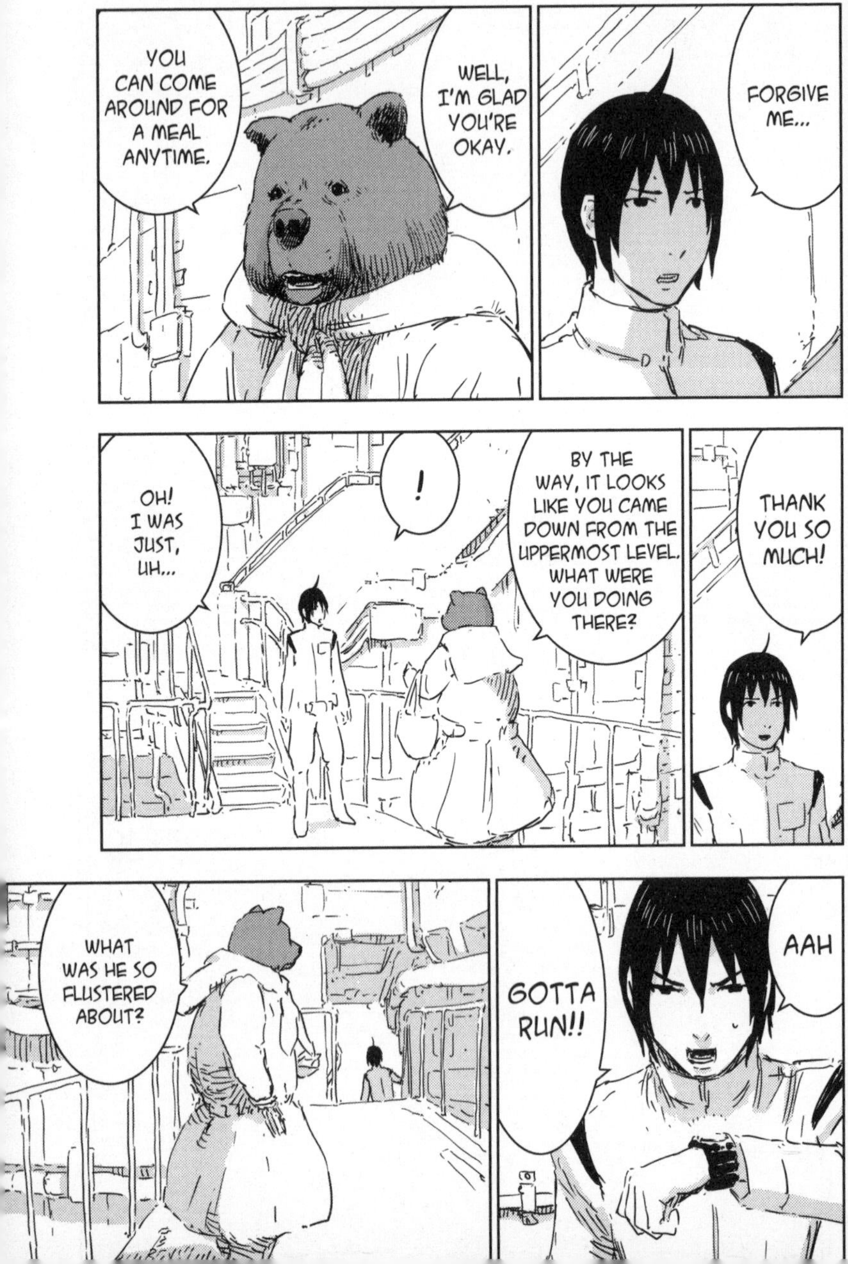
FORGIVE ME...
WELL, I'M GLAD YOU'RE OKAY.
YOU CAN COME AROUND FOR A MEAL ANYTIME.
THANK YOU SO MUCH!
BY THE WAY, IT LOOKS LIKE YOU CAME DOWN FROM THE UPPERMOST LEVEL. WHAT WERE YOU DOING THERE?
!
OH! I WAS JUST, UH...
AAH
GOTTA RUN!!
WHAT WAS HE SO FLUSTERED ABOUT?

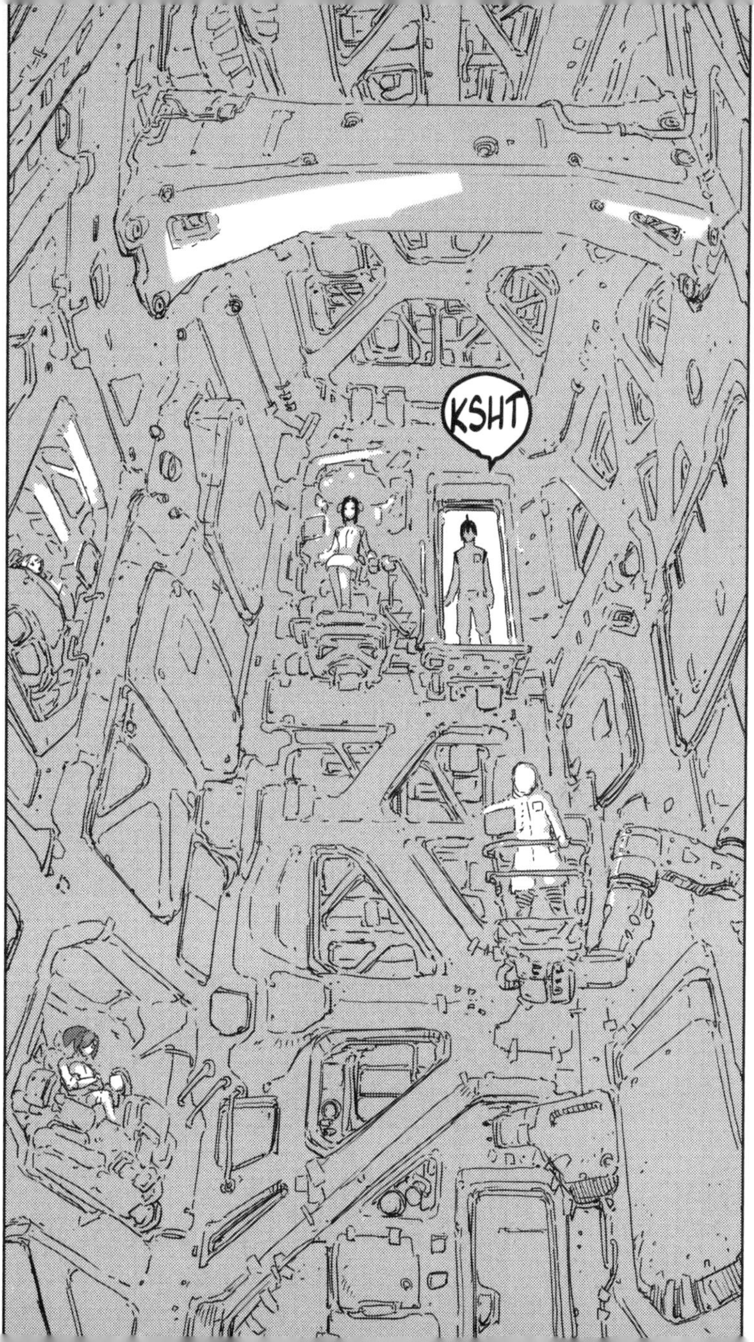
KSHT

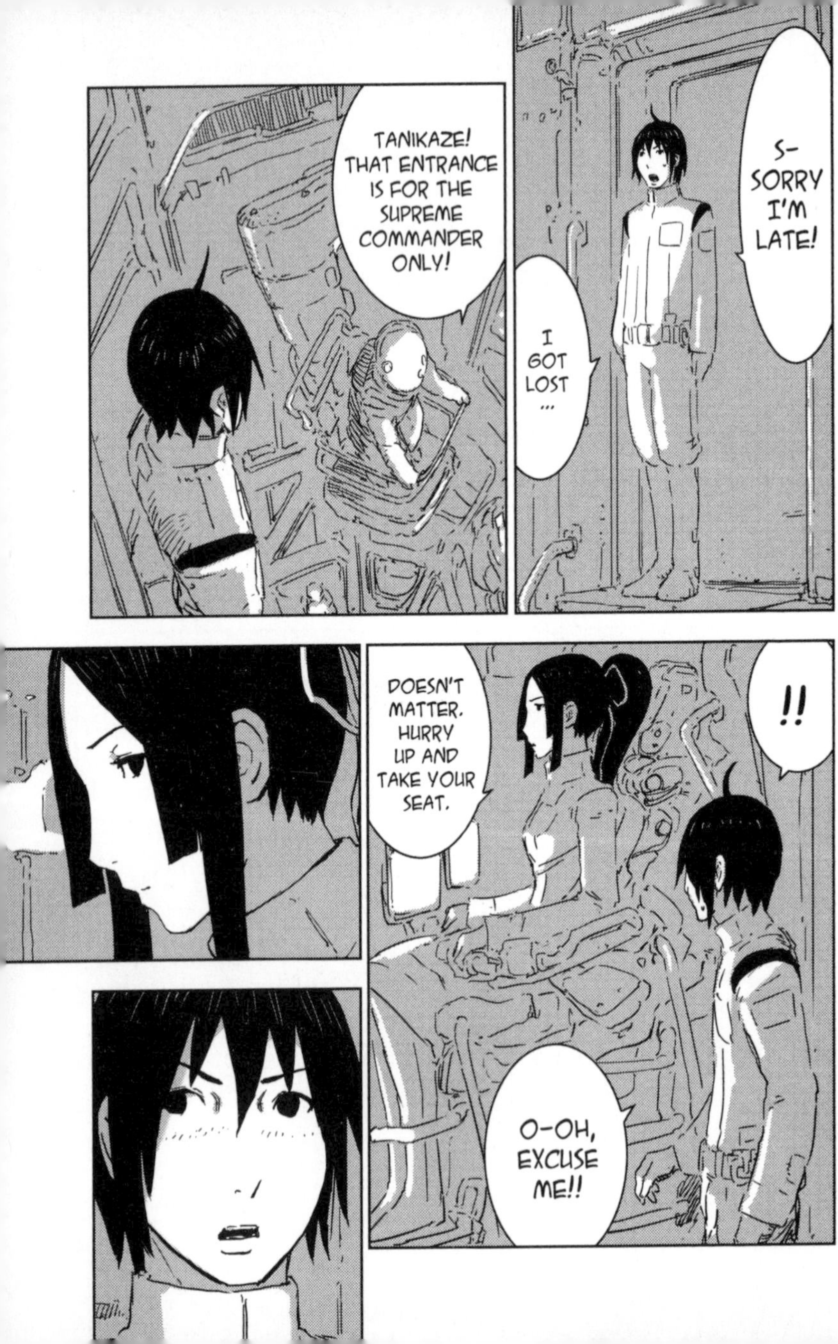
S-SORRY I'M LATE!
I GOT LOST ...
TANIKAZE! THAT ENTRANCE IS FOR THE SUPREME COMMANDER ONLY!
!!
DOESN'T MATTER. HURRY UP AND TAKE YOUR SEAT.
O-OH, EXCUSE ME!!

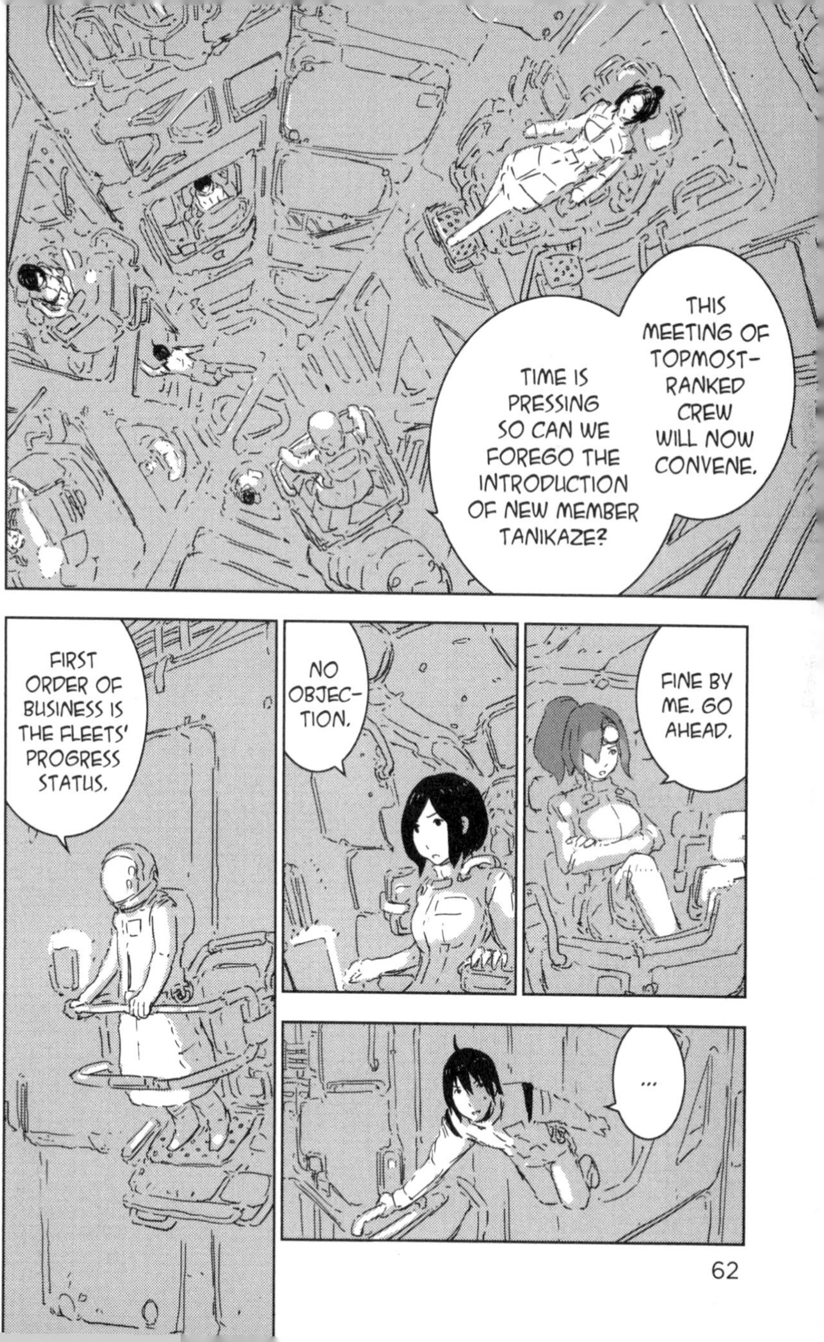
THIS MEETING OF TOPMOST-RANKED CREW WILL NOW CONVENE.
TIME IS PRESSING SO CAN WE FOREGO THE INTRODUCTION OF NEW MEMBER TANIKAZE?
FINE BY ME. GO AHEAD.
NO OBJEC-TION.
...
FIRST ORDER OF BUSINESS IS THE FLEETS' PROGRESS STATUS.

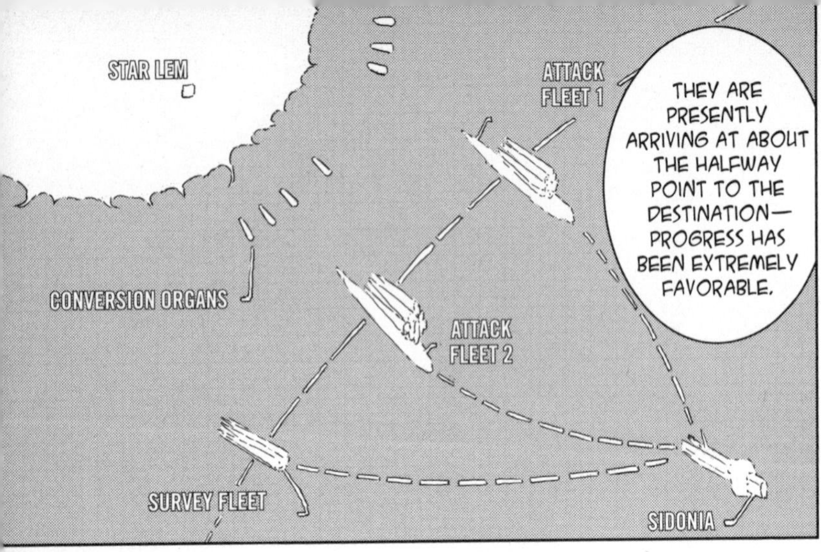
STAR LEM
ATTACK FLEET 1
THEY ARE PRESENTLY ARRIVING AT ABOUT THE HALFWAY POINT TO THE DESTINATION—PROGRESS HAS BEEN EXTREMELY FAVORABLE.
CONVERSION ORGANS
ATTACK FLEET 2
SURVEY FLEET
SIDONIA

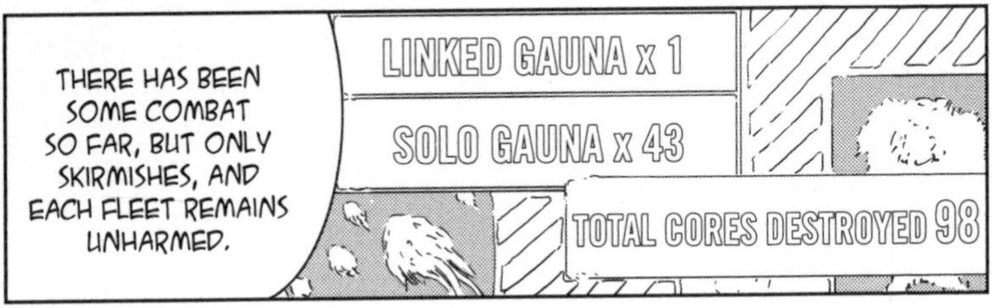
LINKED GAUNA x 1
SOLO GAUNA x 43
TOTAL CORES DESTROYED 98
THERE HAS BEEN SOME COMBAT SO FAR, BUT ONLY SKIRMISHES, AND EACH FLEET REMAINS UNHARMED.

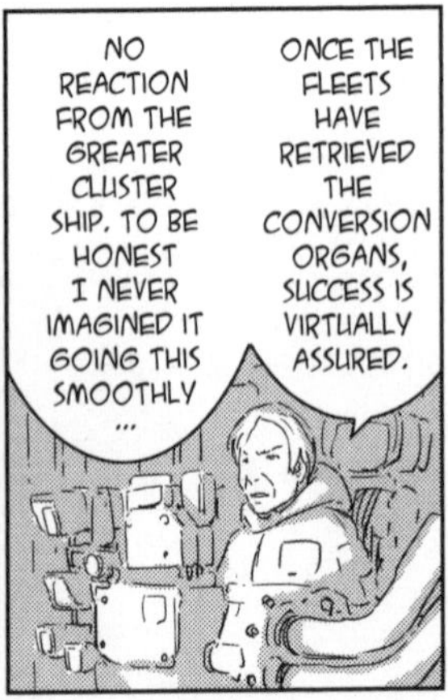
ONCE THE FLEETS HAVE RETRIEVED THE CONVERSION ORGANS, SUCCESS IS VIRTUALLY ASSURED.
NO REACTION FROM THE GREATER CLUSTER SHIP. TO BE HONEST I NEVER IMAGINED IT GOING THIS SMOOTHLY...

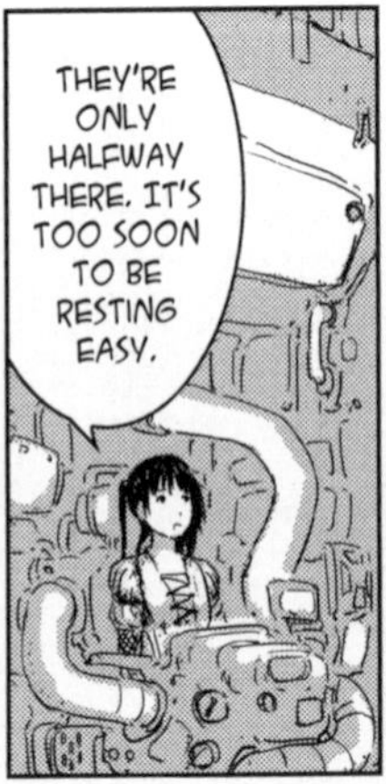
THEY'RE ONLY HALFWAY THERE. IT'S TOO SOON TO BE RESTING EASY.

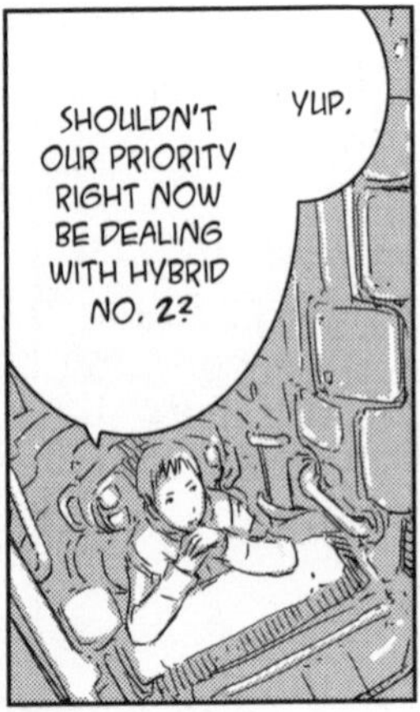
SHOULDN'T OUR PRIORITY RIGHT NOW BE DEALING WITH HYBRID NO. 2?
YUP.

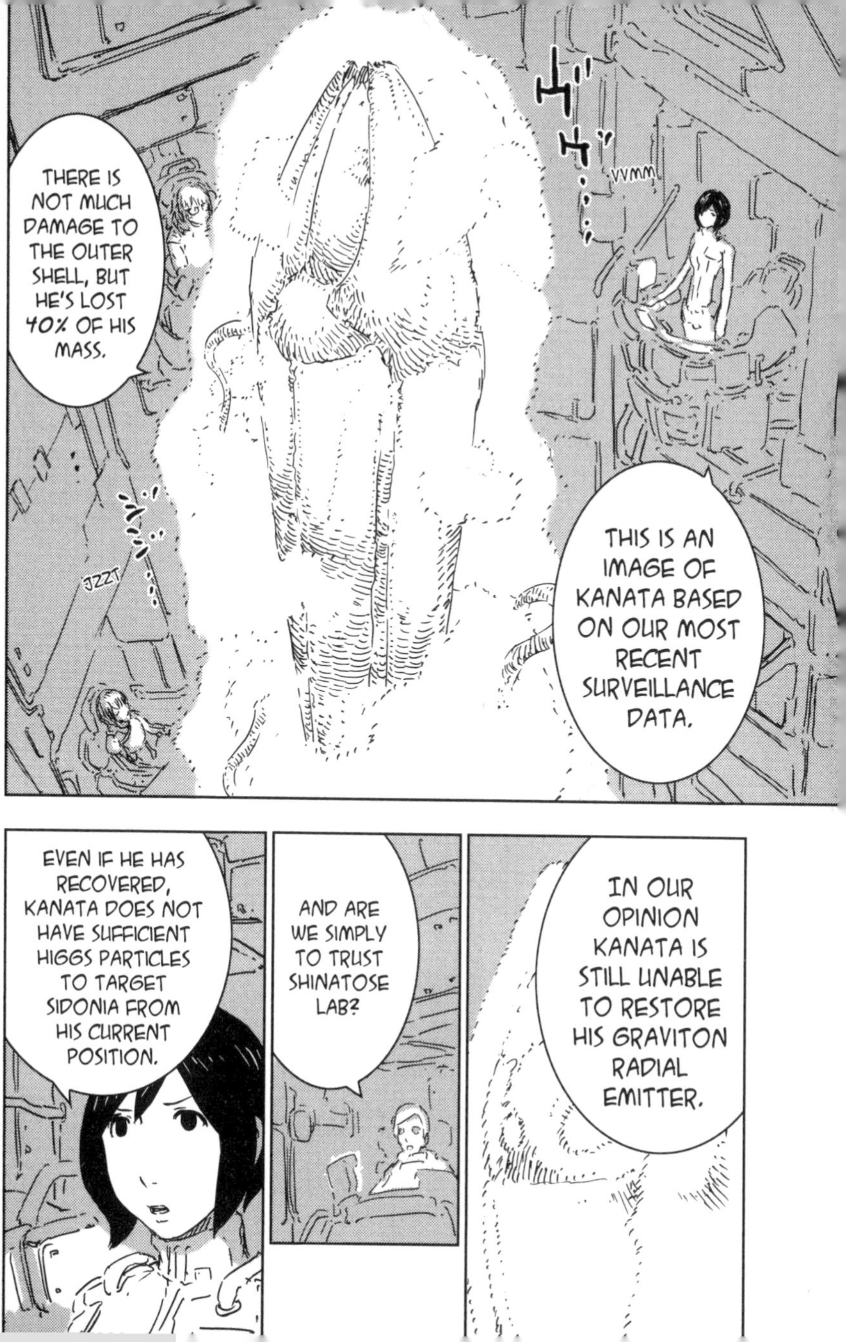
VVMM
THIS IS AN IMAGE OF KANATA BASED ON OUR MOST RECENT SURVEILLANCE DATA.
THERE IS NOT MUCH DAMAGE TO THE OUTER SHELL, BUT HE'S LOST 40% OF HIS MASS.
JZZT
IN OUR OPINION KANATA IS STILL UNABLE TO RESTORE HIS GRAVITON RADIAL EMITTER.
AND ARE WE SIMPLY TO TRUST SHINATOSE LAB?
EVEN IF HE HAS RECOVERED, KANATA DOES NOT HAVE SUFFICIENT HIGGS PARTICLES TO TARGET SIDONIA FROM HIS CURRENT POSITION.

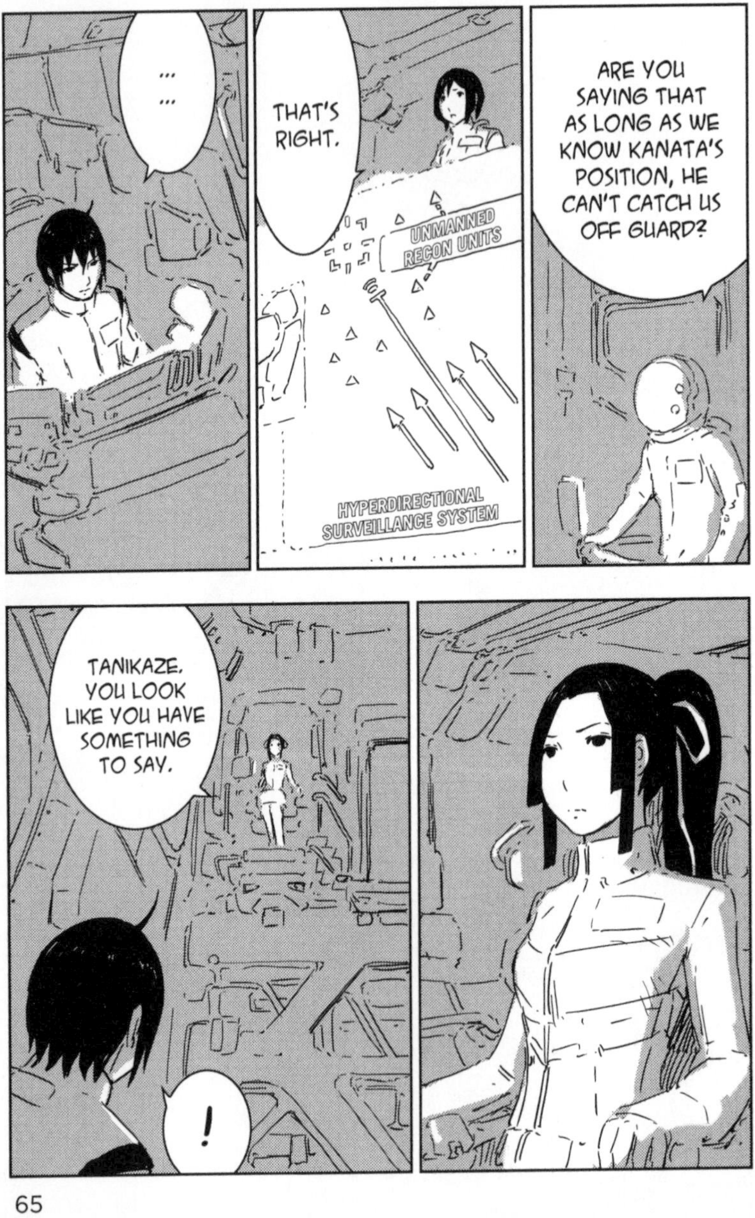
ARE YOU SAYING THAT AS LONG AS WE KNOW KANATA'S POSITION, HE CAN'T CATCH US OFF GUARD?
THAT'S RIGHT.
UNMANNED RECON UNITS
HYPERDIRECTIONAL SURVEILLANCE SYSTEM
...
...
TANIKAZE, YOU LOOK LIKE YOU HAVE SOMETHING TO SAY.
!

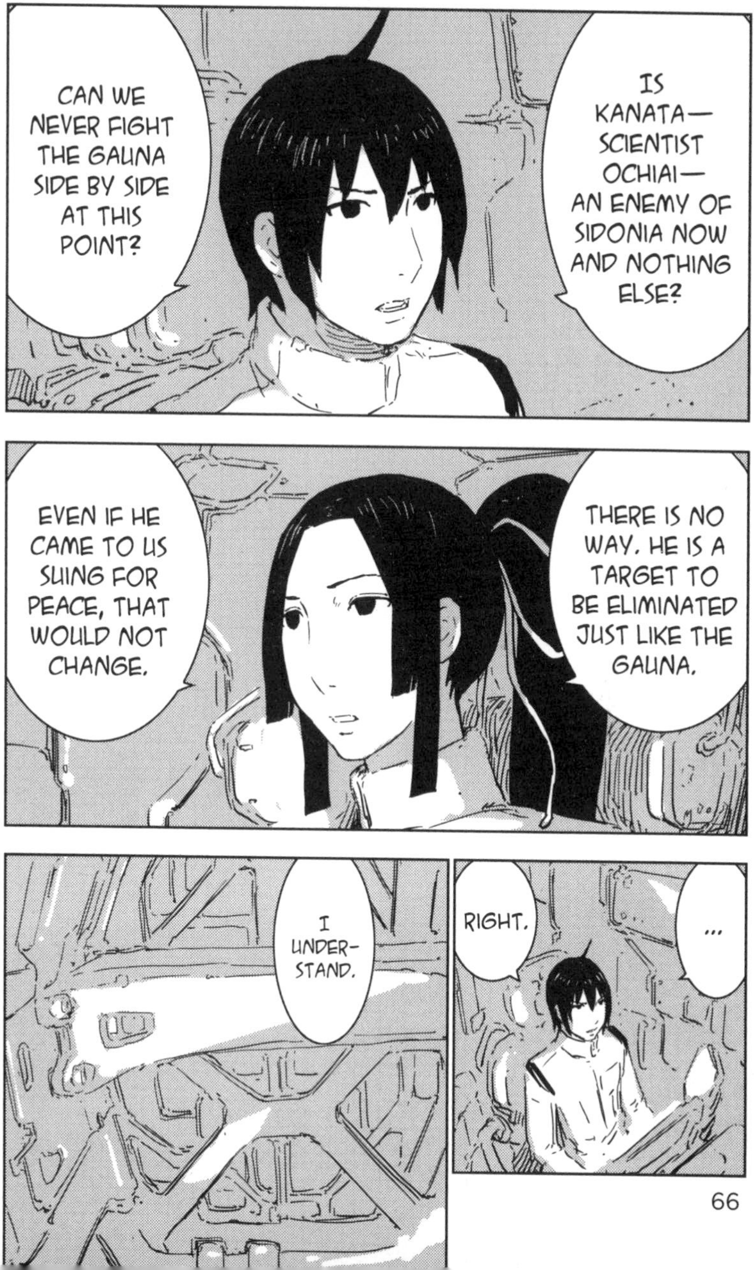
IS KANATA—SCIENTIST OCHIAI—AN ENEMY OF SIDONIA NOW AND NOTHING ELSE?
CAN WE NEVER FIGHT THE GAUNA SIDE BY SIDE AT THIS POINT?
THERE IS NO WAY. HE IS A TARGET TO BE ELIMINATED JUST LIKE THE GAUNA.
EVEN IF HE CAME TO US SUING FOR PEACE, THAT WOULD NOT CHANGE.
...
RIGHT.
I UNDER-STAND.

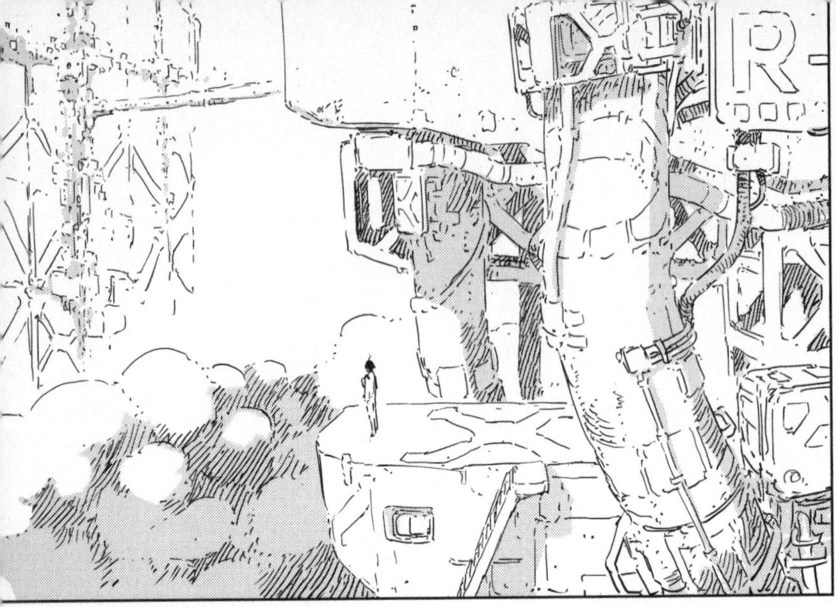
R-
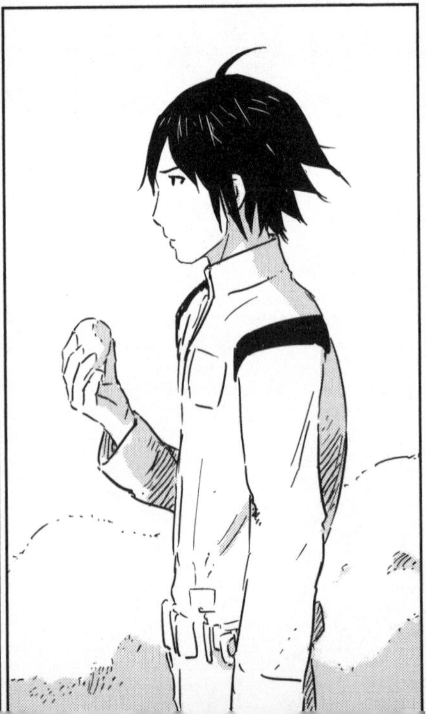
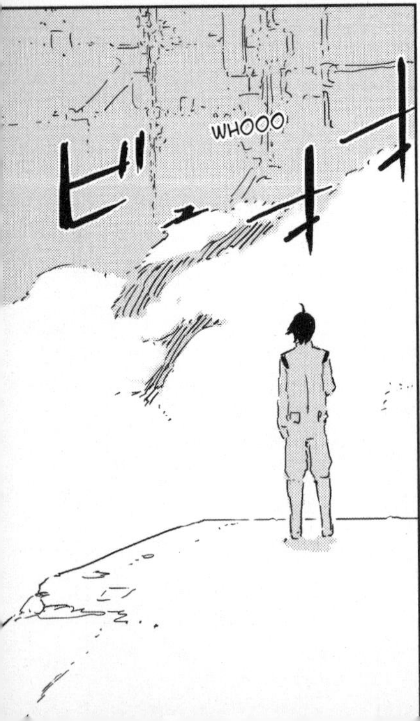
WHOOO
ビュオオ

ゴゴ
GWRR
オオオ
RRR
BEEEP
BEEEP
!!!
A SPATIAL ANOMALY HAS APPEARED 100,000 KILO UNITS TO OUR REAR!!
IT'S HEADING STRAIGHT TOWARDS US!!

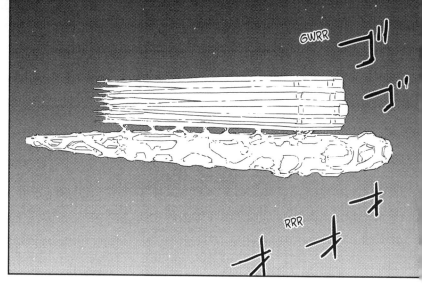

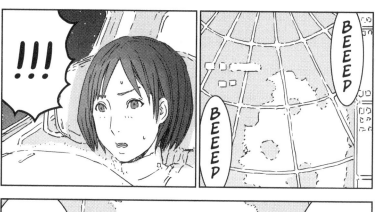

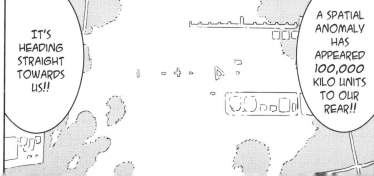

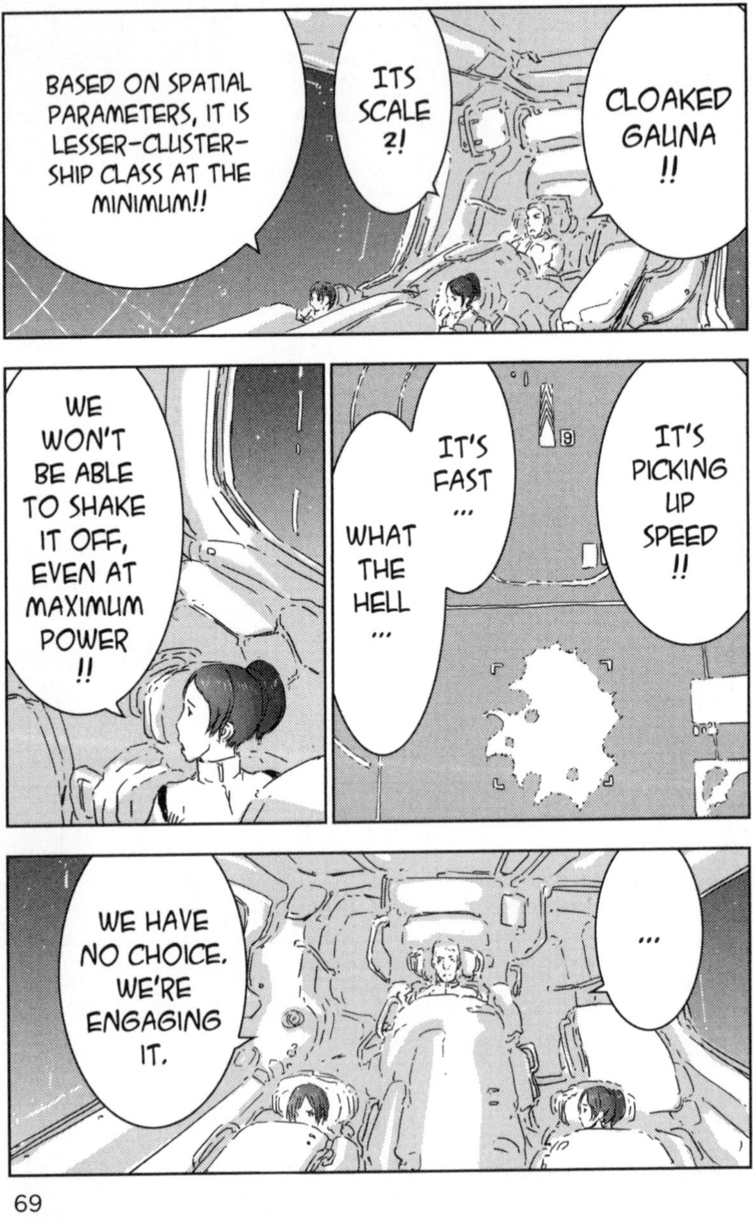
CLOAKED GAUNA !!
ITS SCALE ?!
BASED ON SPATIAL PARAMETERS, IT IS LESSER-CLUSTER-SHIP CLASS AT THE MINIMUM!!
IT'S PICKING UP SPEED !!
IT'S FAST ...
WHAT THE HELL ...
WE WON'T BE ABLE TO SHAKE IT OFF, EVEN AT MAXIMUM POWER !!
...
WE HAVE NO CHOICE. WE'RE ENGAGING IT.

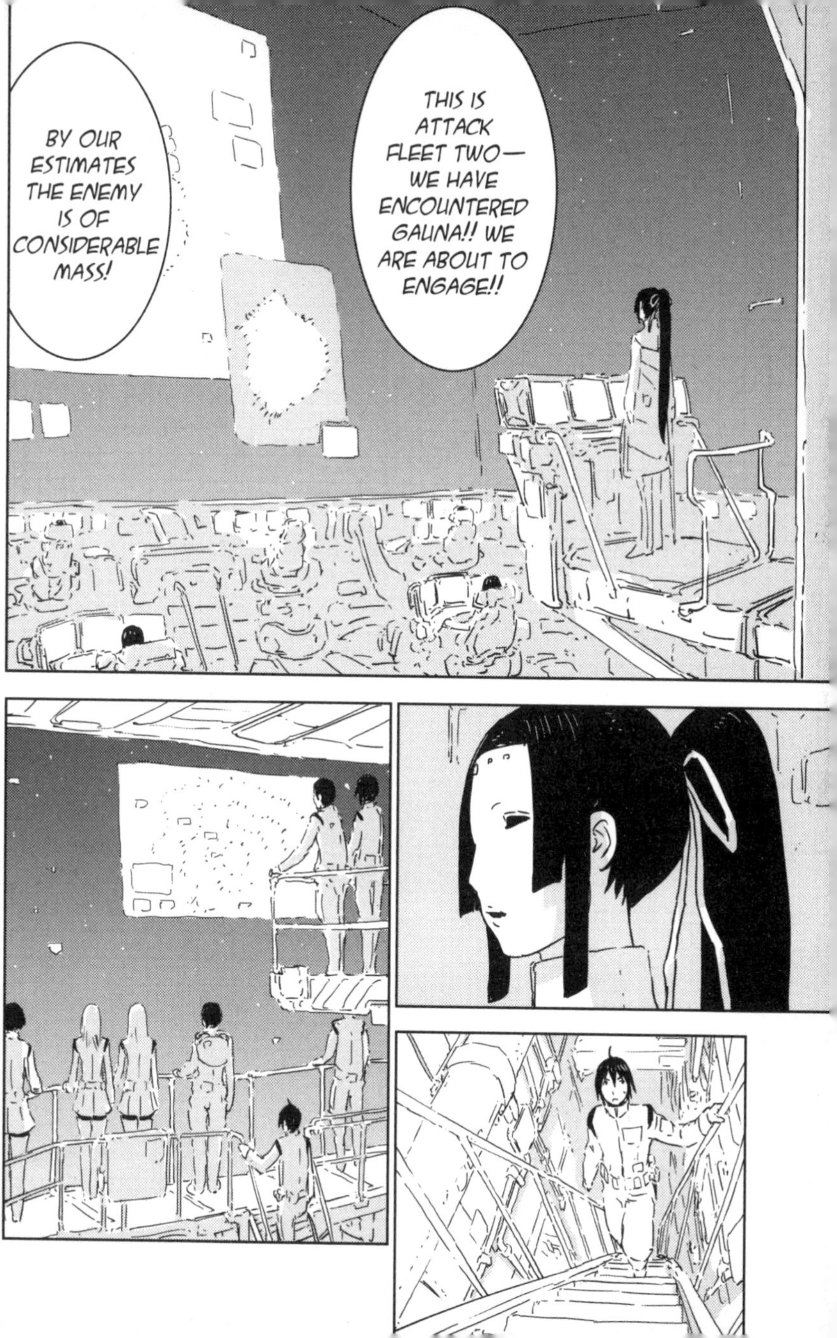
THIS IS ATTACK FLEET TWO— WE HAVE ENCOUNTERED GAUNA!! WE ARE ABOUT TO ENGAGE!!
BY OUR ESTIMATES THE ENEMY IS OF CONSIDERABLE MASS!

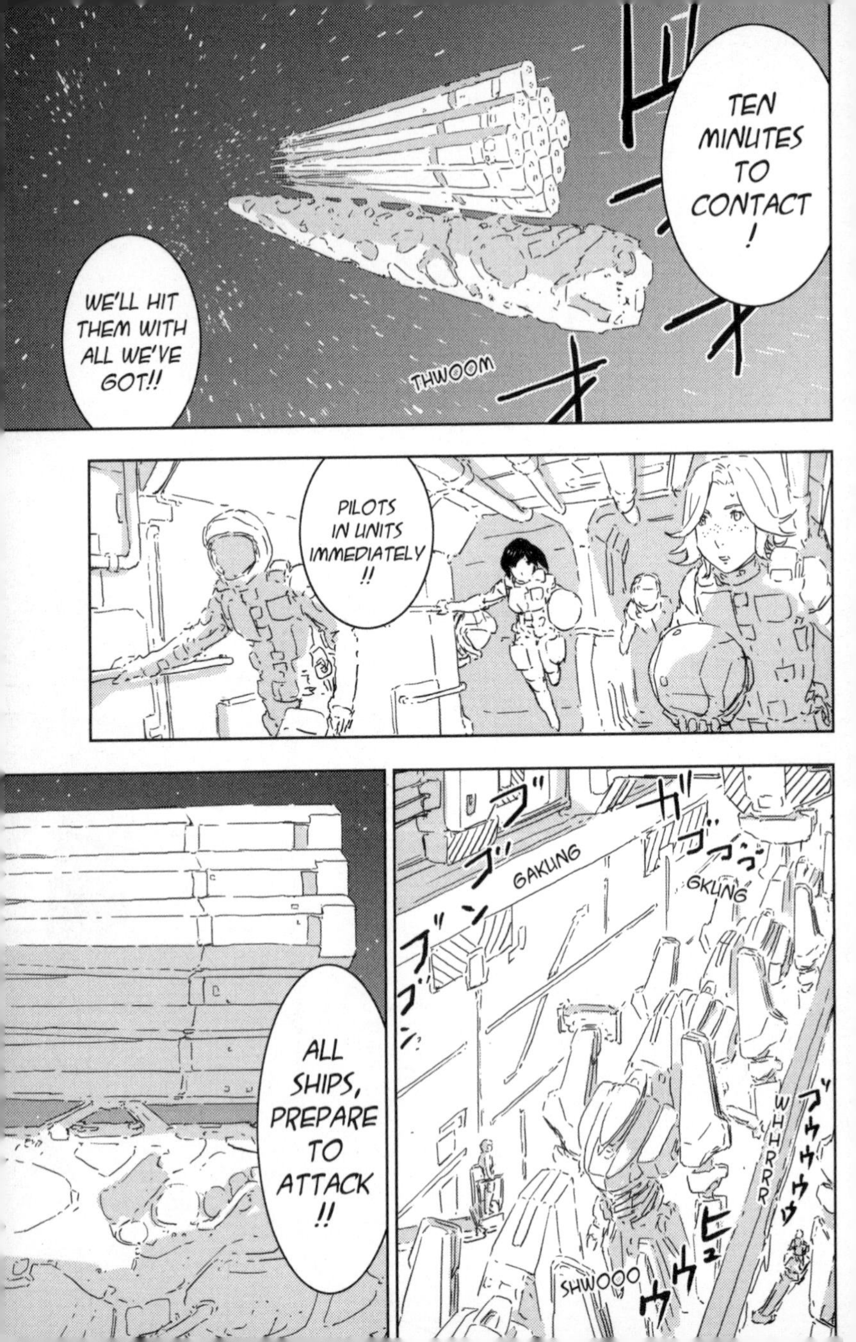
TEN MINUTES TO CONTACT!
WE'LL HIT THEM WITH ALL WE'VE GOT!!
THWOOM
PILOTS IN UNITS IMMEDIATELY!!
GAKUNG
GKUNG
WHHRRR
SHWOOO
ALL SHIPS, PREPARE TO ATTACK!!

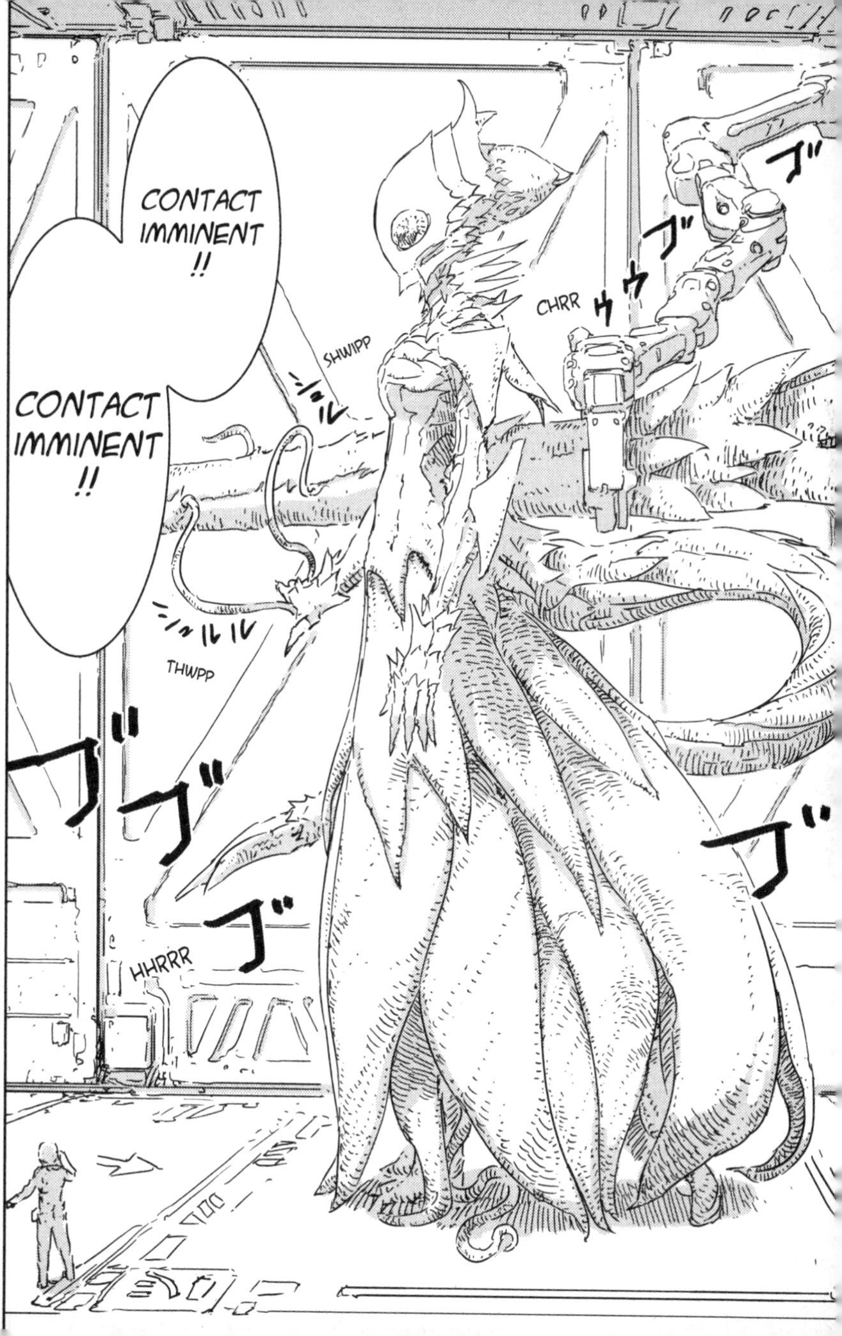

CONTACT IMMINENT !!
CONTACT IMMINENT !!
ゴゴウ
CHRR
シュル
SHWIPP
シュルルル
THWPP
ゴ
ゴゴゴ
HHRRR

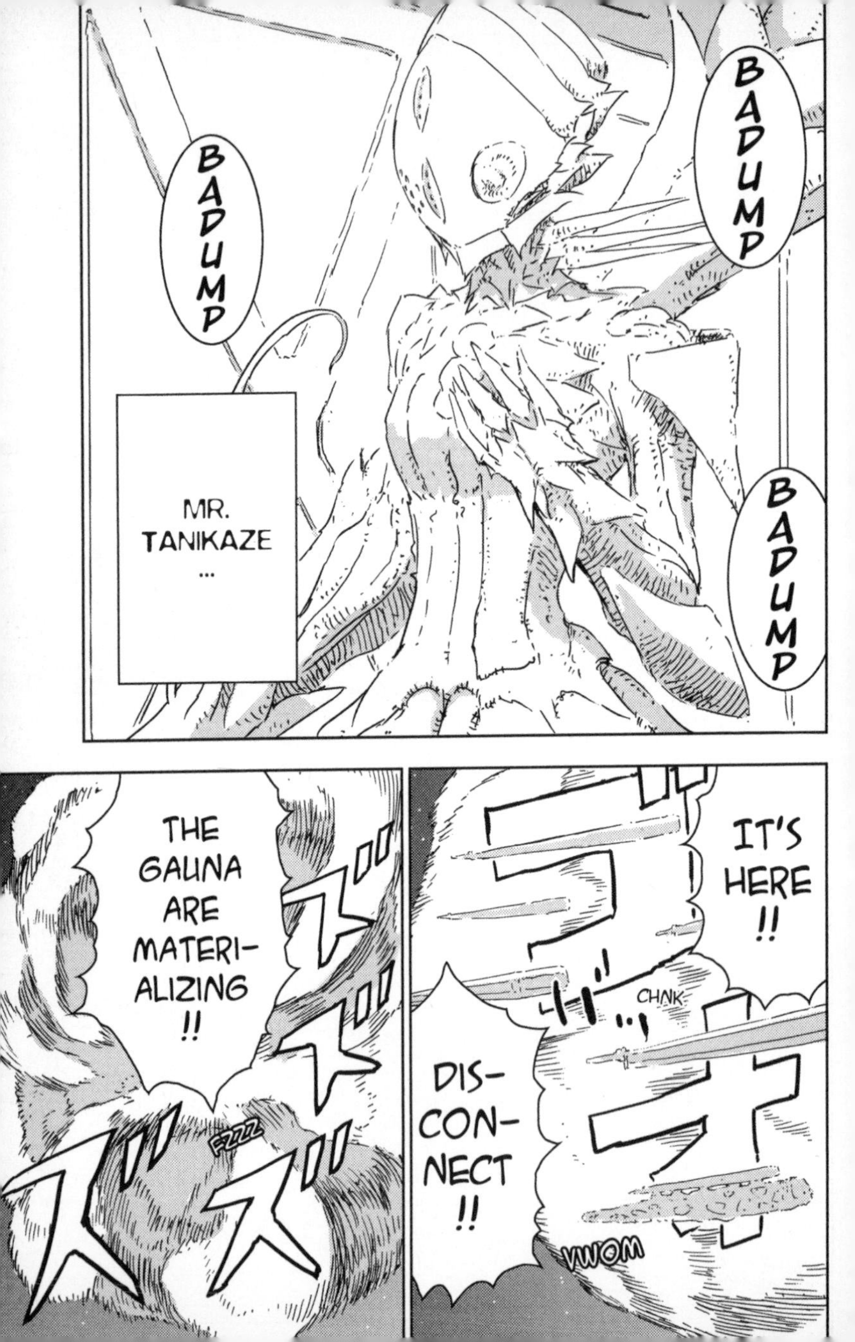
BADUMP
BADUMP
MR. TANIKAZE ...
BADUMP
IT'S HERE!!
CHNK
DIS-CON-NECT!!
VWOM
THE GAUNA ARE MATERI-ALIZING!!
FZZZ

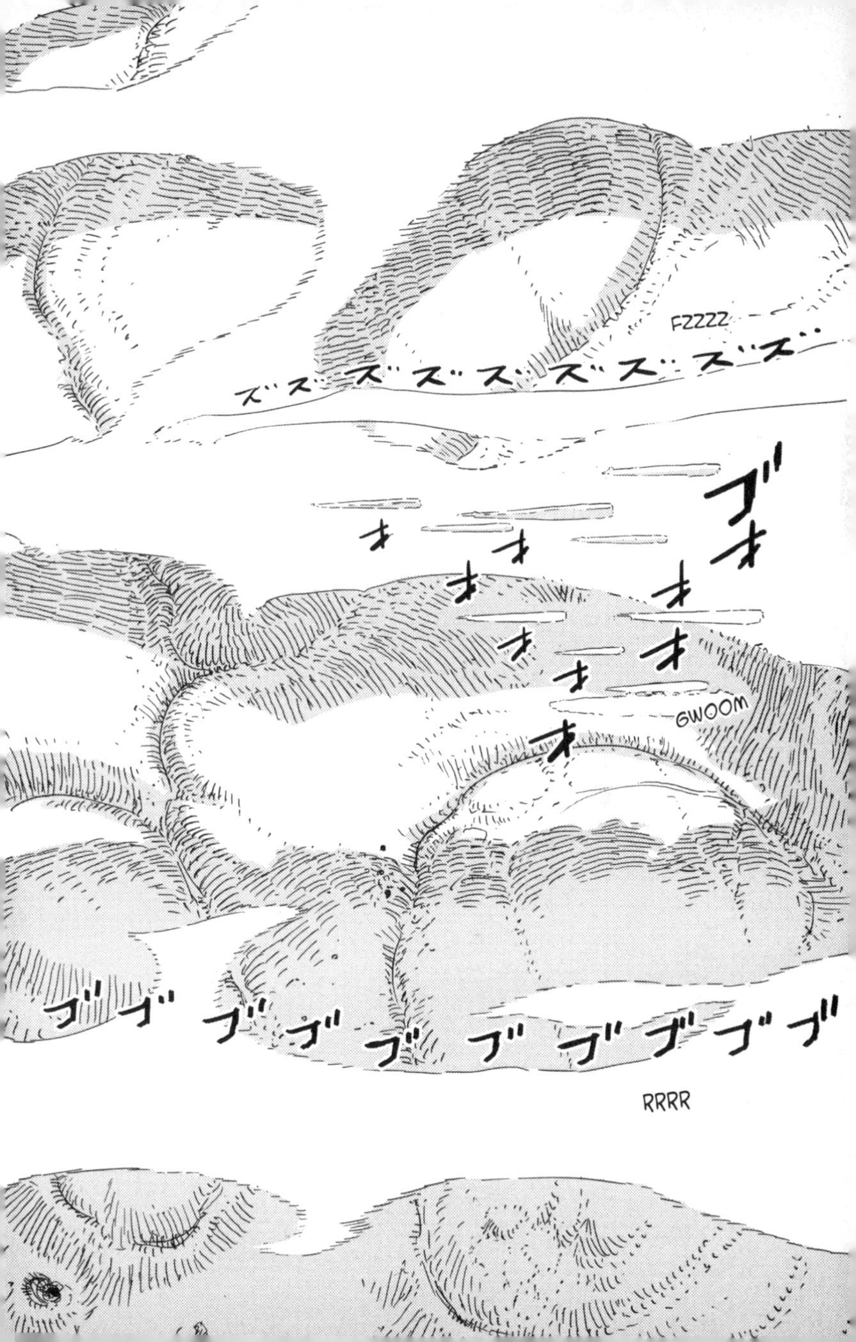
ズズズズズズズズズ
FZZZZ
ゴォォォォォォォォォ
GWOOM
ゴゴブブブブブブゴブ
RRRR

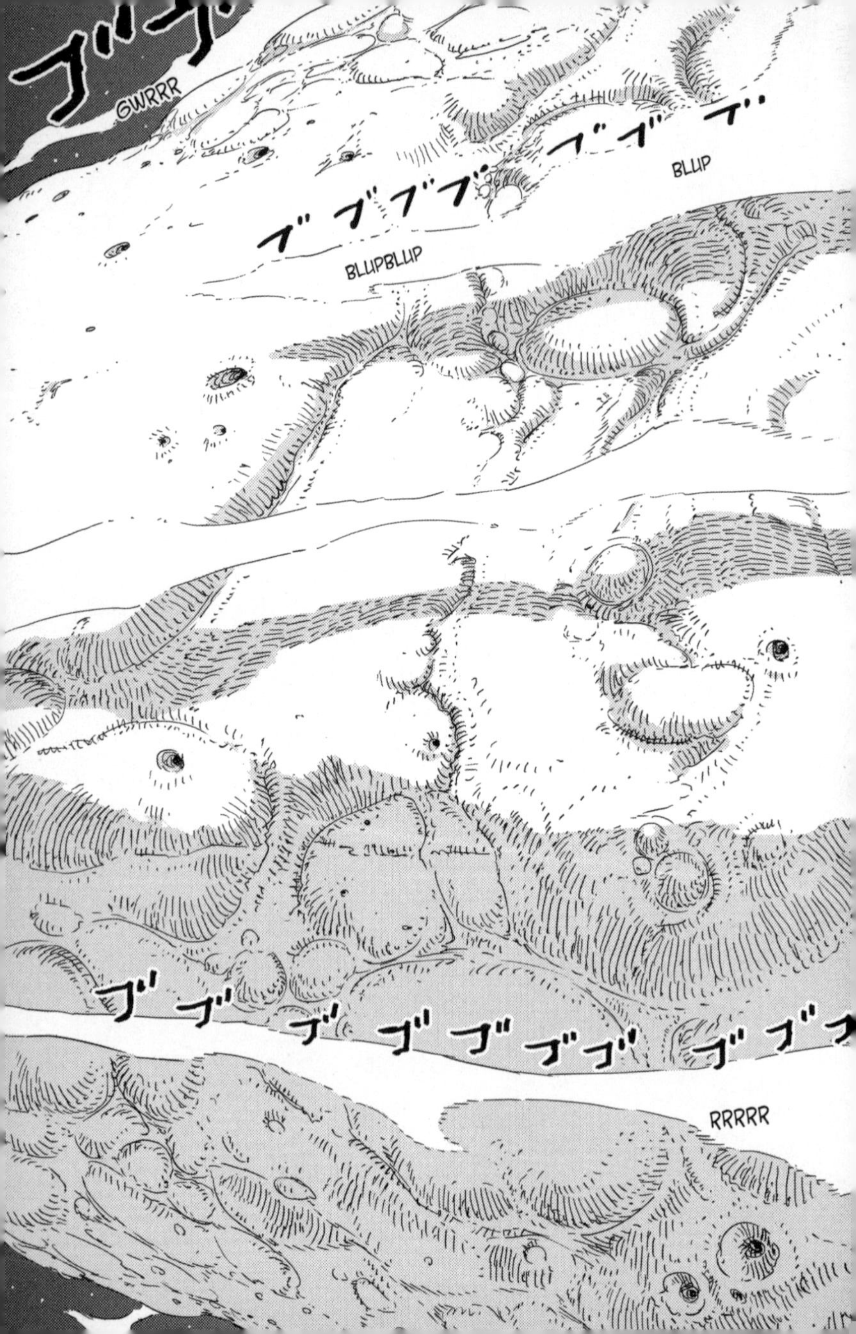
GWRRR
BLUP
BLUPBLUP
RRRRR

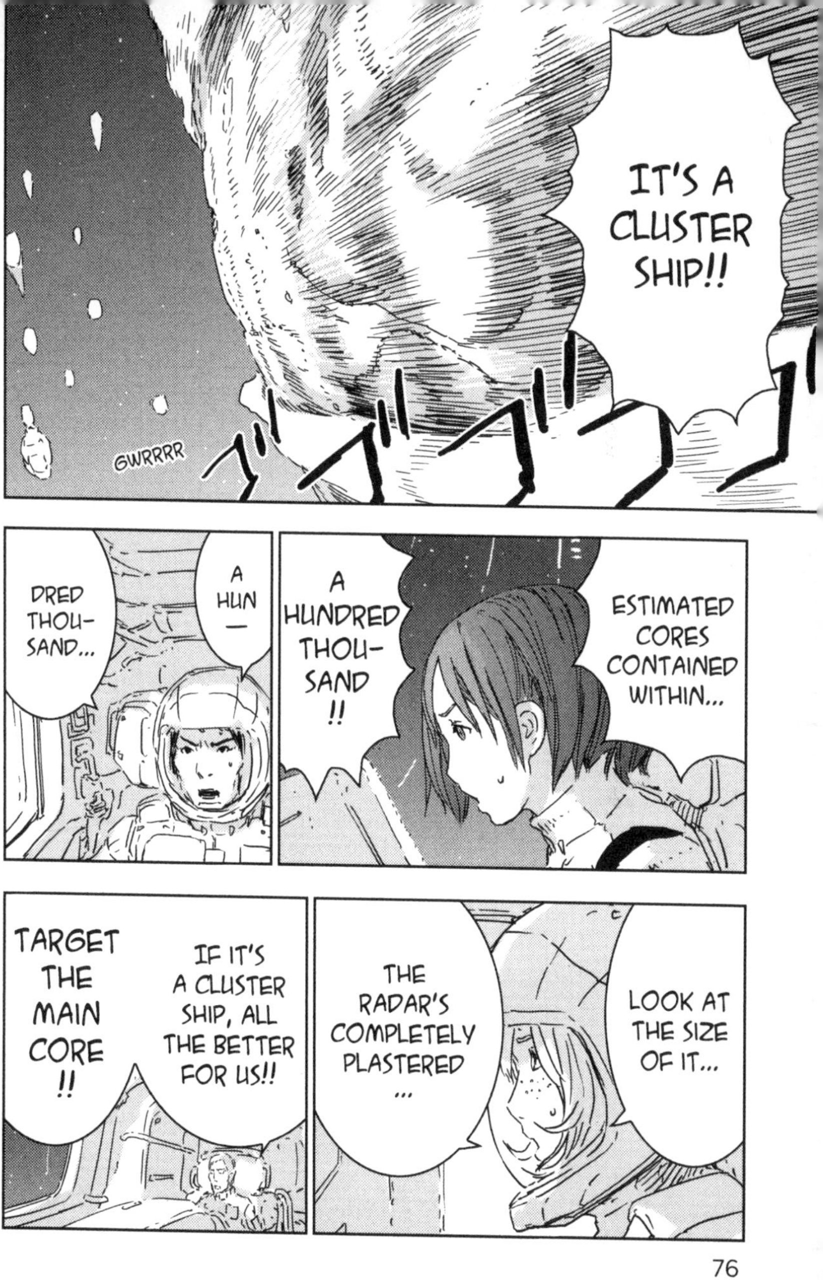
IT'S A CLUSTER SHIP!!
GWRRRR
ESTIMATED CORES CONTAINED WITHIN...
A HUNDRED THOUSAND!!
A HUN—
DRED THOUSAND...
LOOK AT THE SIZE OF IT...
THE RADAR'S COMPLETELY PLASTERED...
IF IT'S A CLUSTER SHIP, ALL THE BETTER FOR US!!
TARGET THE MAIN CORE!!

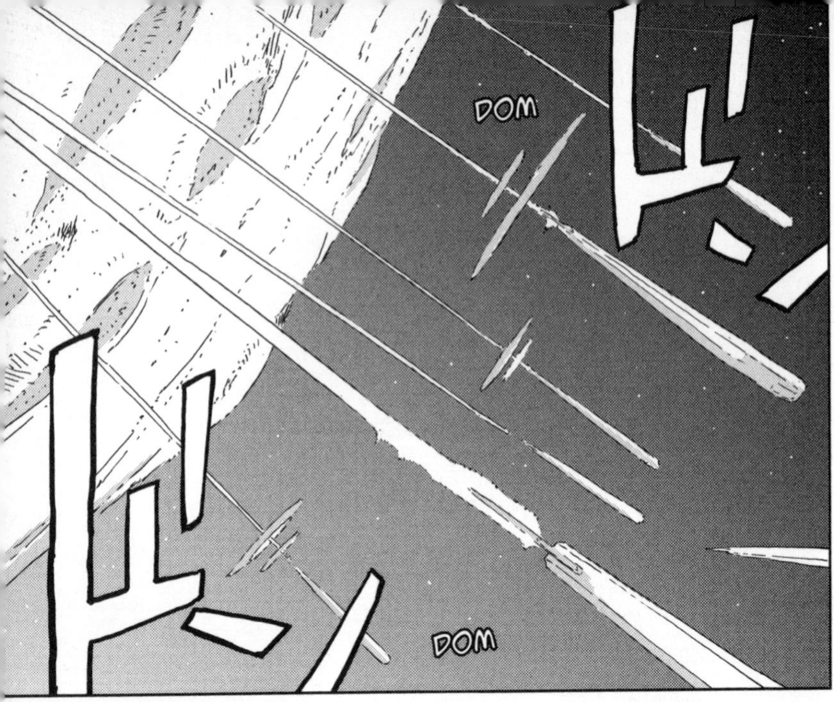
DOM
DOM
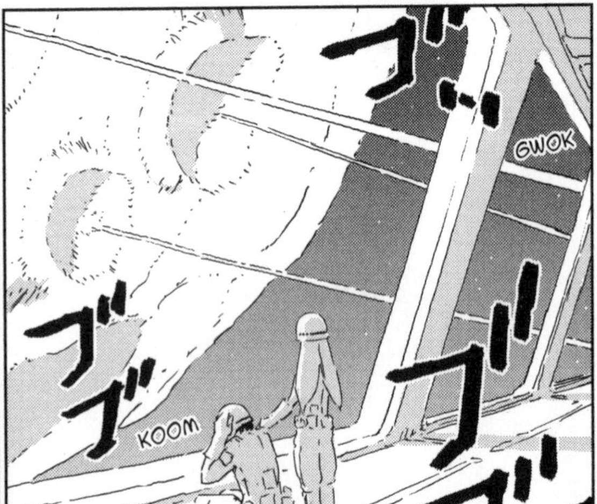
GWOK
KOOM
KOOM
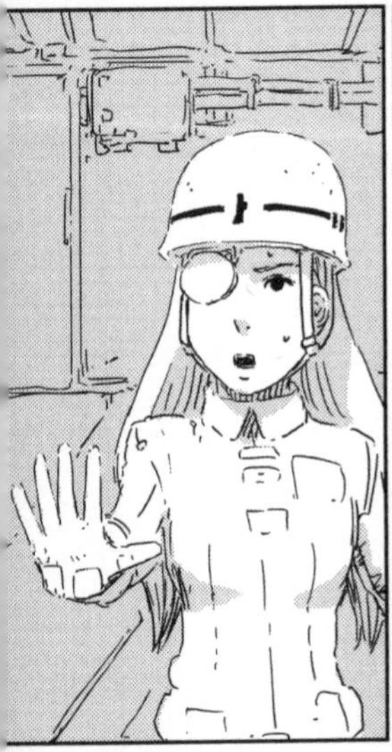

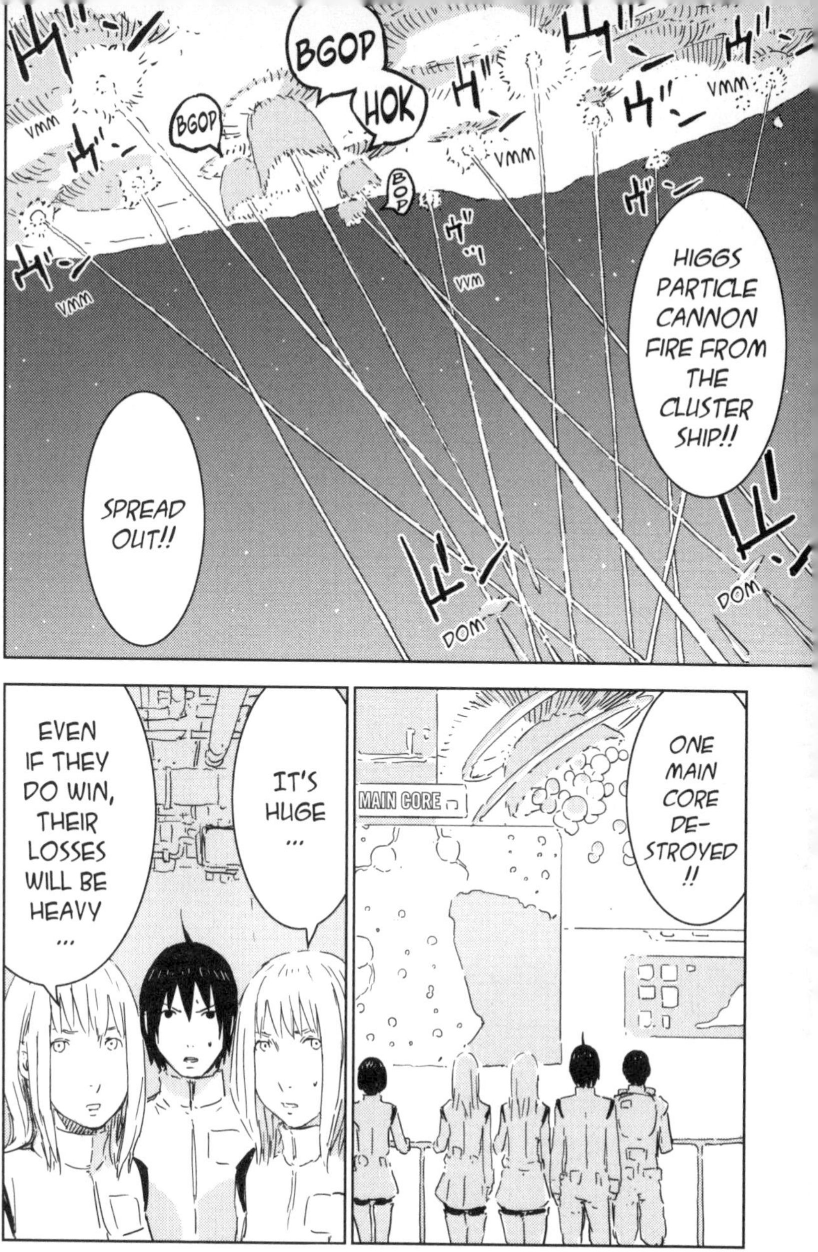
BGOP
HOK
BGOP
BOP
VMM
VMM
VMM
VMM
VMM
HIGGS PARTICLE CANNON FIRE FROM THE CLUSTER SHIP!!
SPREAD OUT!!
DOM
DOM
MAIN CORE
ONE MAIN CORE DE-STROYED!!
IT'S HUGE...
EVEN IF THEY DO WIN, THEIR LOSSES WILL BE HEAVY...

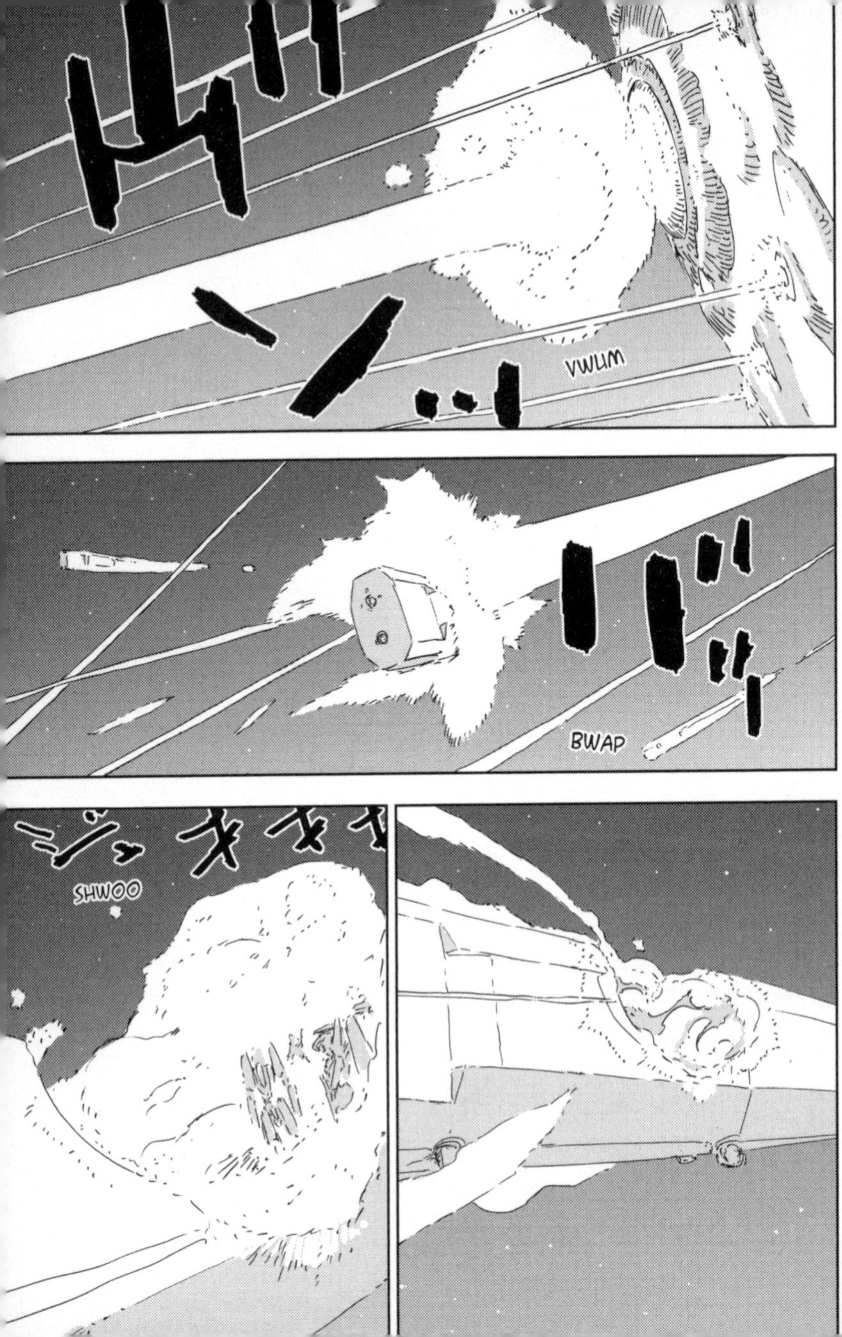
VWUM
BWAP
SHWOO

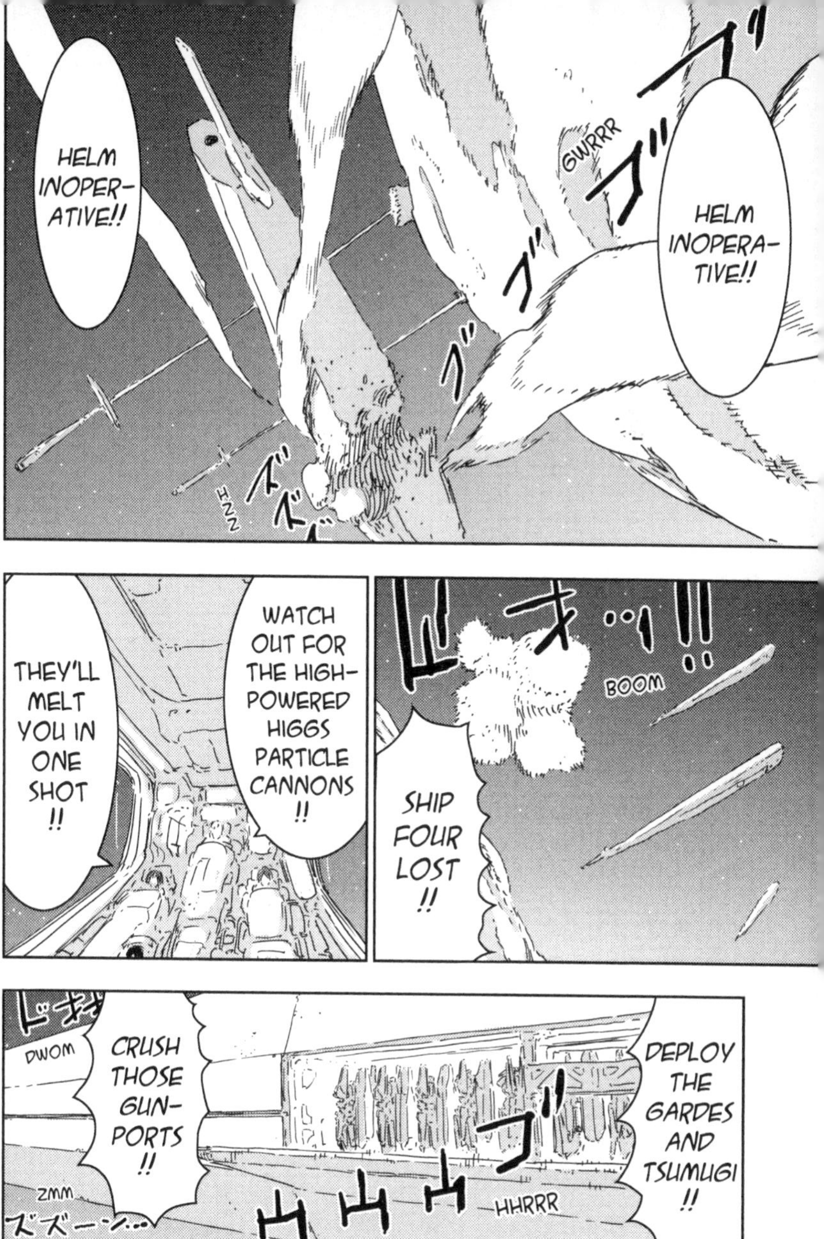
GWRRR
HELM INOPERA-TIVE!!
HELM INOPER-ATIVE!!
BOOM
SHIP FOUR LOST!!
WATCH OUT FOR THE HIGH-POWERED HIGGS PARTICLE CANNONS!!
THEY'LL MELT YOU IN ONE SHOT!!
DEPLOY THE GARDES AND TSUMUGI!!
HHRRR
CRUSH THOSE GUN-PORTS!!
DWOM
ZMM

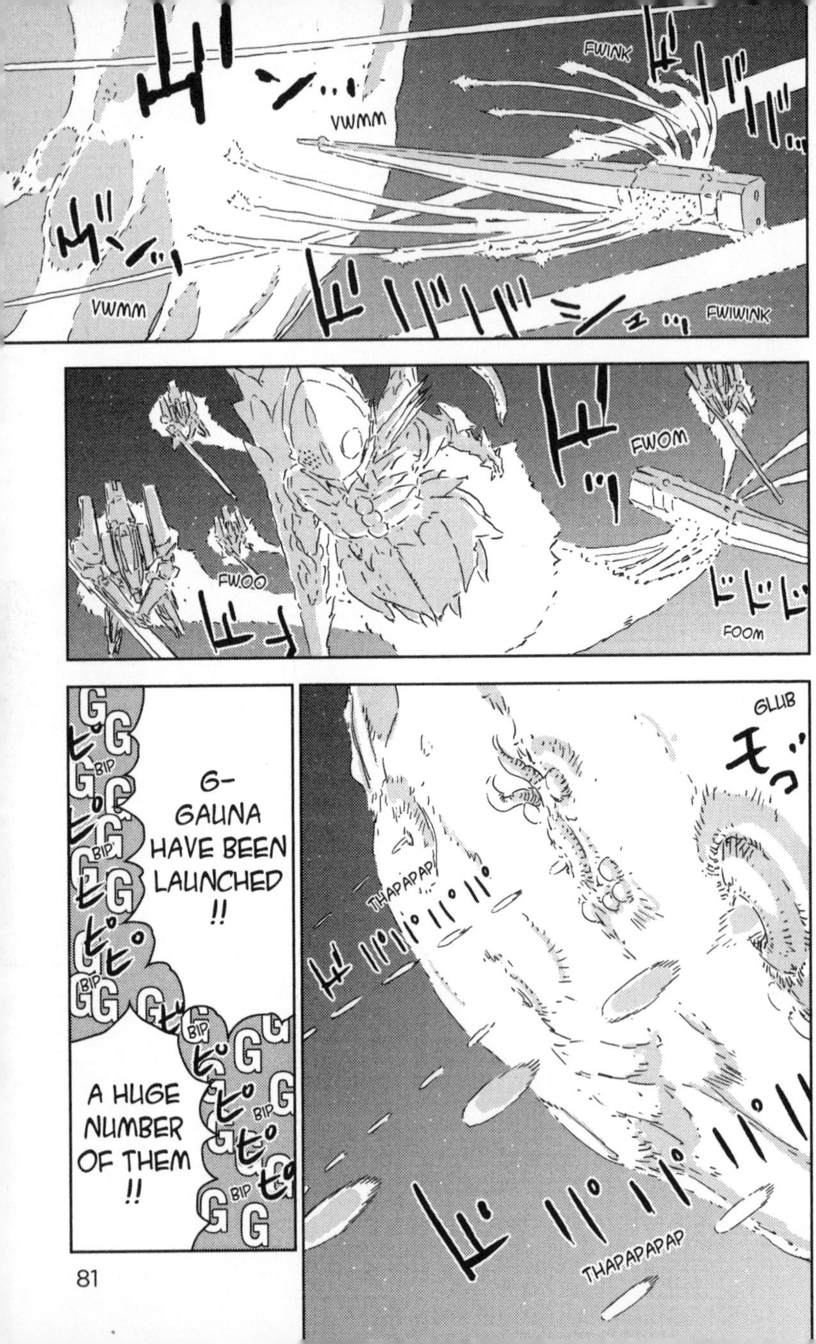
FWINK
VWMM
VWMM
FWIWINK
FWOM
FWOO
FOOM
GLUB
THAPAPAP
THAPAPAPAP
G-GAUNA HAVE BEEN LAUNCHED!!
A HUGE NUMBER OF THEM!!
BIP

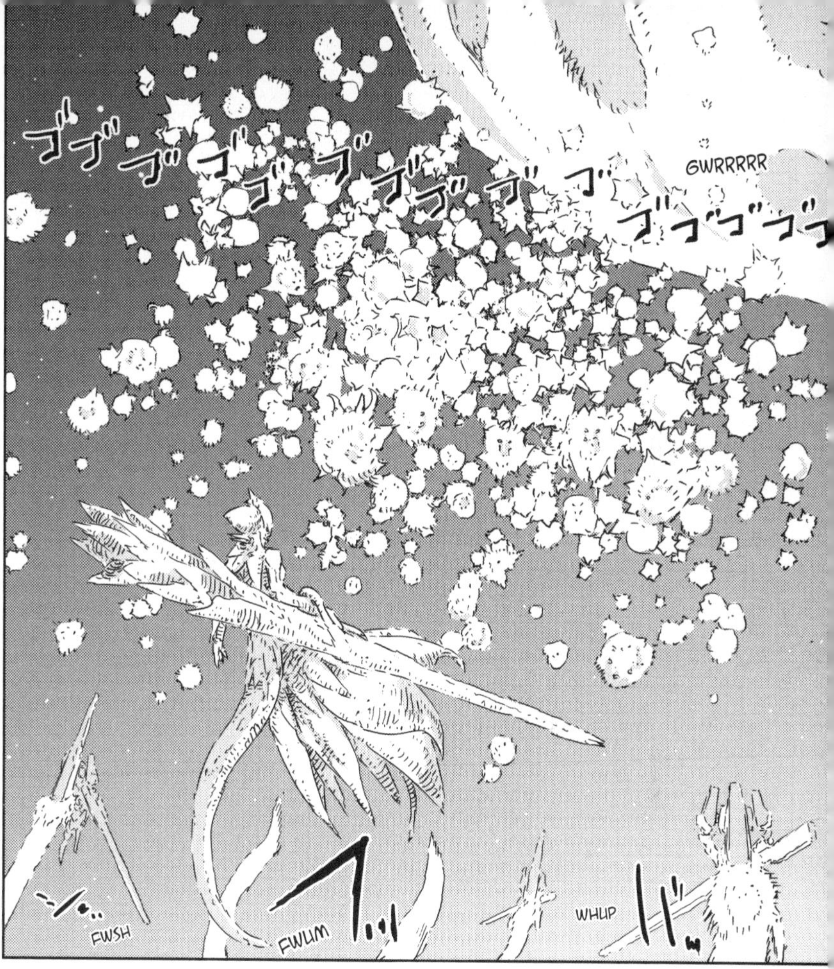
GWRRRRR
WHUP
FWUM
FWSH

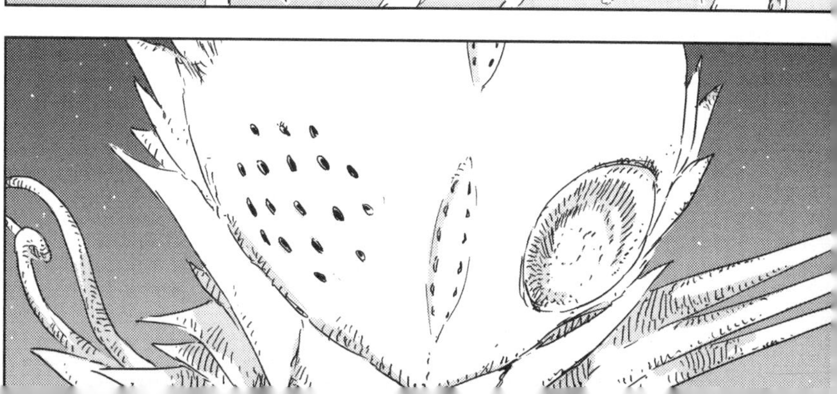

Chapter 68: Nagate Tanikaze's Restlessness

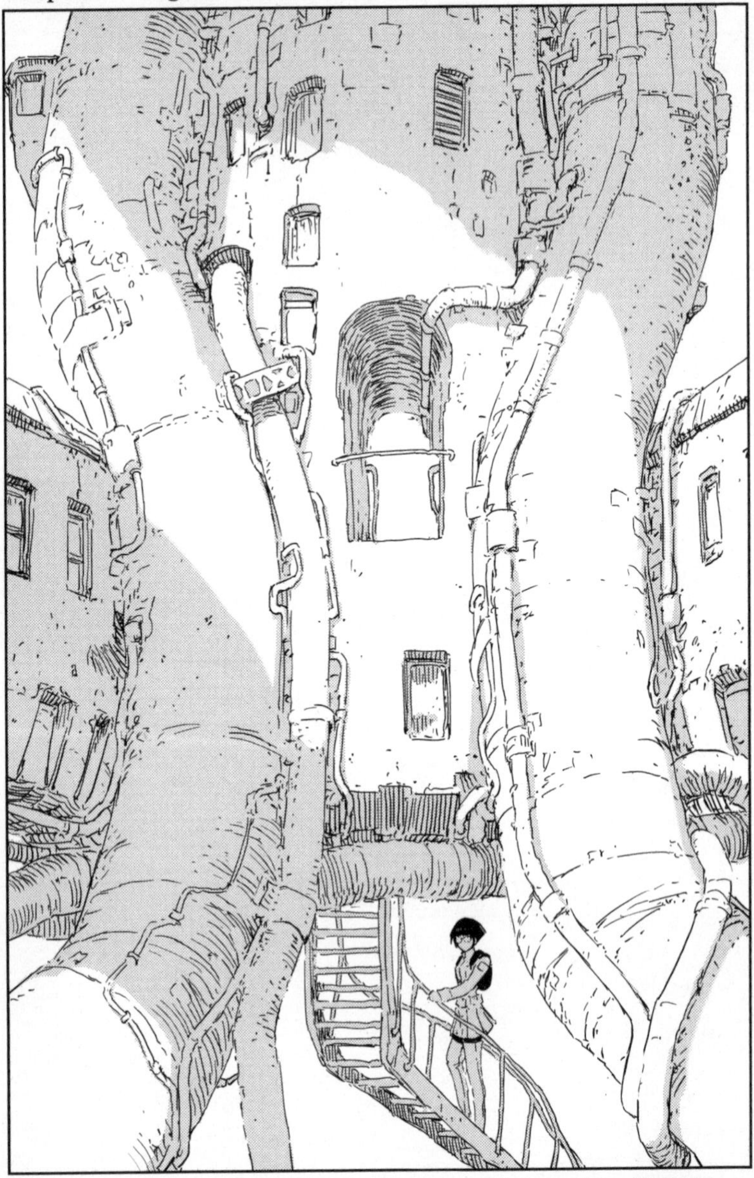

One Hundred Sights of Sidonia Part Fifty-Two:
Pilots' Dorm, Ward F

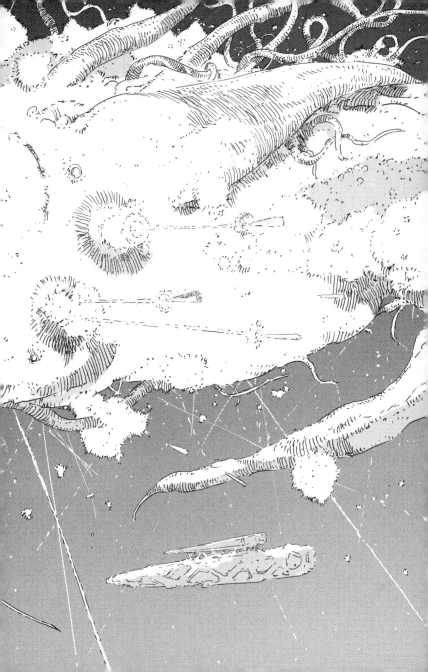

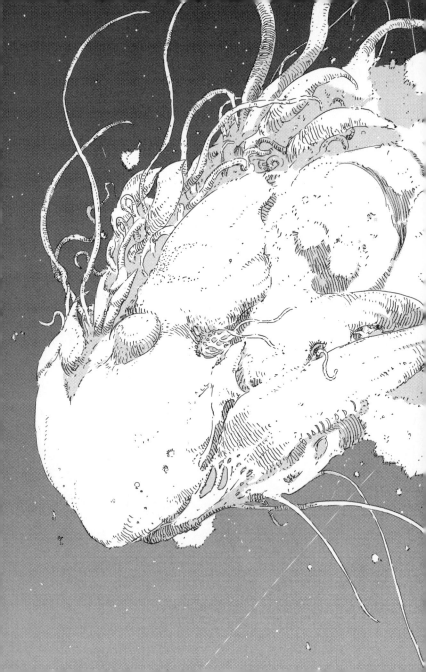

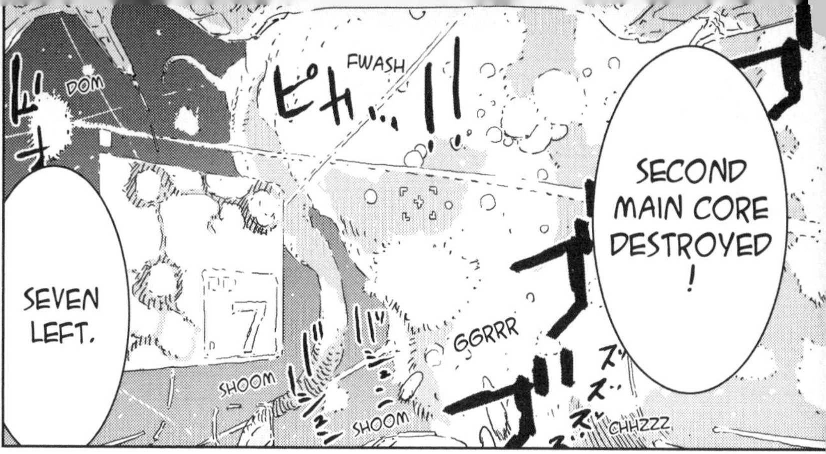
SECOND MAIN CORE DESTROYED !
FWASH
ピカ…!!
GGRRR
CHHZZZ
SHOOM
SHOOM
DOM
SEVEN LEFT.
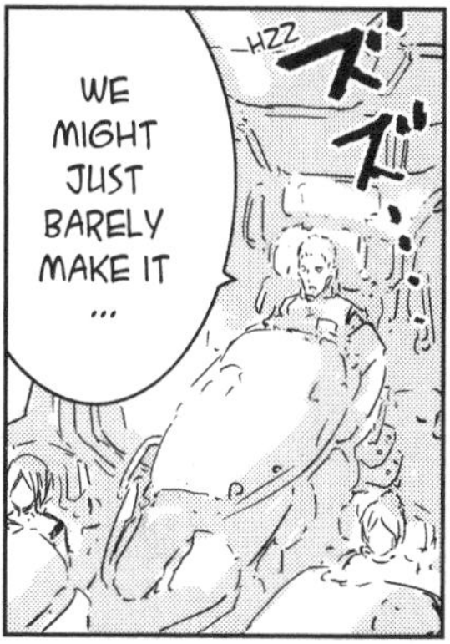
HZZ
WE MIGHT JUST BARELY MAKE IT ...
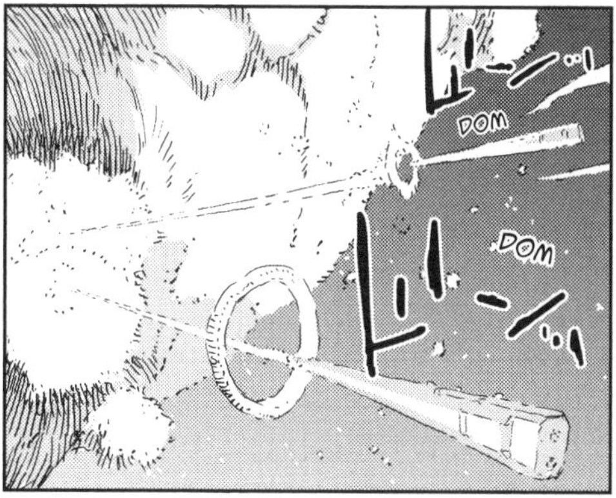
DOM
DOM
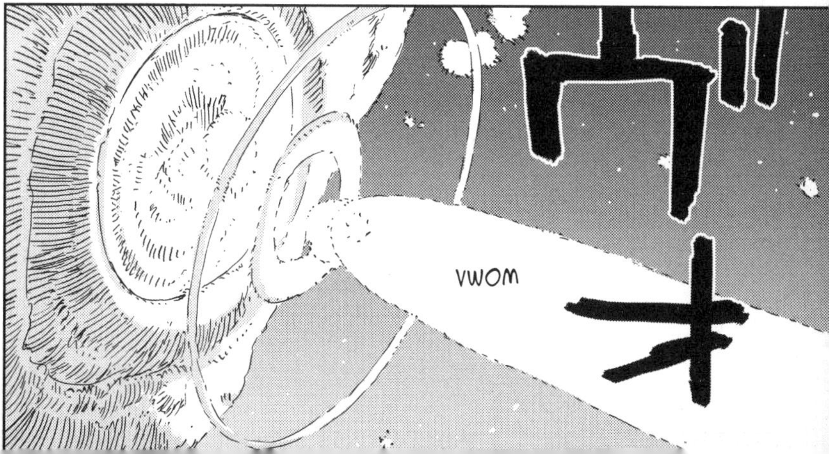
VWOM

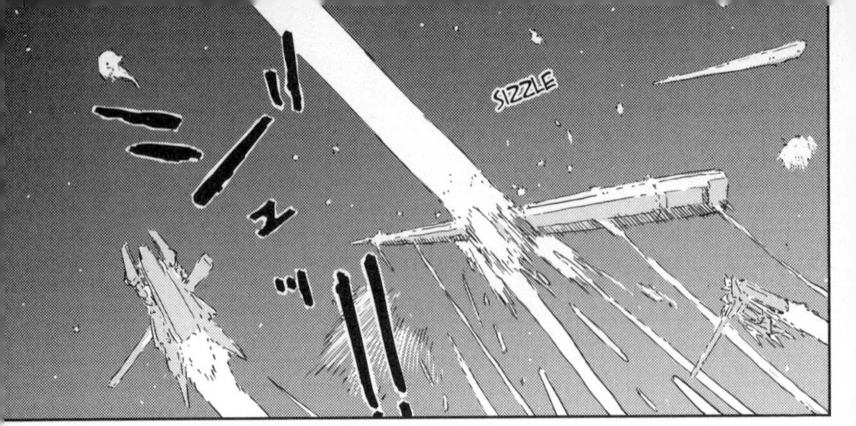
SIZZLE
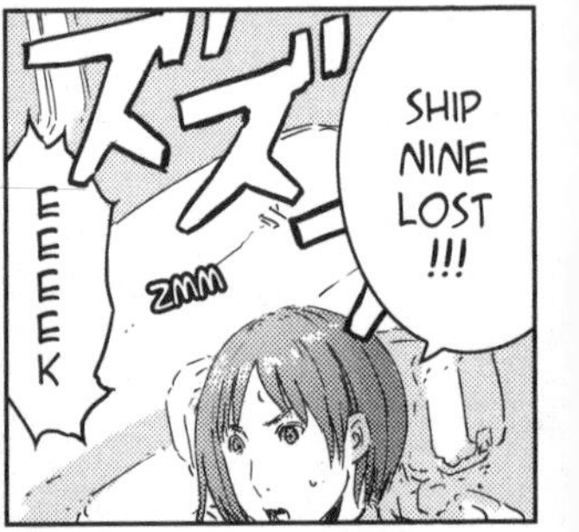
SHIP NINE LOST !!!
EEEEEK
ZMM
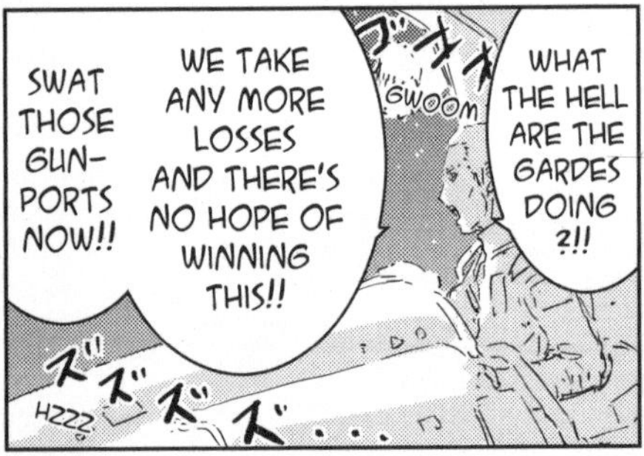
WHAT THE HELL ARE THE GARDES DOING ?!!
GWOOM
WE TAKE ANY MORE LOSSES AND THERE'S NO HOPE OF WINNING THIS!!
SWAT THOSE GUN-PORTS NOW!!
HZZZ
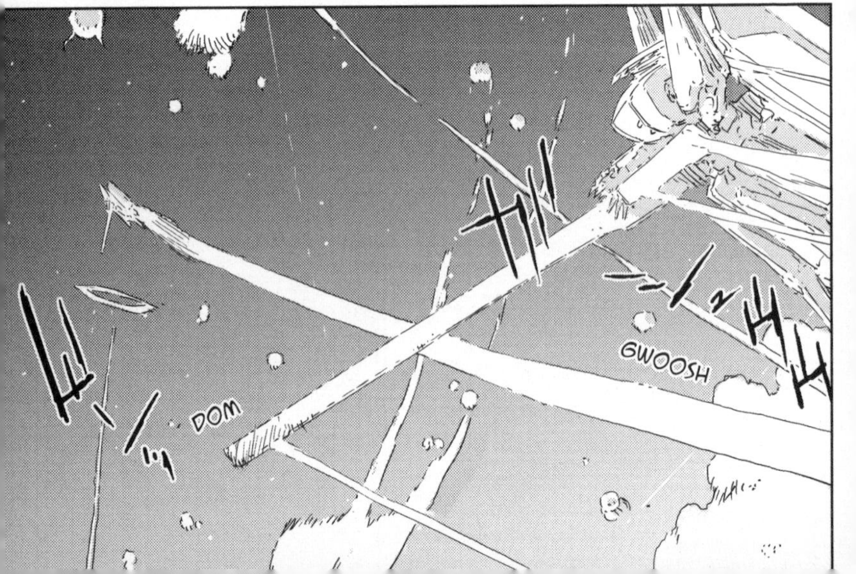
GWOOSH
DOM

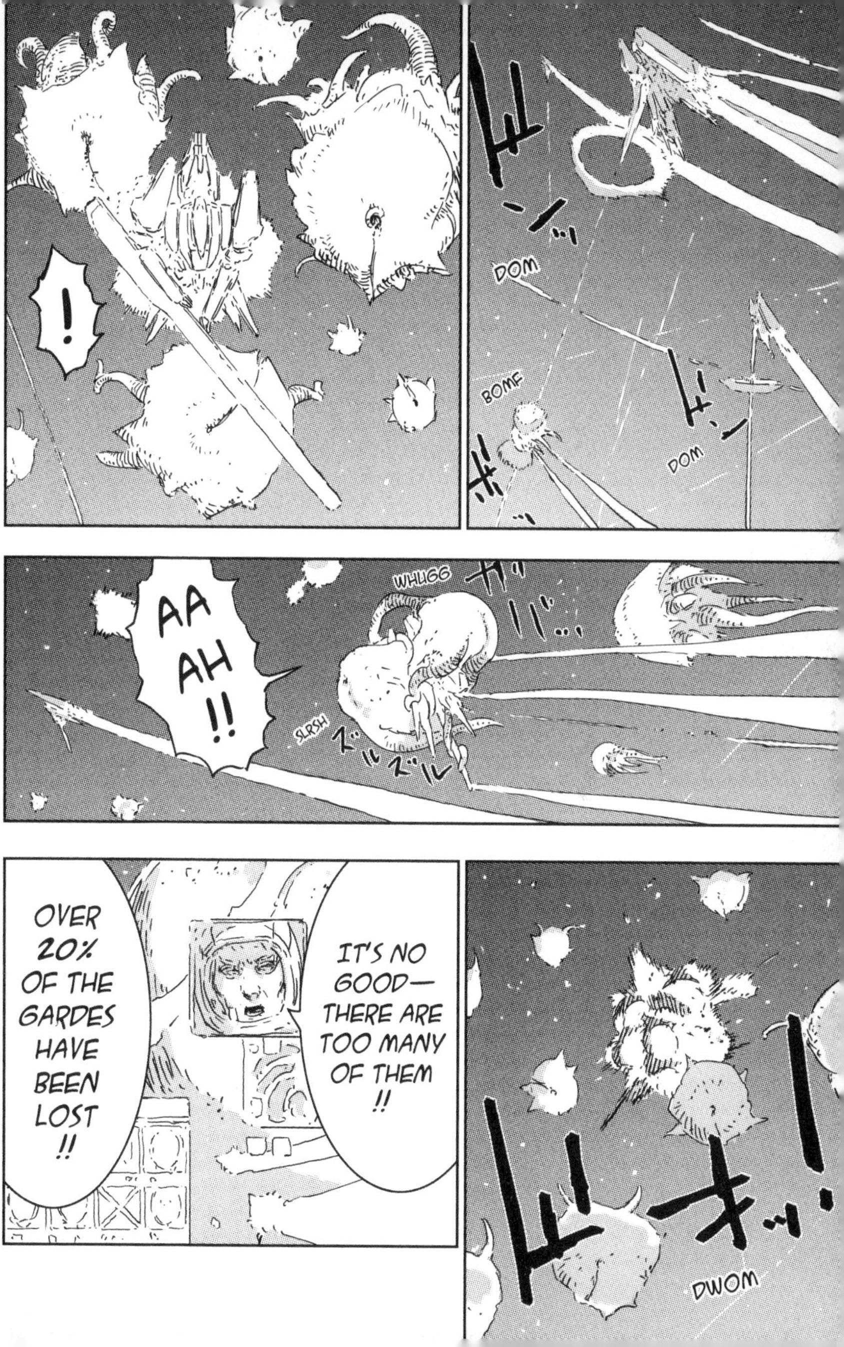
DOM
BOMF
DOM
!
WHUGG
AA AH !!
SLRSH
DWOM
IT'S NO GOOD— THERE ARE TOO MANY OF THEM !!
OVER 20% OF THE GARDES HAVE BEEN LOST !!

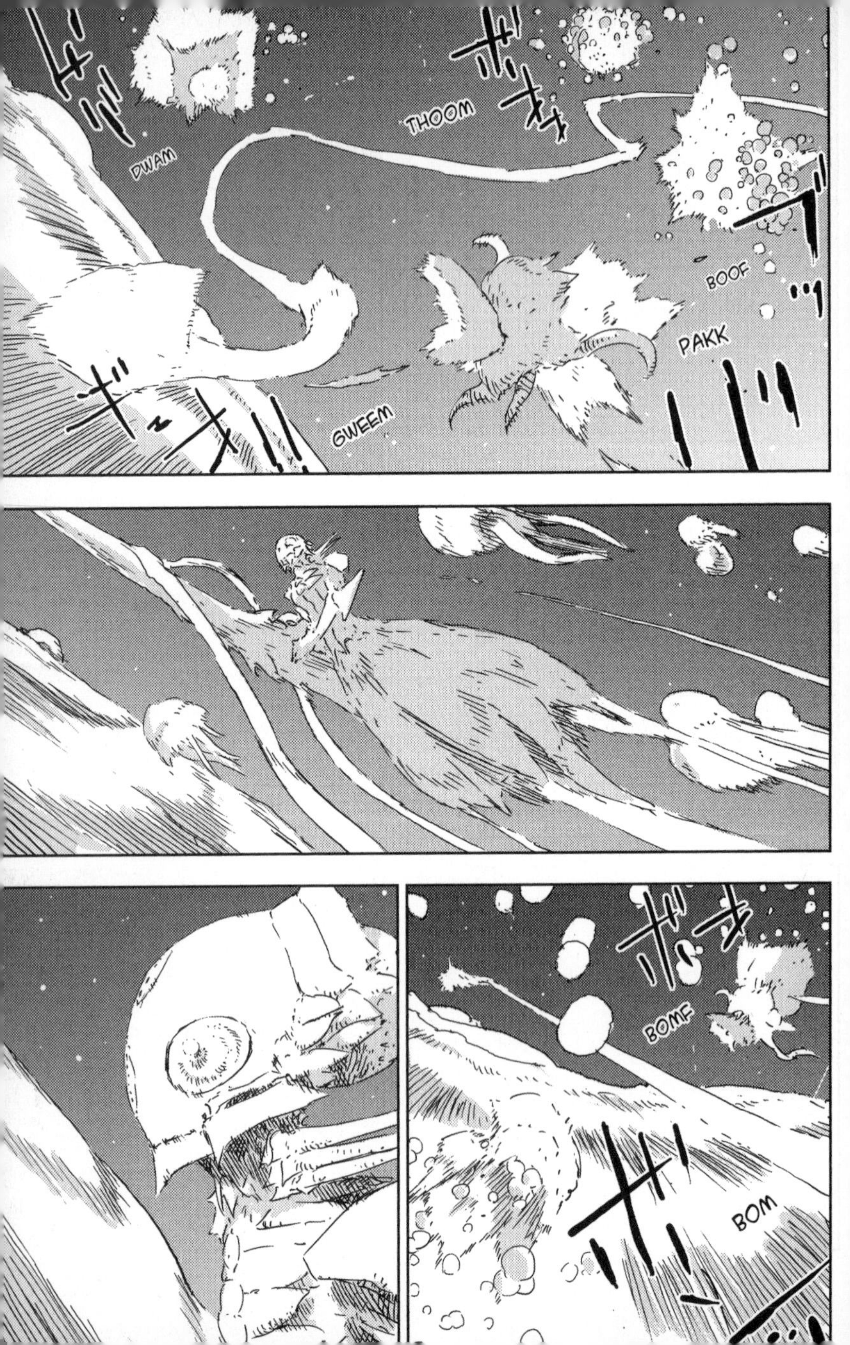
THOOM
DWAM
BOOF
PAKK
GWEEM
BOMF
BOM

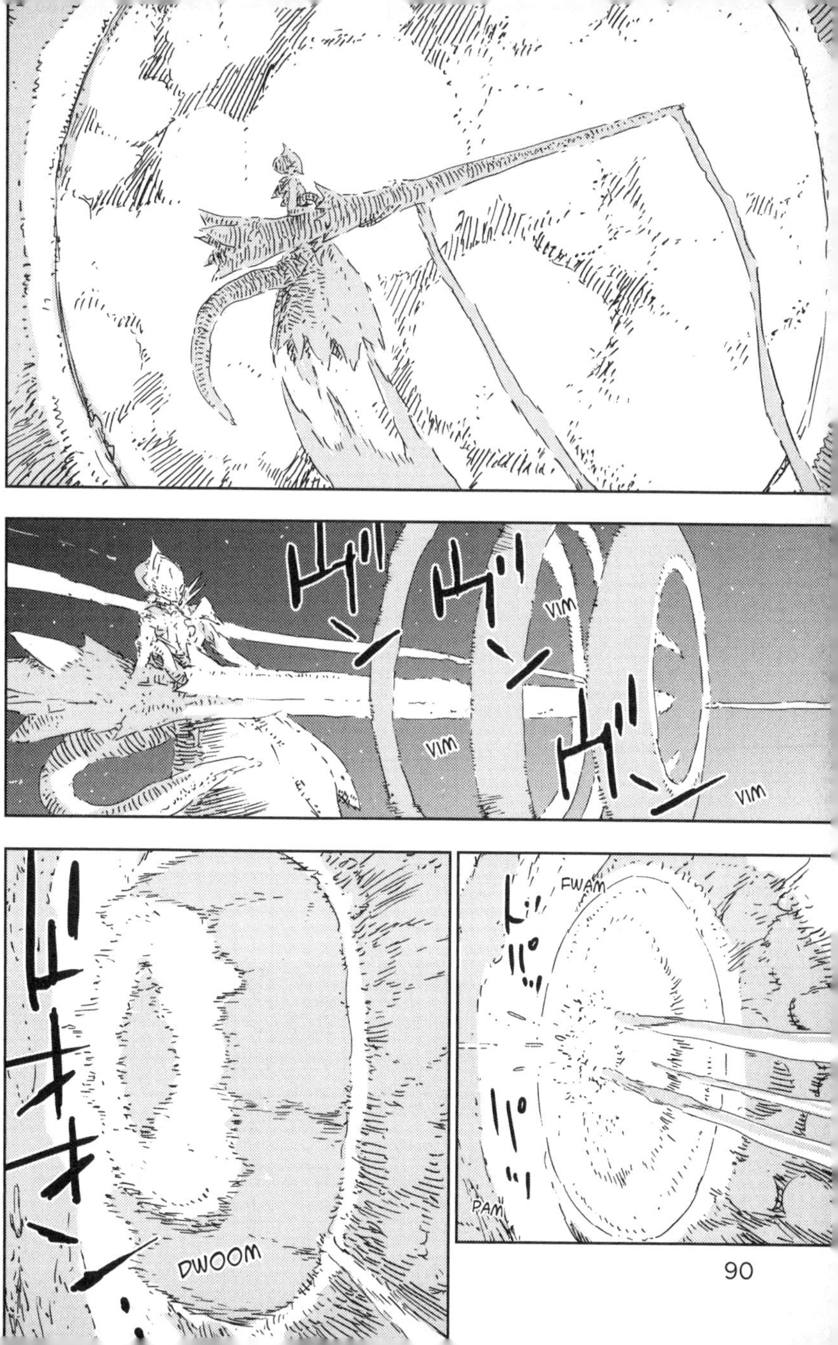
VIM
VIM
VIM
FWAM
PAM
DWOOM

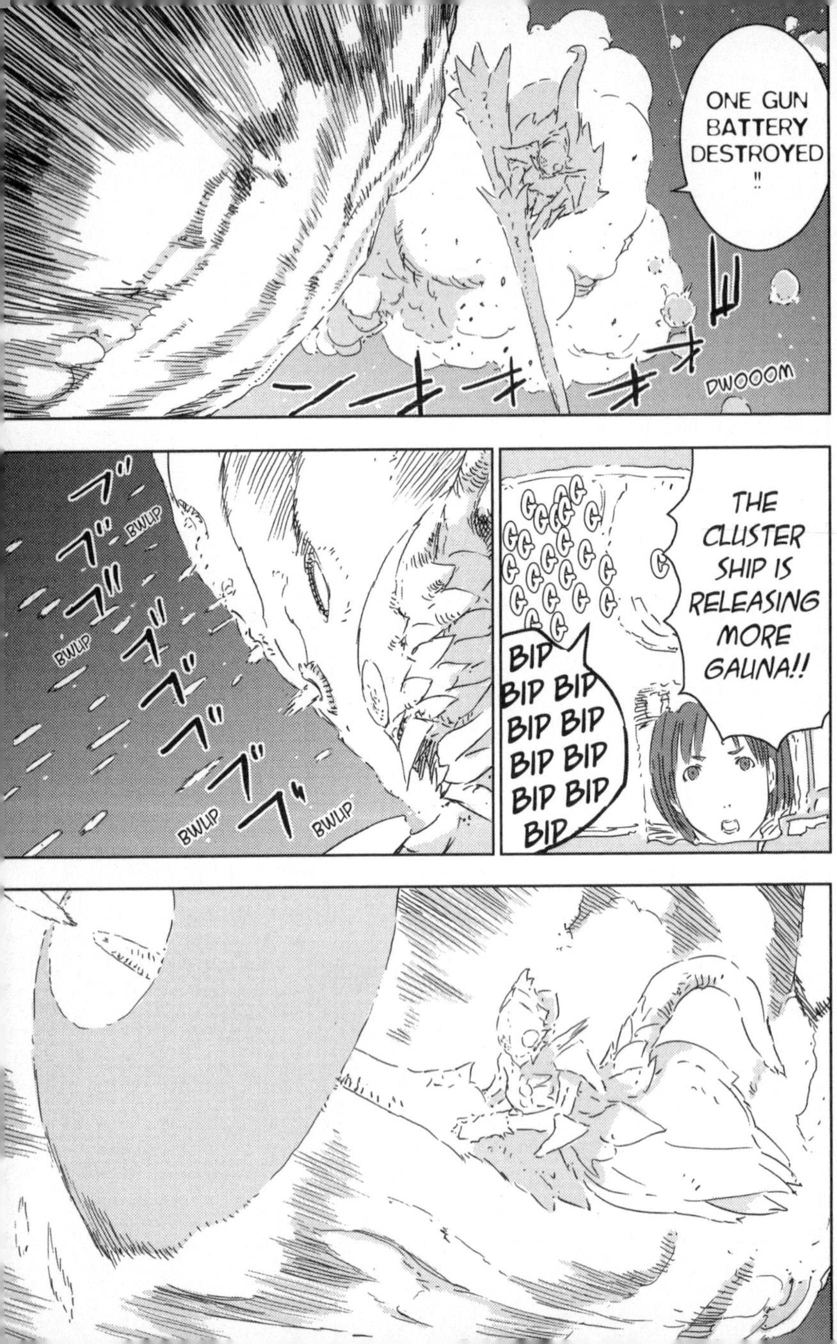
ONE GUN BATTERY DESTROYED !!
DWOOOM
THE CLUSTER SHIP IS RELEASING MORE GAUNA!!
BIP BIP BIP BIP BIP BIP BIP BIP BIP BIP BIP
BWLIP
BWLIP
BWLIP
BWLIP

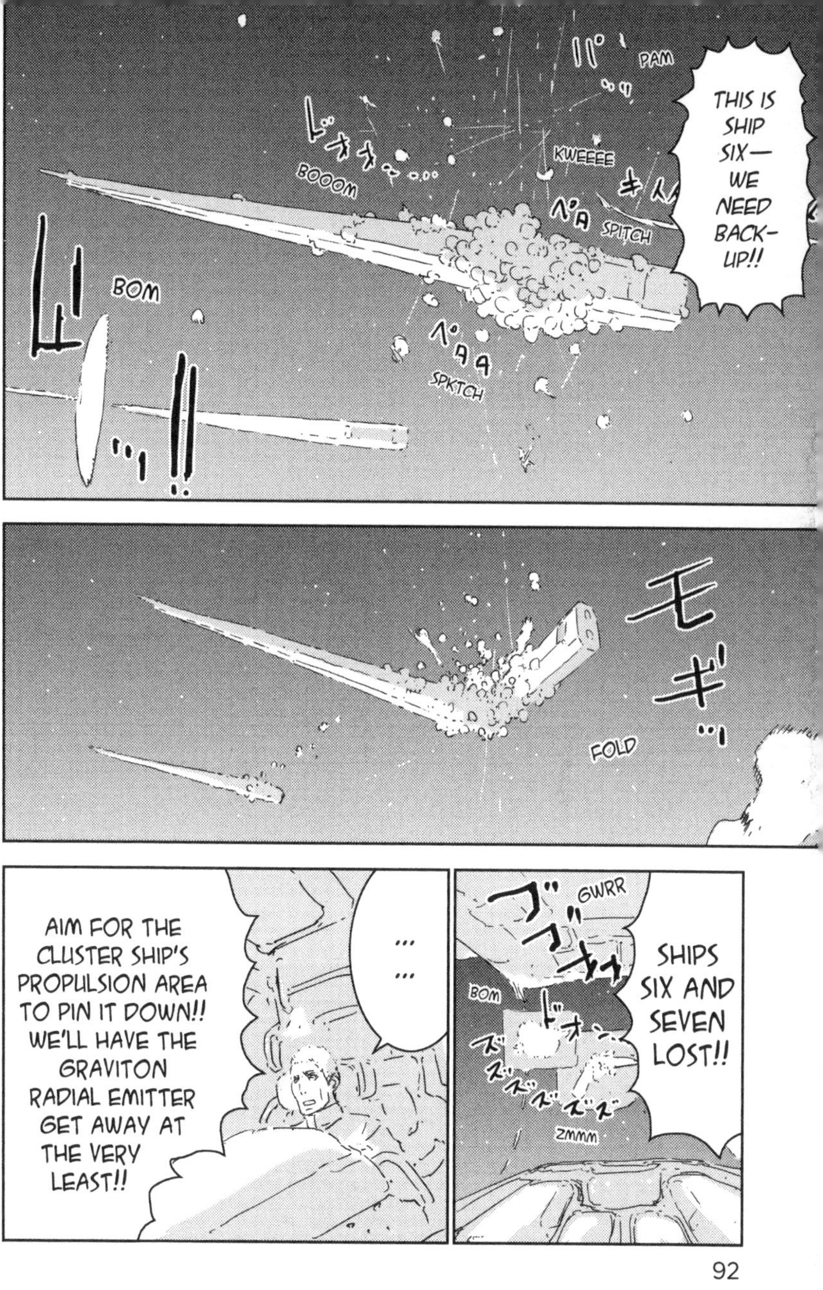
THIS IS SHIP SIX— WE NEED BACK-UP!!
PAM
KWEEEE
SPITCH
BOOOM
SPKTCH
BOM
FOLD
GWRR
SHIPS SIX AND SEVEN LOST!!
BOM
ZMMM
… …
AIM FOR THE CLUSTER SHIP'S PROPULSION AREA TO PIN IT DOWN!! WE'LL HAVE THE GRAVITON RADIAL EMITTER GET AWAY AT THE VERY LEAST!!

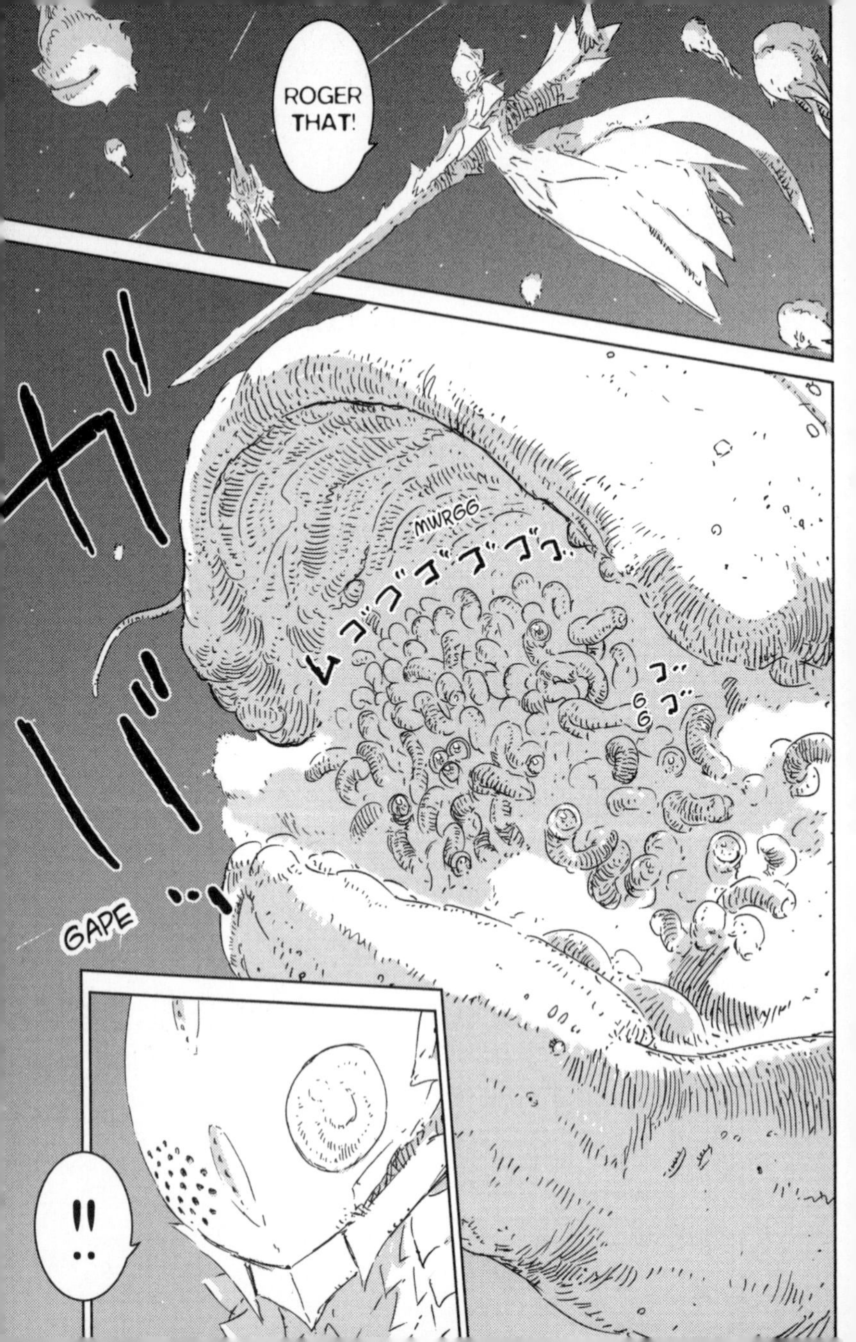
ROGER THAT!
MWRGG
ムゴゴゴゴ
ゴ.. ゴ..
GG
ガバ...
GAPE
!!

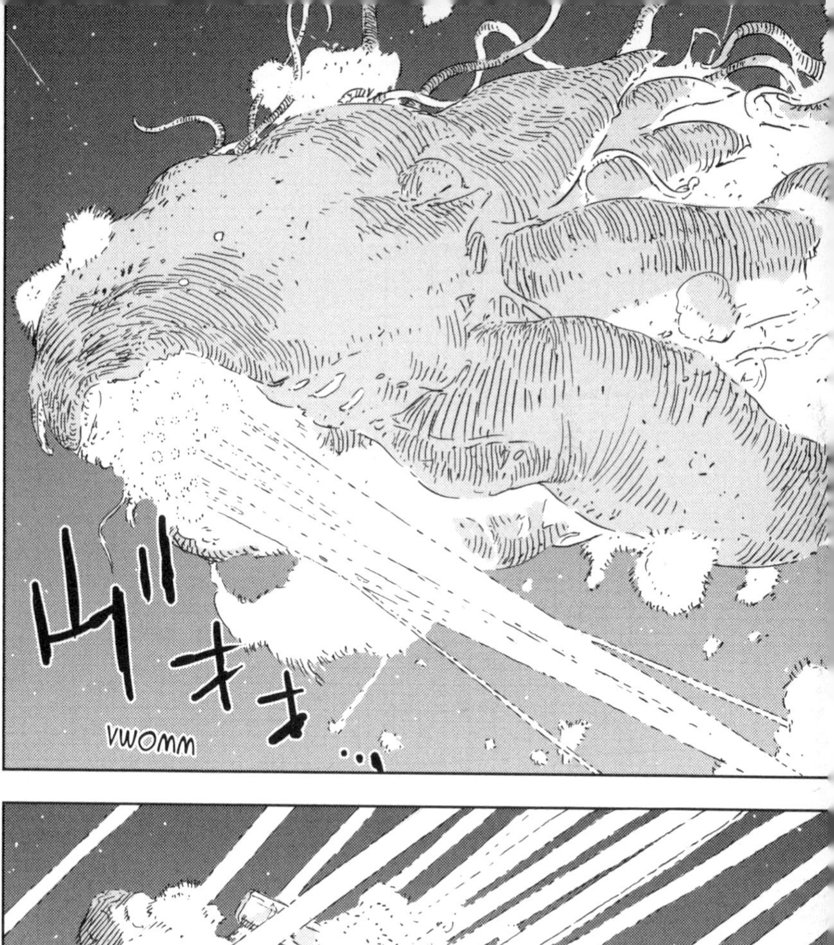
ヴォォ…
VWOMM
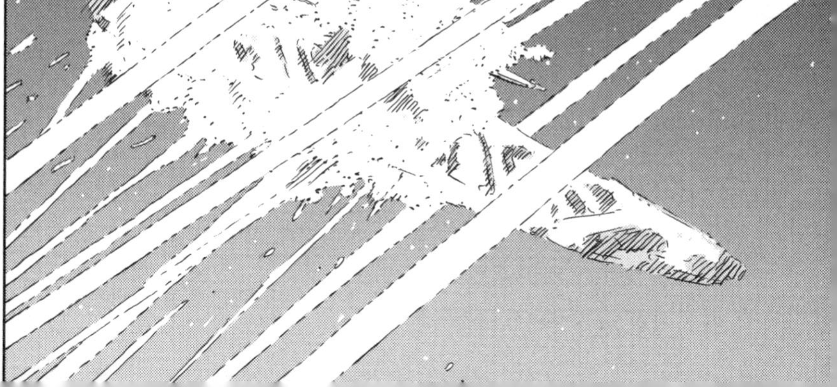

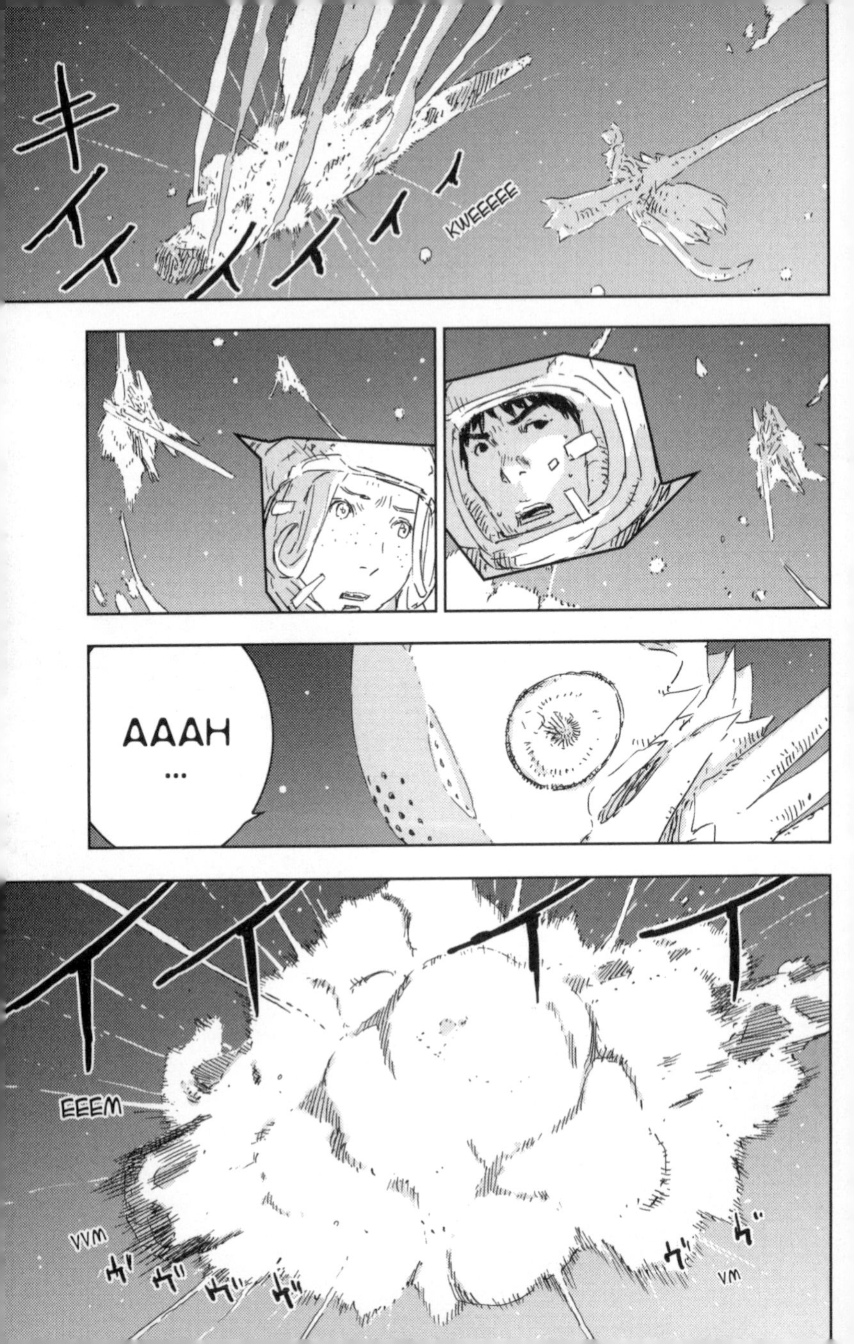
キイイイイイイ
KWEEEEE
AAAH
...
イイイイ
EEEM
VVM
ヴヴヴヴ
ヴヴ
VM

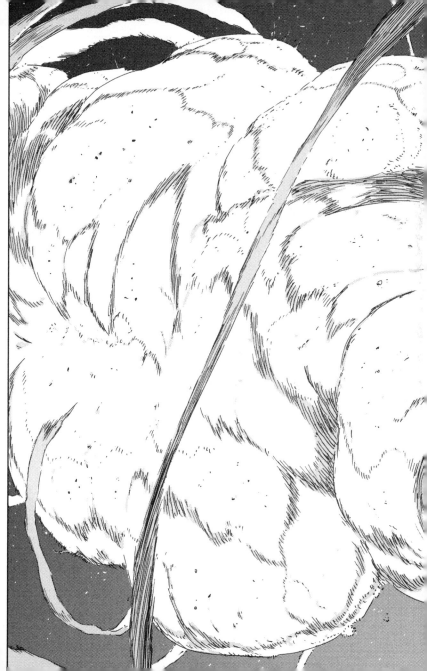

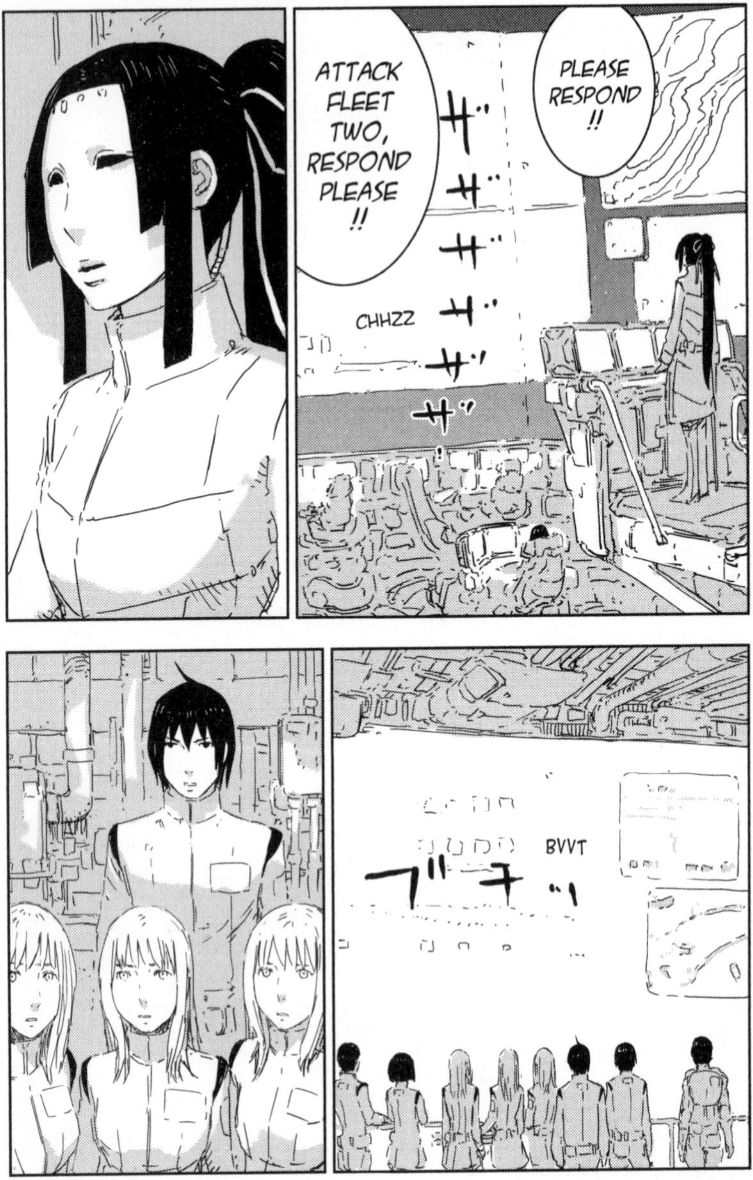
PLEASE RESPOND !!
ATTACK FLEET TWO, RESPOND PLEASE !!
CHHZZ
BVVT

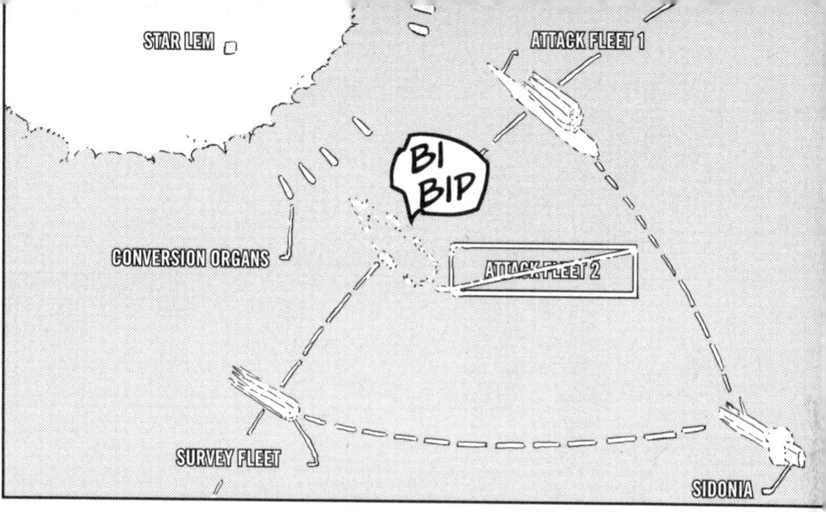
STAR LEM
ATTACK FLEET 1
BI BIP
CONVERSION ORGANS
ATTACK FLEET 2
SURVEY FLEET
SIDONIA

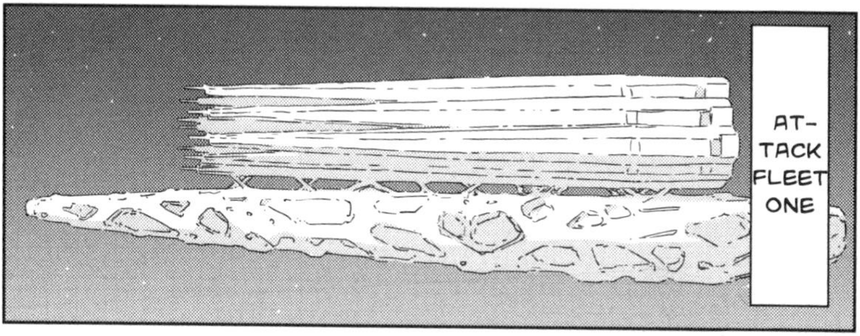
AT-TACK FLEET ONE

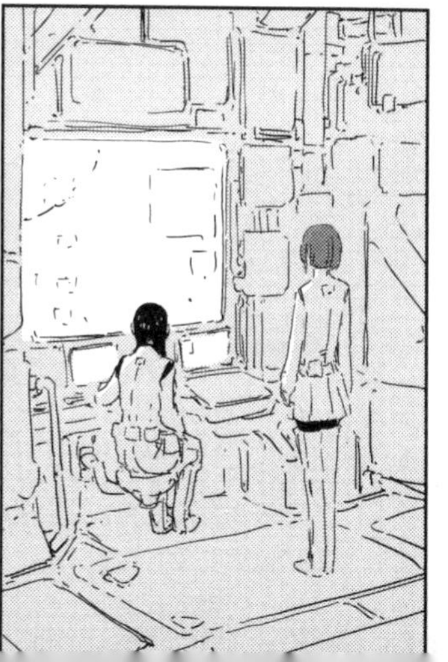

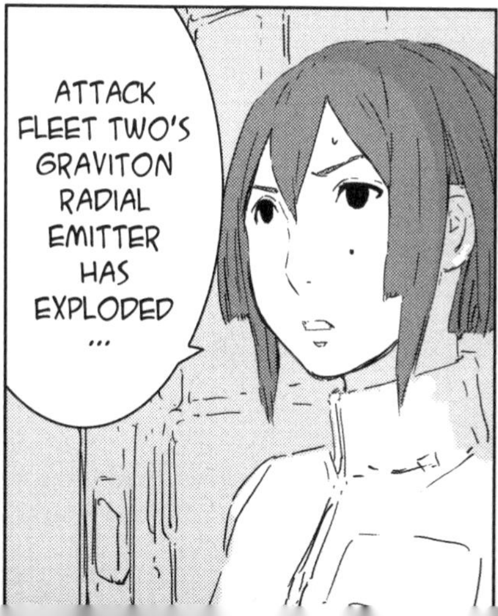
ATTACK FLEET TWO'S GRAVITON RADIAL EMITTER HAS EXPLODED ...

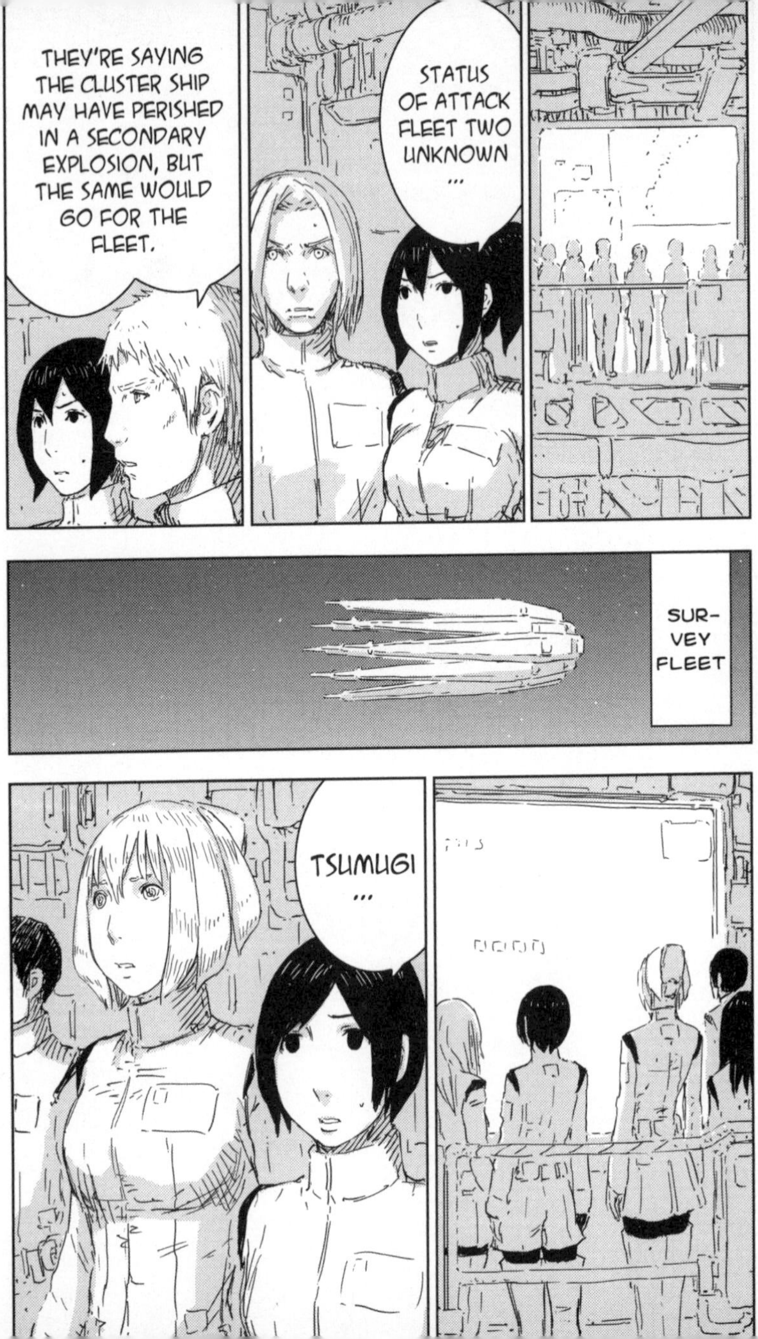
STATUS OF ATTACK FLEET TWO UNKNOWN ...
THEY'RE SAYING THE CLUSTER SHIP MAY HAVE PERISHED IN A SECONDARY EXPLOSION, BUT THE SAME WOULD GO FOR THE FLEET.
SUR-VEY FLEET
TSUMUGI ...

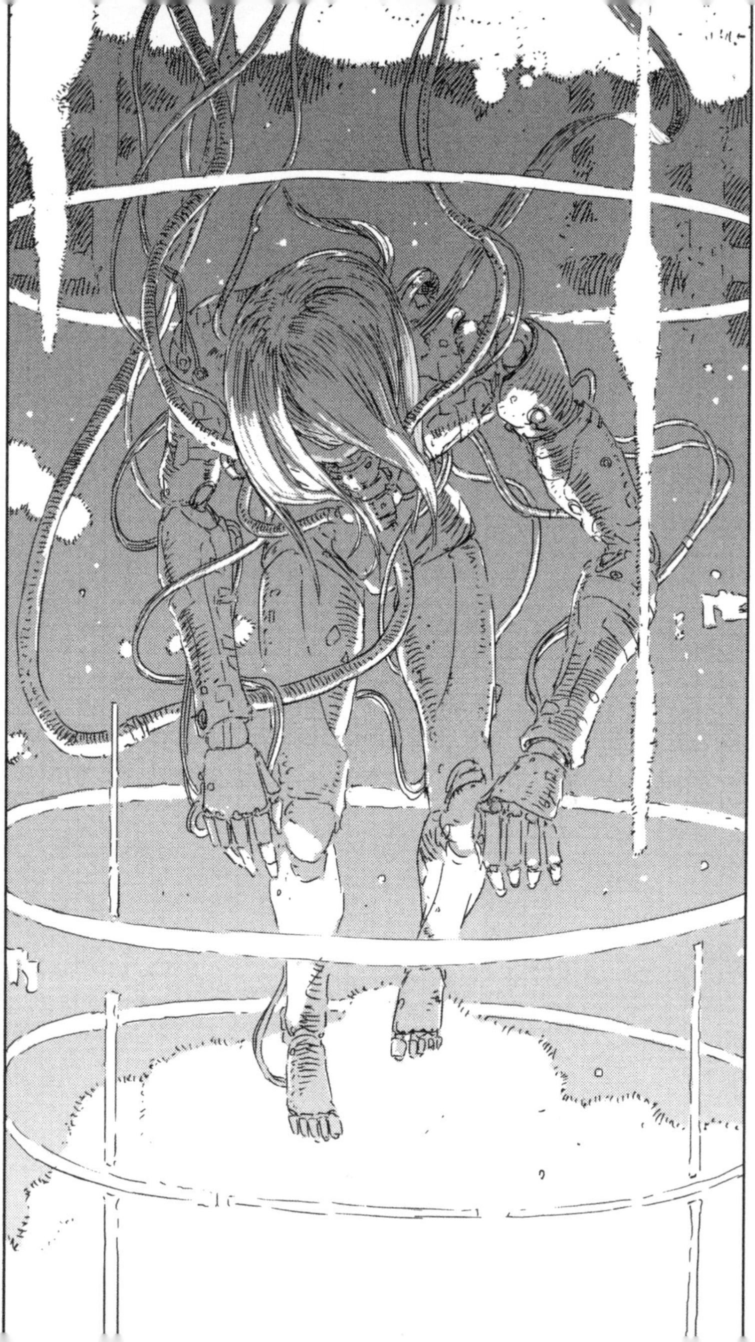

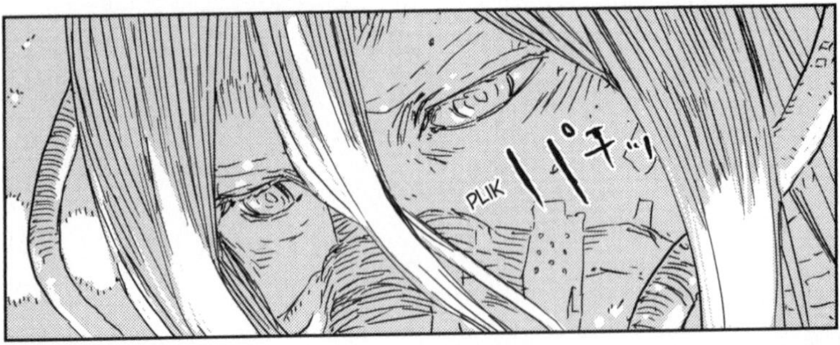
パキッ
PLIK
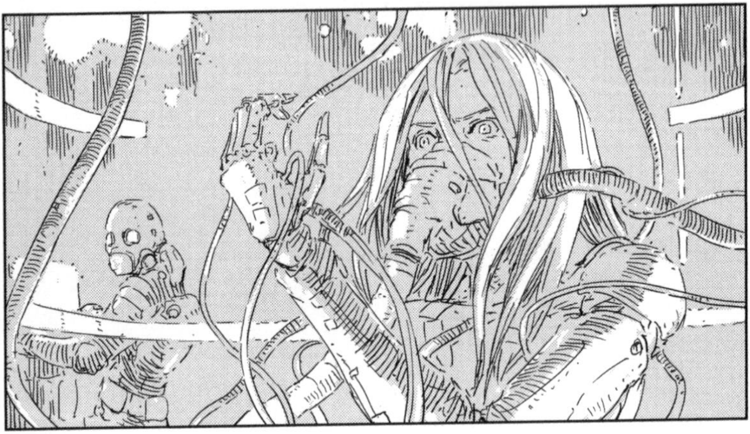
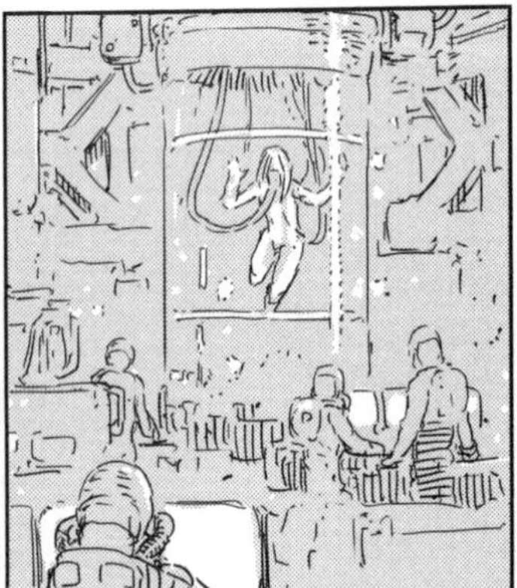
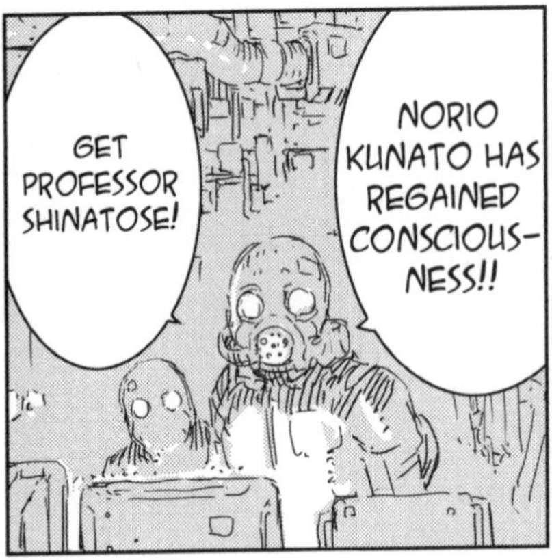
NORIO KUNATO HAS REGAINED CONSCIOUS-NESS!!
GET PROFESSOR SHINATOSE!

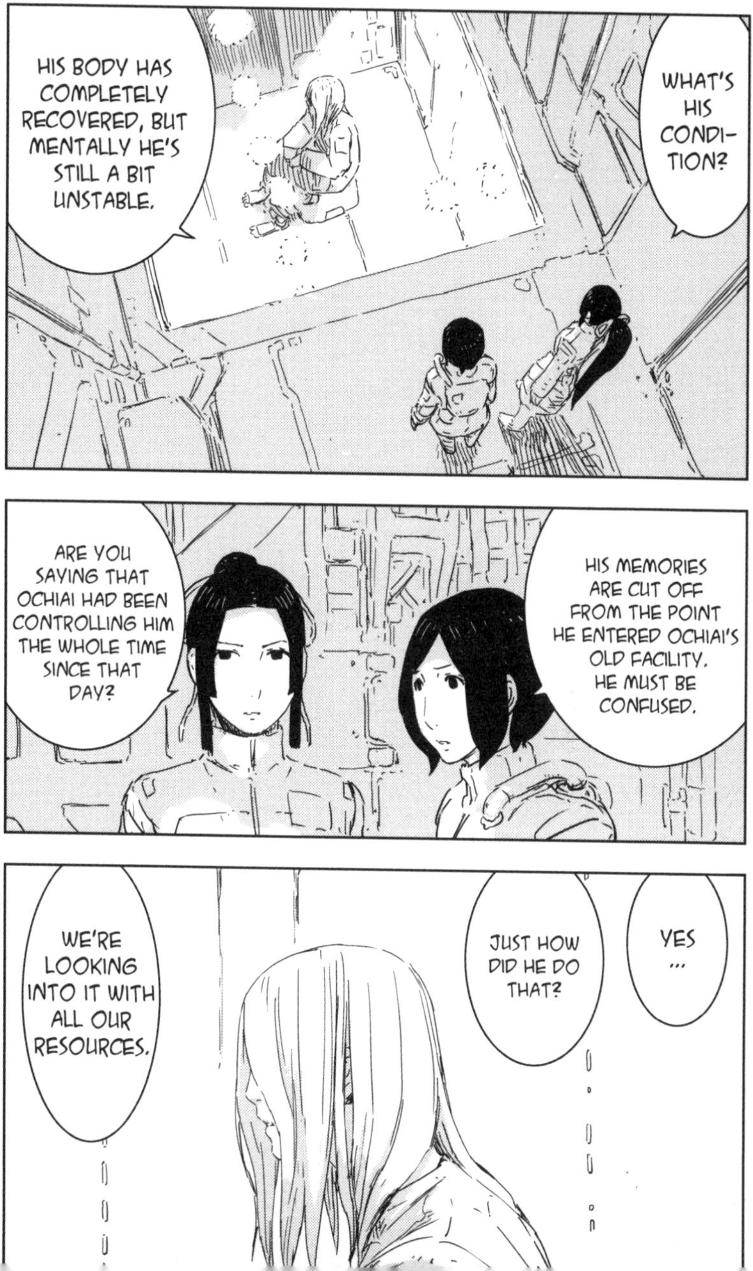
WHAT'S HIS CONDITION?
HIS BODY HAS COMPLETELY RECOVERED, BUT MENTALLY HE'S STILL A BIT UNSTABLE.
HIS MEMORIES ARE CUT OFF FROM THE POINT HE ENTERED OCHIAI'S OLD FACILITY. HE MUST BE CONFUSED.
ARE YOU SAYING THAT OCHIAI HAD BEEN CONTROLLING HIM THE WHOLE TIME SINCE THAT DAY?
YES ...
JUST HOW DID HE DO THAT?
WE'RE LOOKING INTO IT WITH ALL OUR RESOURCES.

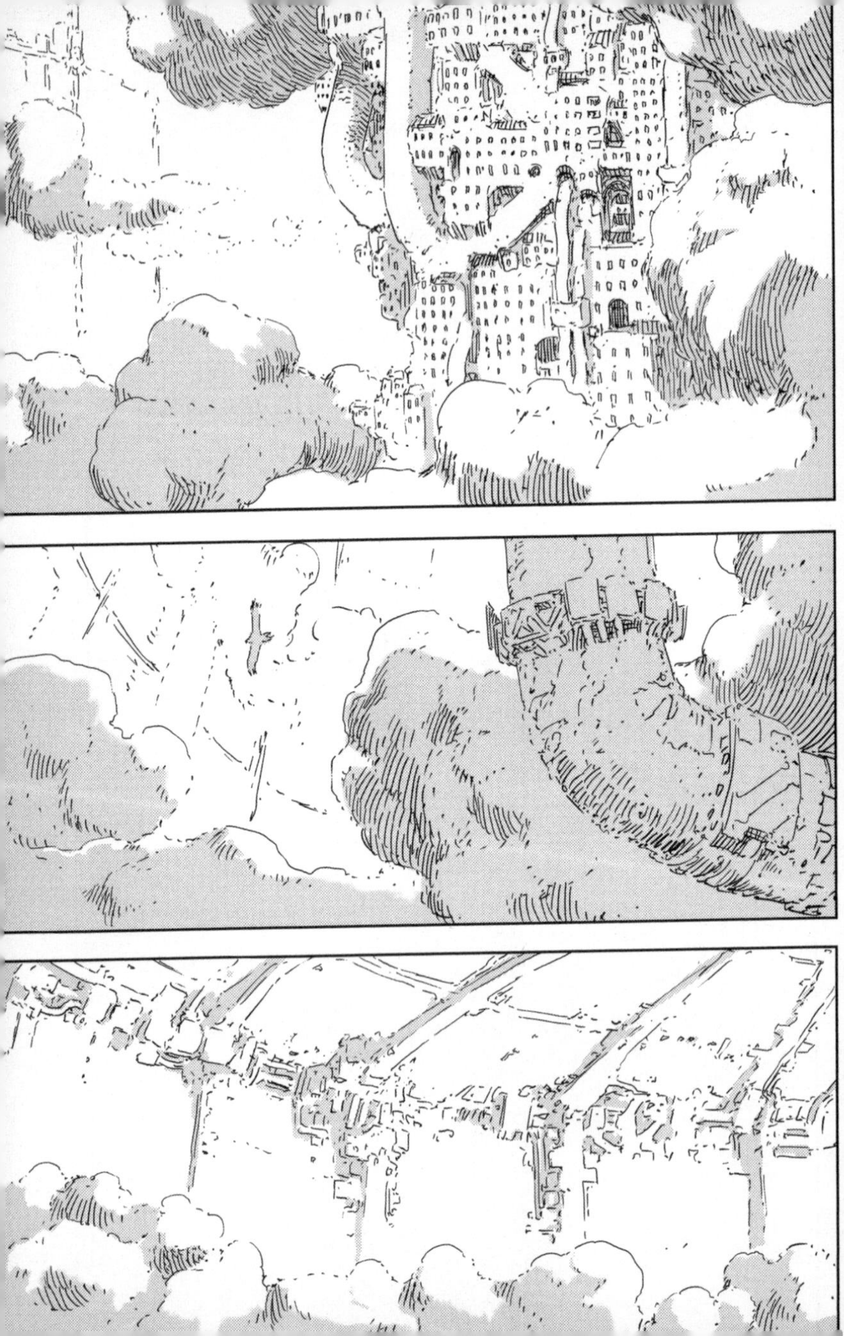

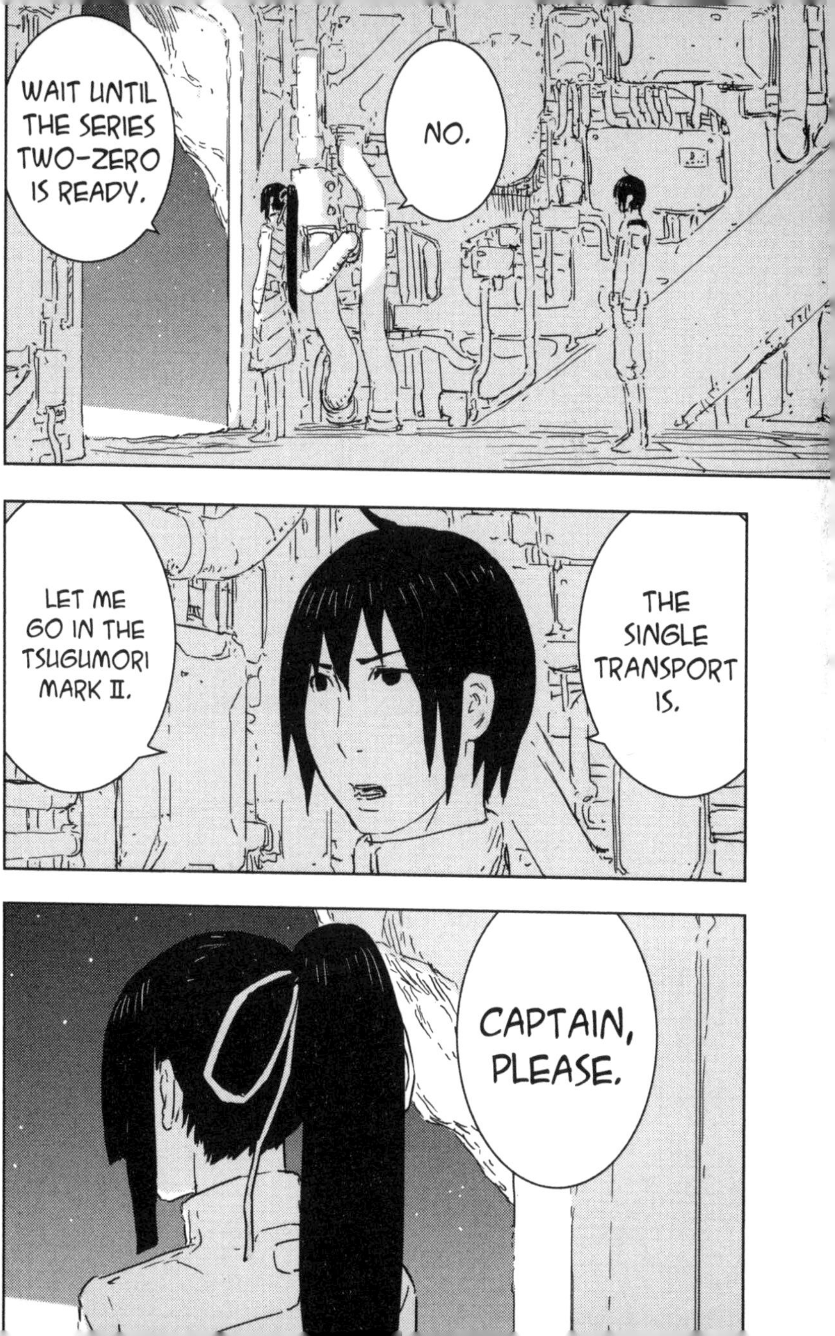
NO.
WAIT UNTIL THE SERIES TWO-ZERO IS READY.
THE SINGLE TRANSPORT IS.
LET ME GO IN THE TSUGUMORI MARK II.
CAPTAIN, PLEASE.

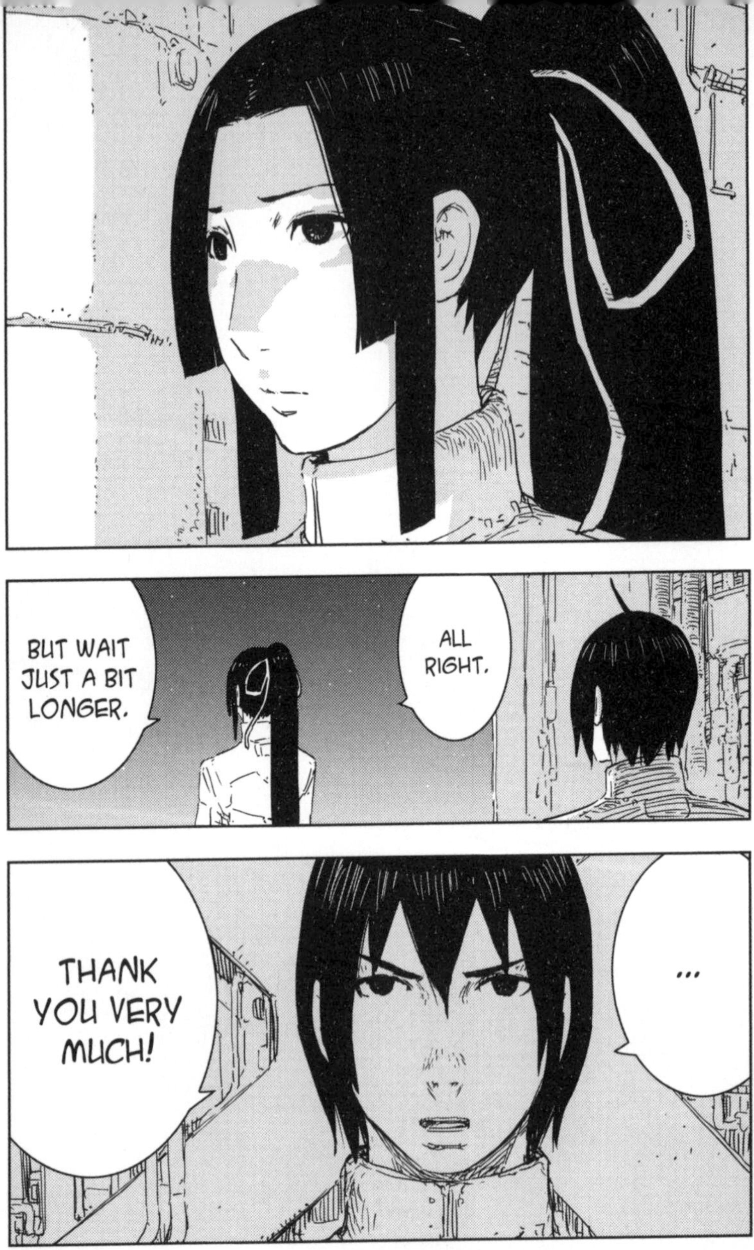
ALL RIGHT.
BUT WAIT JUST A BIT LONGER.
...
THANK YOU VERY MUCH!

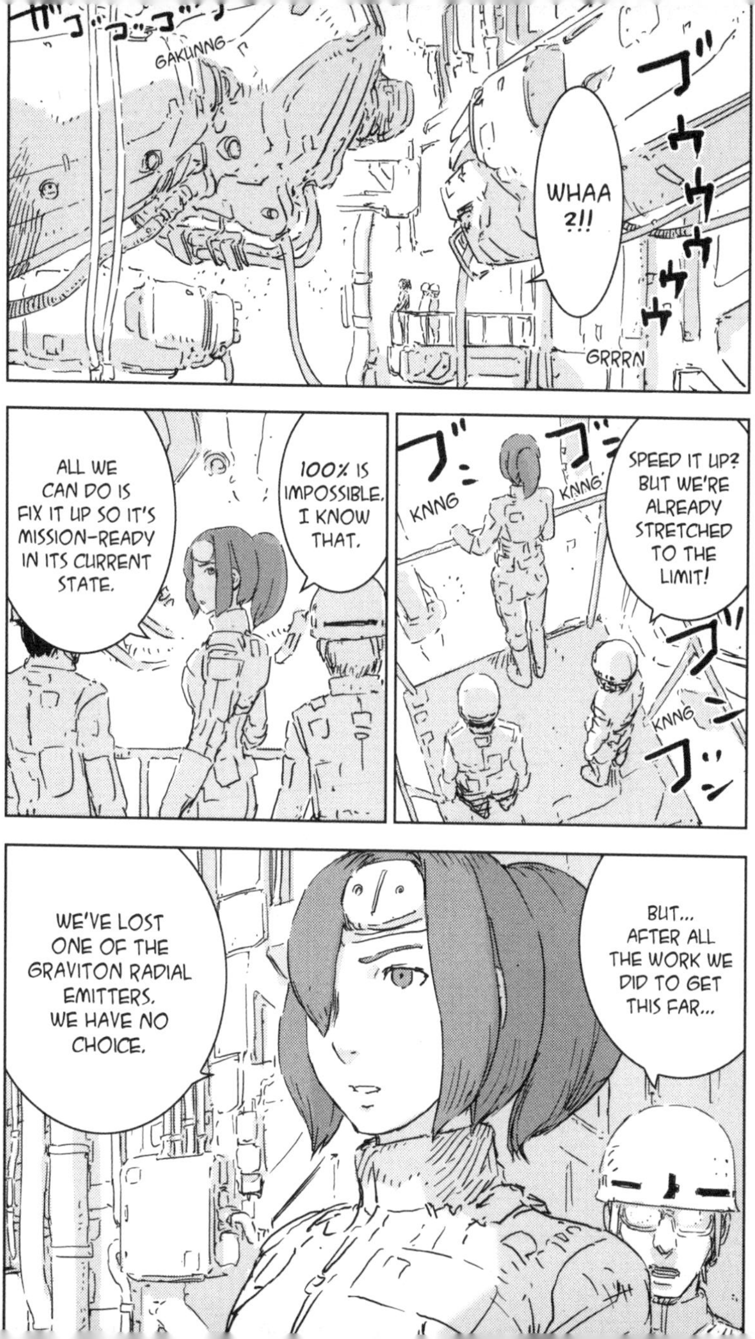
GAKUNNG
WHAA?!!
GRRRN
KNNG
SPEED IT UP? BUT WE'RE ALREADY STRETCHED TO THE LIMIT!
KNNG
KNNG
100% IS IMPOSSIBLE, I KNOW THAT.
ALL WE CAN DO IS FIX IT UP SO IT'S MISSION-READY IN ITS CURRENT STATE.
BUT... AFTER ALL THE WORK WE DID TO GET THIS FAR...
WE'VE LOST ONE OF THE GRAVITON RADIAL EMITTERS. WE HAVE NO CHOICE.

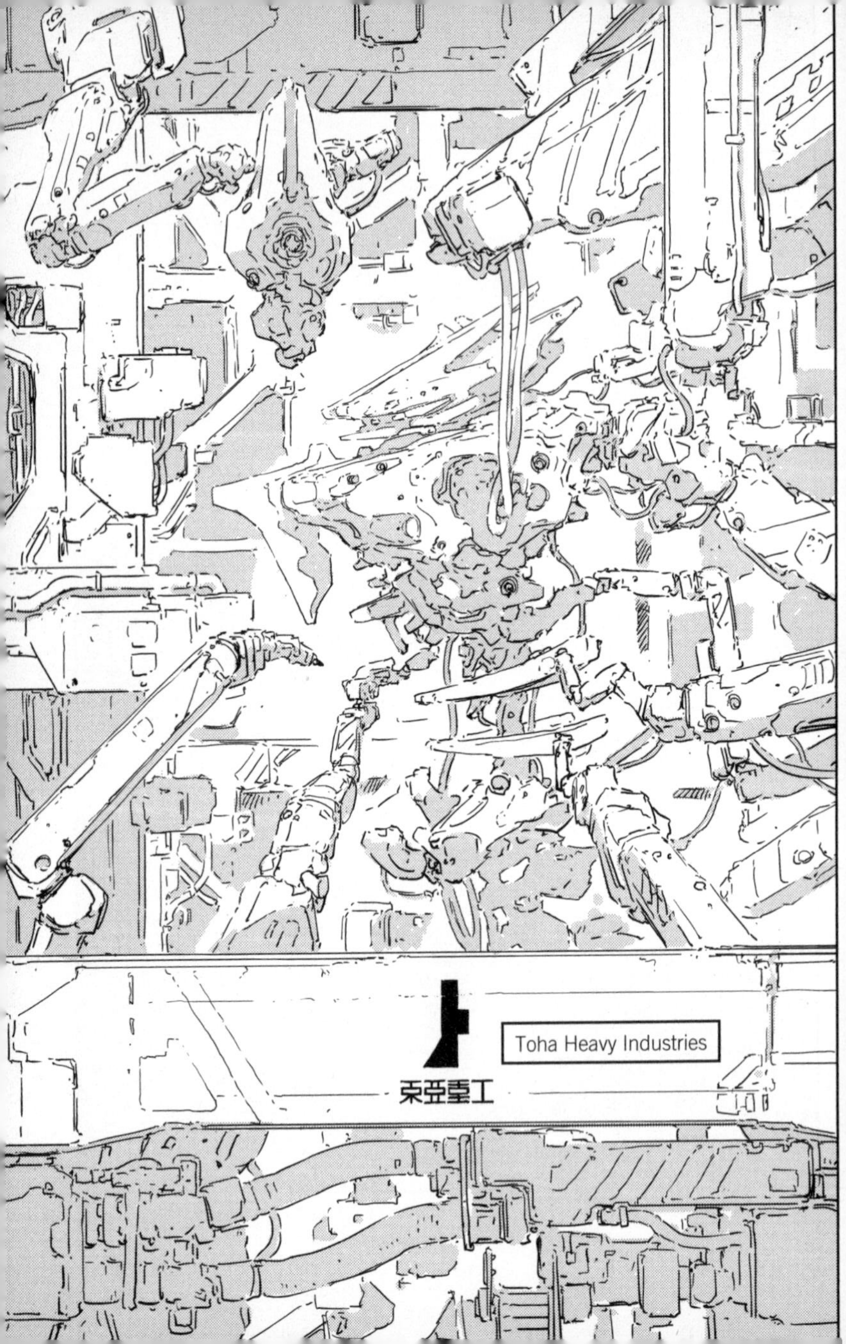
Toha Heavy Industries
東亜重工

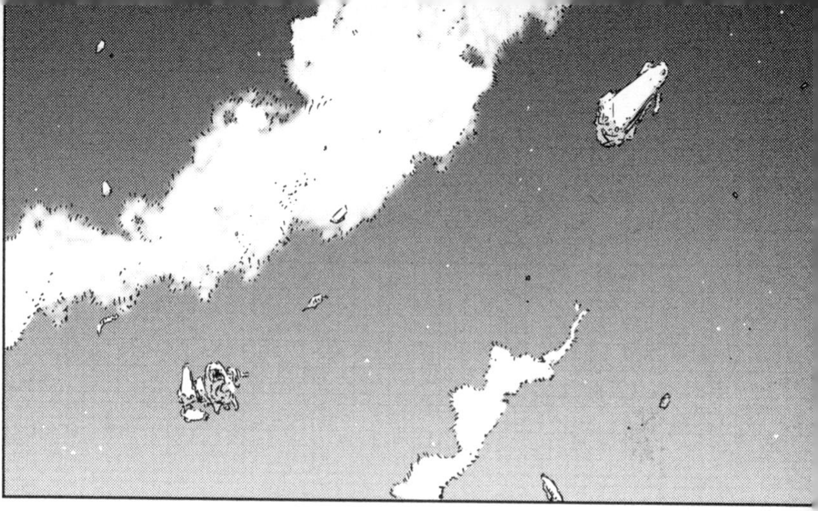
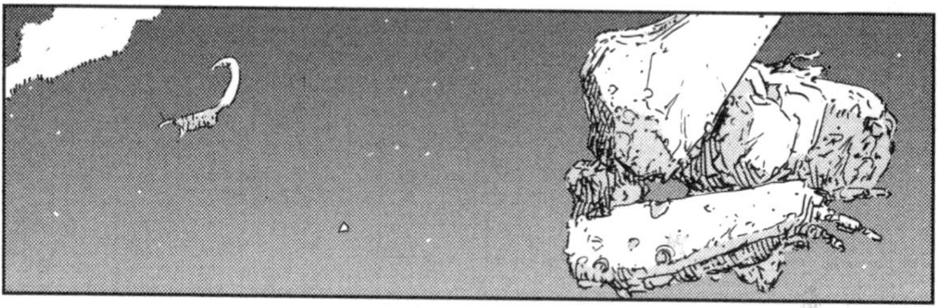
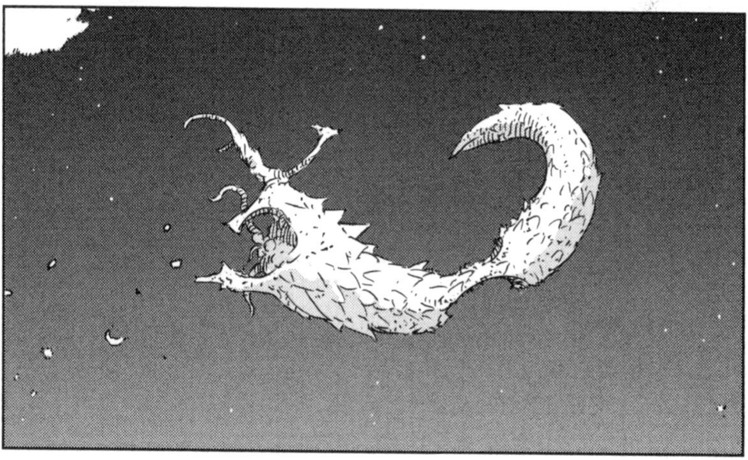

Chapter 68: END

シドニアの騎士

KNIGHTS OF SIDONIA

REJECTED COVER SKETCH FOR VOL. 14

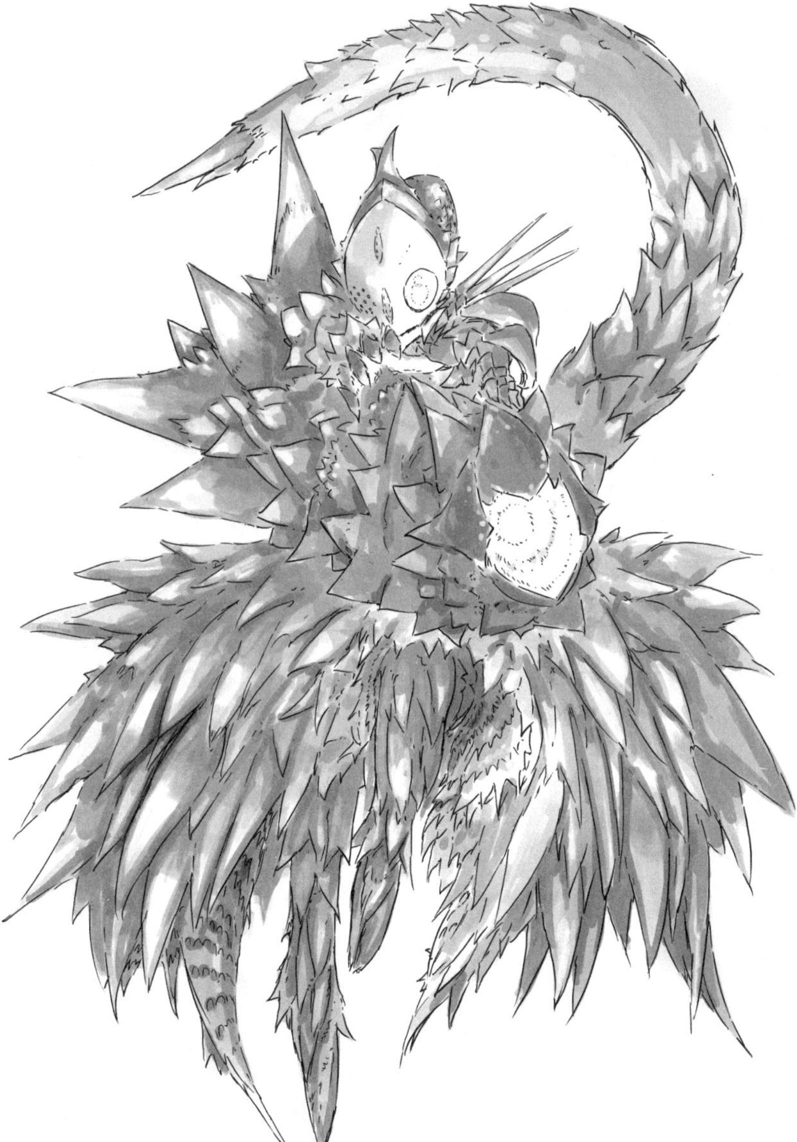

Chapter 69: Norio Kunato's Comeback

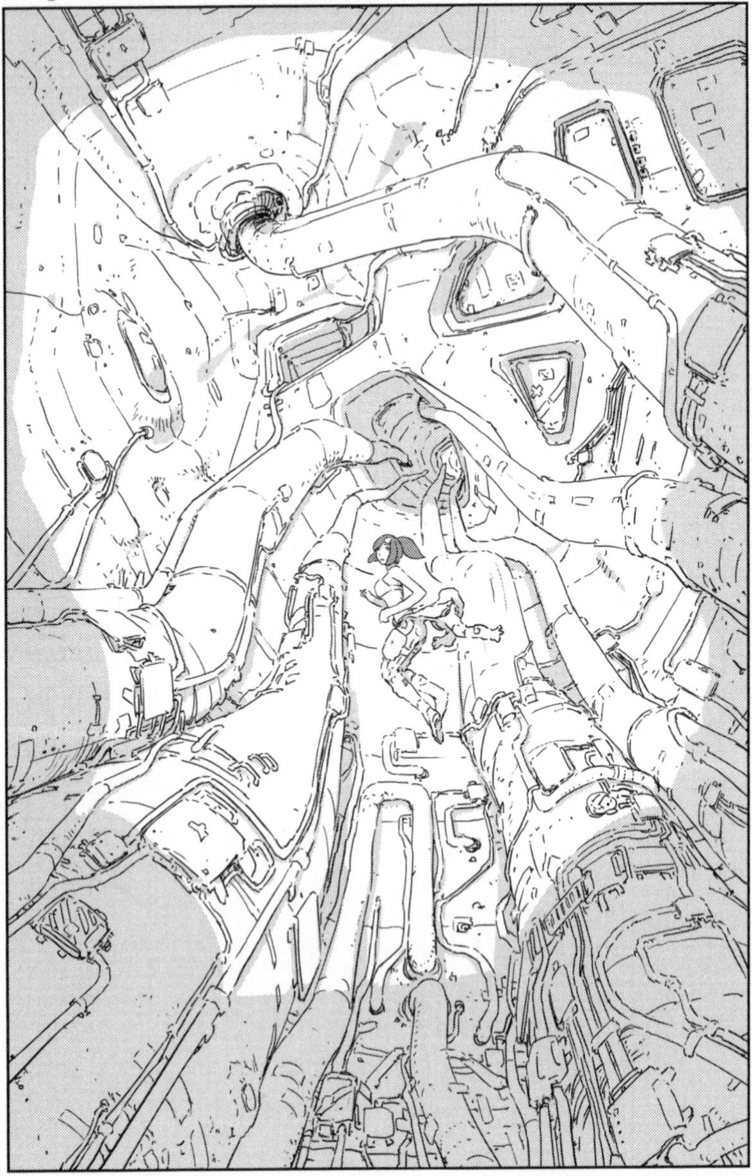

One Hundred Sights of Sidonia Part Fifty-Three:
Toha Heavy Industries Power Flow Channel

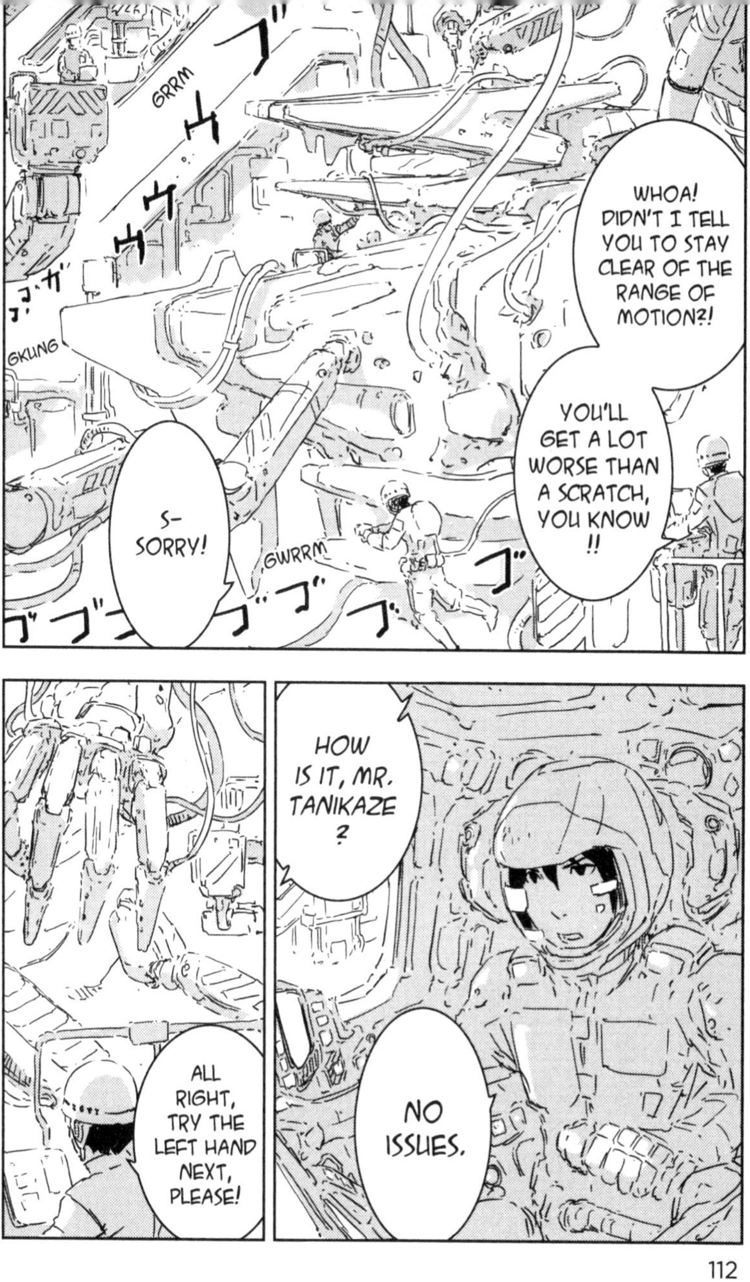
WHOA! DIDN'T I TELL YOU TO STAY CLEAR OF THE RANGE OF MOTION?!
YOU'LL GET A LOT WORSE THAN A SCRATCH, YOU KNOW!!
GRRM
GKUNG
S-SORRY!
GWRRM
HOW IS IT, MR. TANIKAZE?
NO ISSUES.
ALL RIGHT, TRY THE LEFT HAND NEXT, PLEASE!

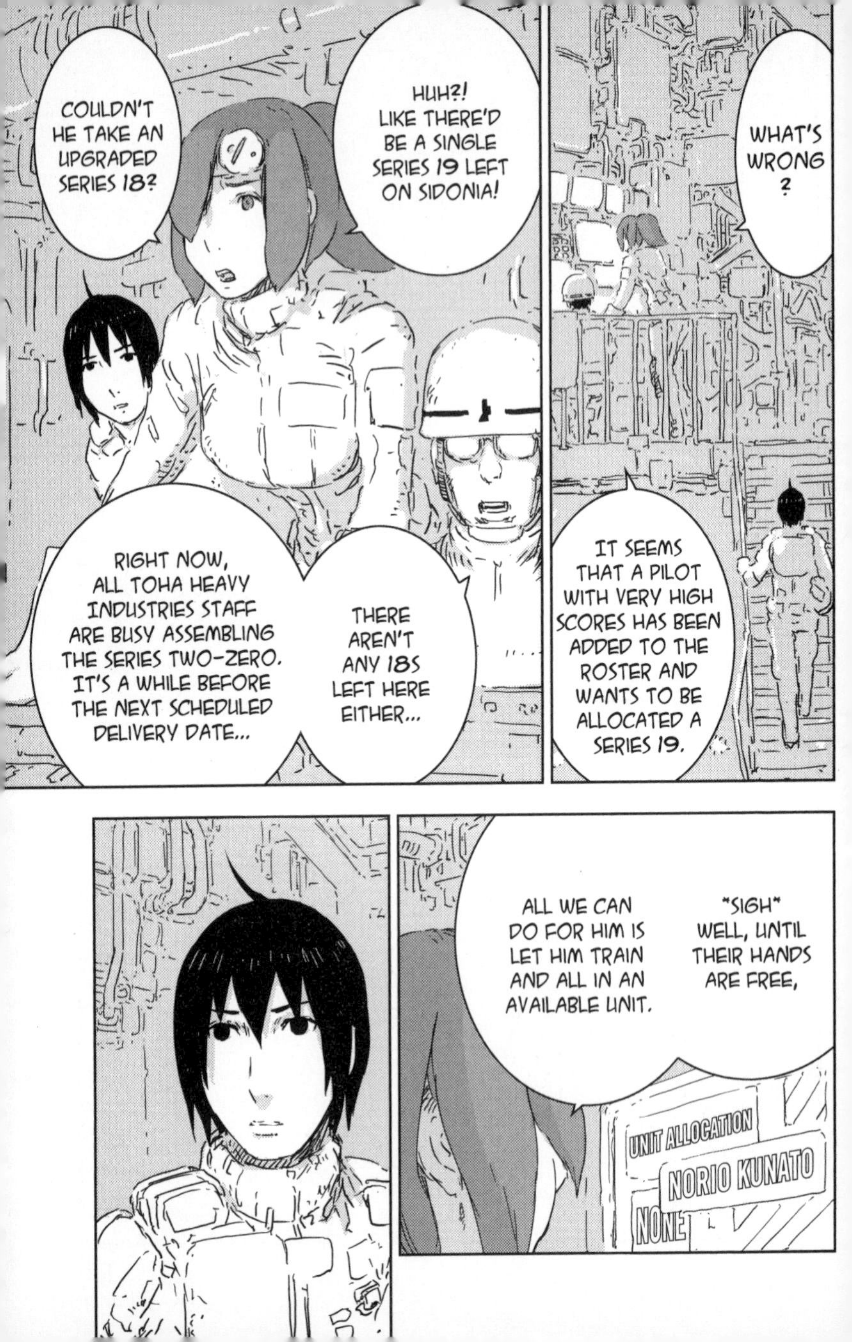
WHAT'S WRONG?
IT SEEMS THAT A PILOT WITH VERY HIGH SCORES HAS BEEN ADDED TO THE ROSTER AND WANTS TO BE ALLOCATED A SERIES 19.
HUH?! LIKE THERE'D BE A SINGLE SERIES 19 LEFT ON SIDONIA!
COULDN'T HE TAKE AN UPGRADED SERIES 18?
THERE AREN'T ANY 18S LEFT HERE EITHER...
RIGHT NOW, ALL TOHA HEAVY INDUSTRIES STAFF ARE BUSY ASSEMBLING THE SERIES TWO-ZERO. IT'S A WHILE BEFORE THE NEXT SCHEDULED DELIVERY DATE...
SIGH WELL, UNTIL THEIR HANDS ARE FREE,
ALL WE CAN DO FOR HIM IS LET HIM TRAIN AND ALL IN AN AVAILABLE UNIT.
UNIT ALLOCATION
NORIO KUNATO
NONE

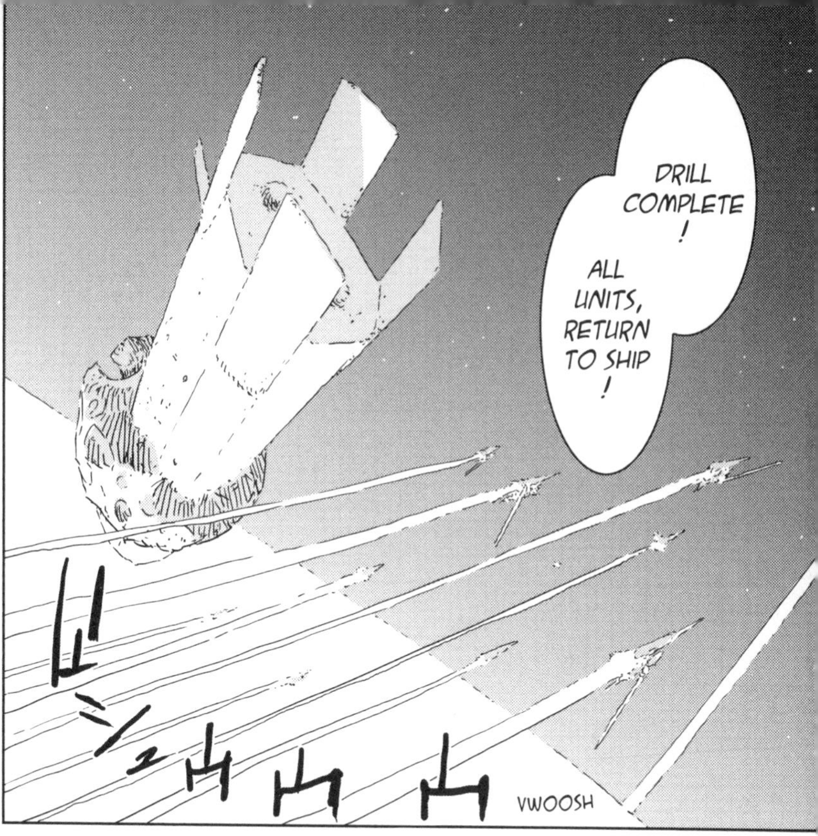
DRILL COMPLETE !
ALL UNITS, RETURN TO SHIP !
VWOOSH

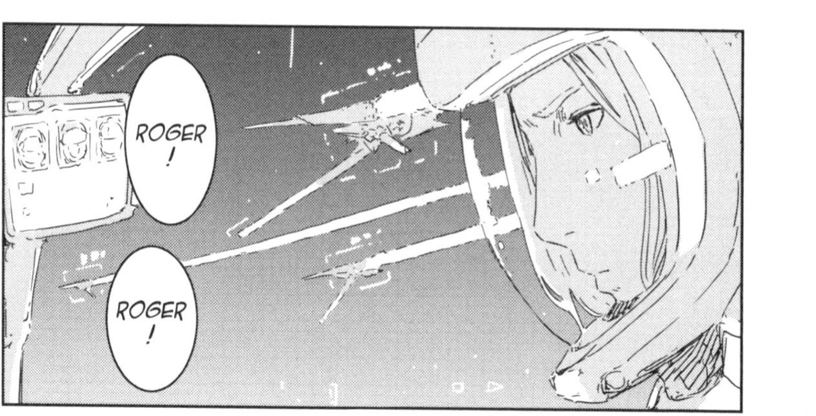
ROGER !
ROGER !

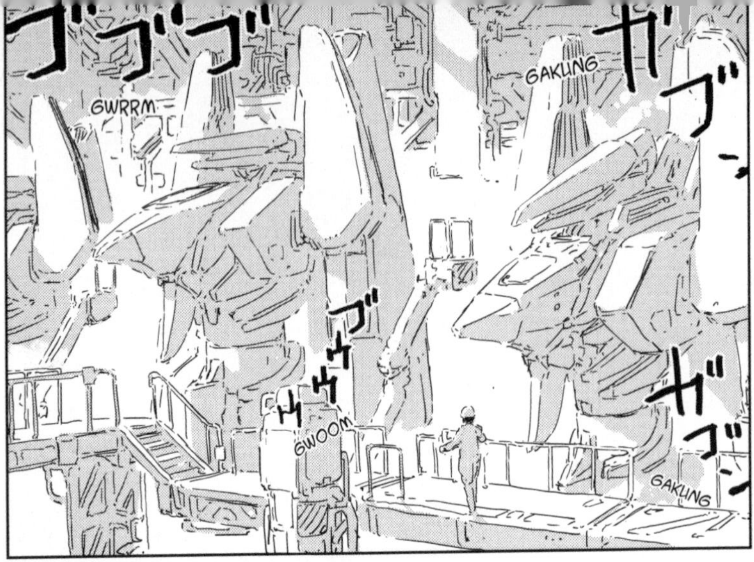
ゴゴゴ
GWRRM
GAKUNG
ガゴッ
GWOOM
ガゴン
GAKUNG

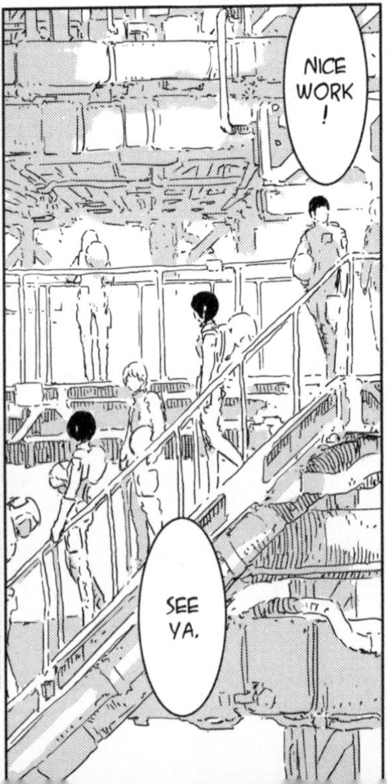
NICE WORK!
SEE YA.

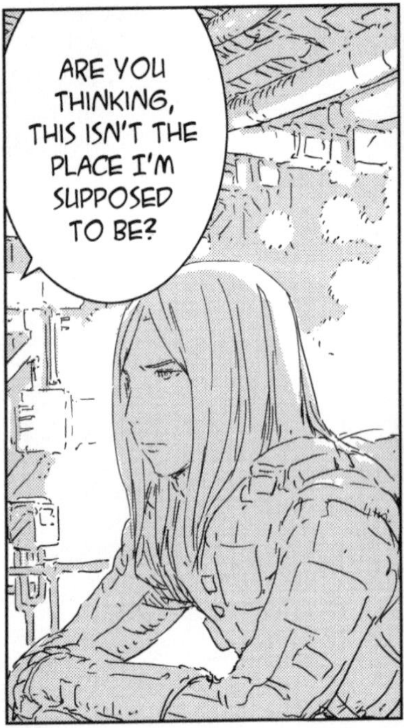
ARE YOU THINKING, THIS ISN'T THE PLACE I'M SUPPOSED TO BE?

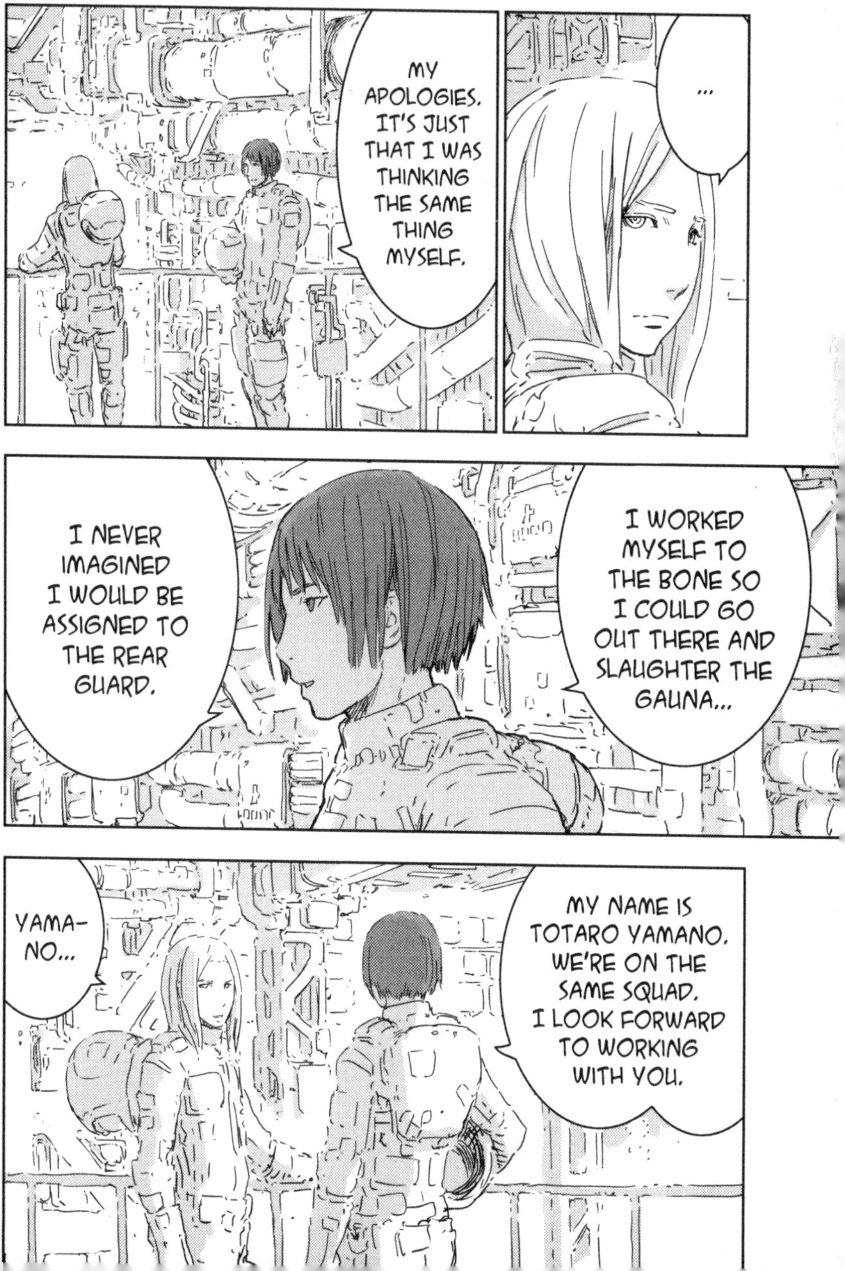
...
MY APOLOGIES. IT'S JUST THAT I WAS THINKING THE SAME THING MYSELF.
I WORKED MYSELF TO THE BONE SO I COULD GO OUT THERE AND SLAUGHTER THE GAUNA...
I NEVER IMAGINED I WOULD BE ASSIGNED TO THE REAR GUARD.
MY NAME IS TOTARO YAMANO. WE'RE ON THE SAME SQUAD. I LOOK FORWARD TO WORKING WITH YOU.
YAMA-NO...

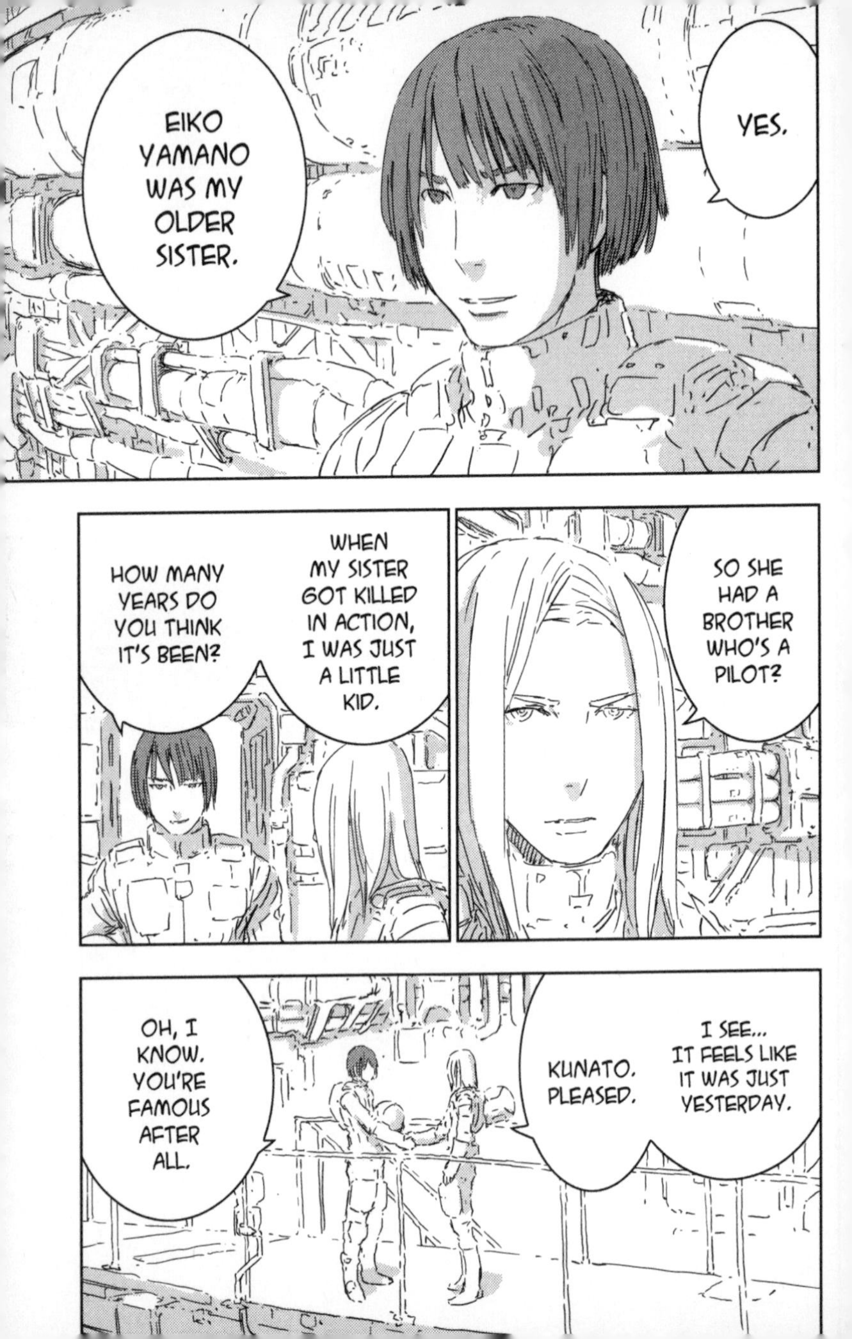
YES.
EIKO YAMANO WAS MY OLDER SISTER.
SO SHE HAD A BROTHER WHO'S A PILOT?
WHEN MY SISTER GOT KILLED IN ACTION, I WAS JUST A LITTLE KID.
HOW MANY YEARS DO YOU THINK IT'S BEEN?
I SEE... IT FEELS LIKE IT WAS JUST YESTERDAY.
KUNATO. PLEASED.
OH, I KNOW. YOU'RE FAMOUS AFTER ALL.

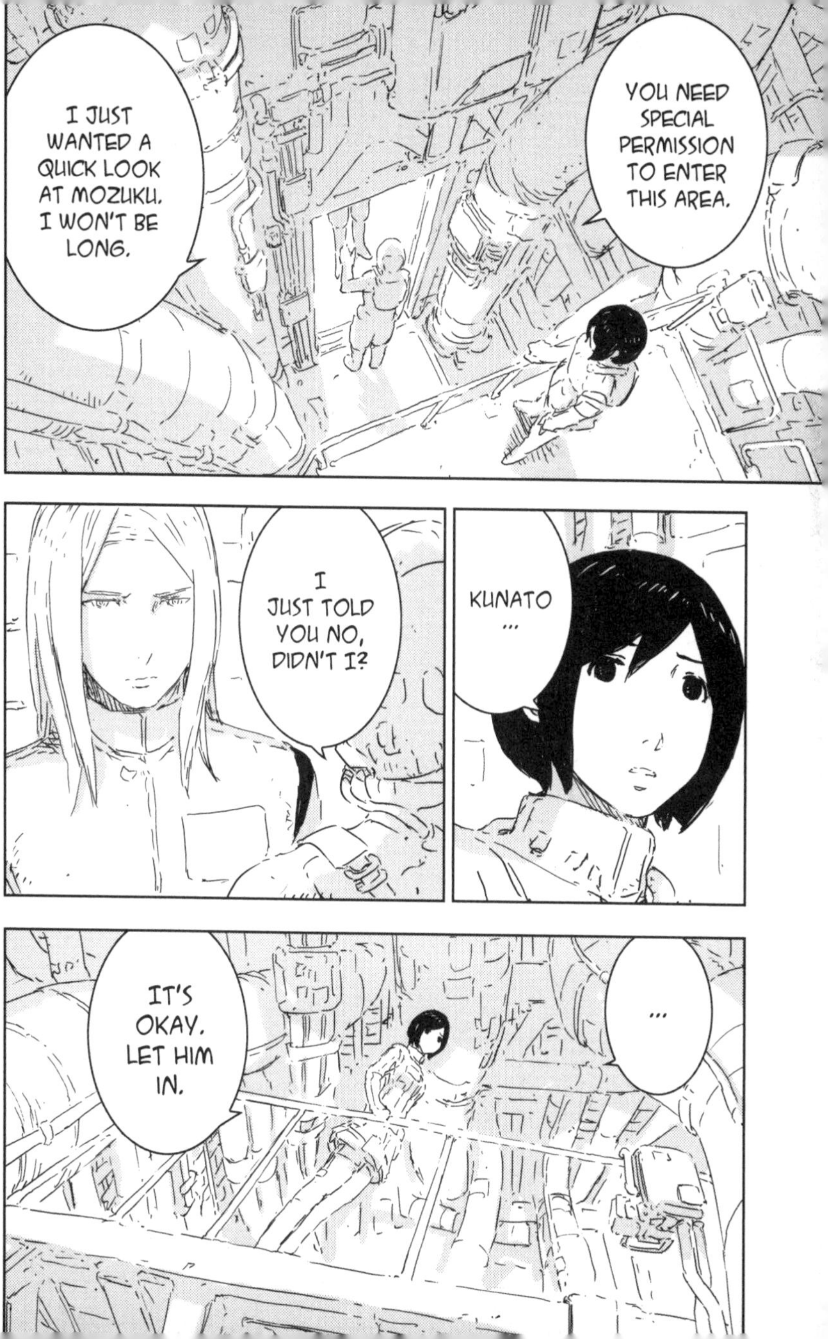
YOU NEED SPECIAL PERMISSION TO ENTER THIS AREA.
I JUST WANTED A QUICK LOOK AT MOZUKU. I WON'T BE LONG.
KUNATO ...
I JUST TOLD YOU NO, DIDN'T I?
...
IT'S OKAY. LET HIM IN.

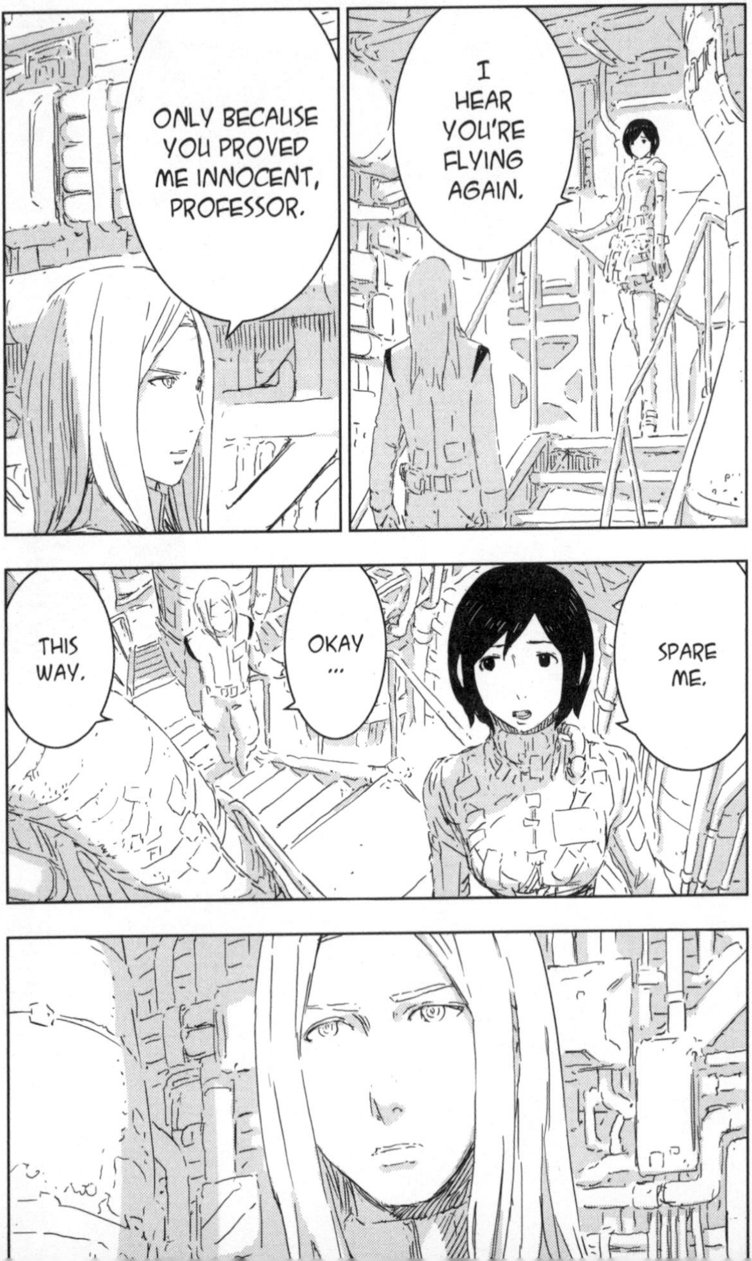
I HEAR YOU'RE FLYING AGAIN.
ONLY BECAUSE YOU PROVED ME INNOCENT, PROFESSOR.
SPARE ME.
OKAY ...
THIS WAY.

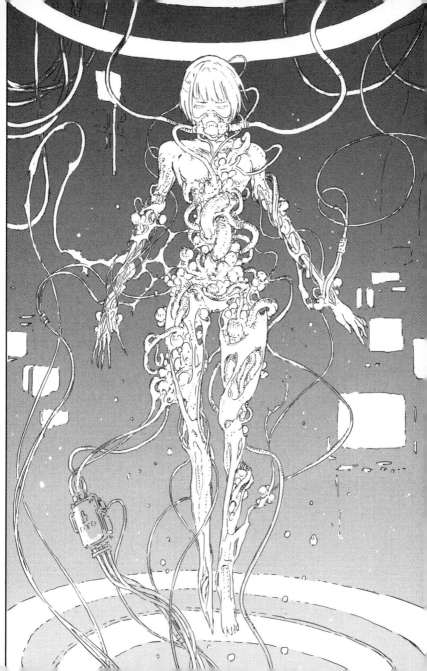

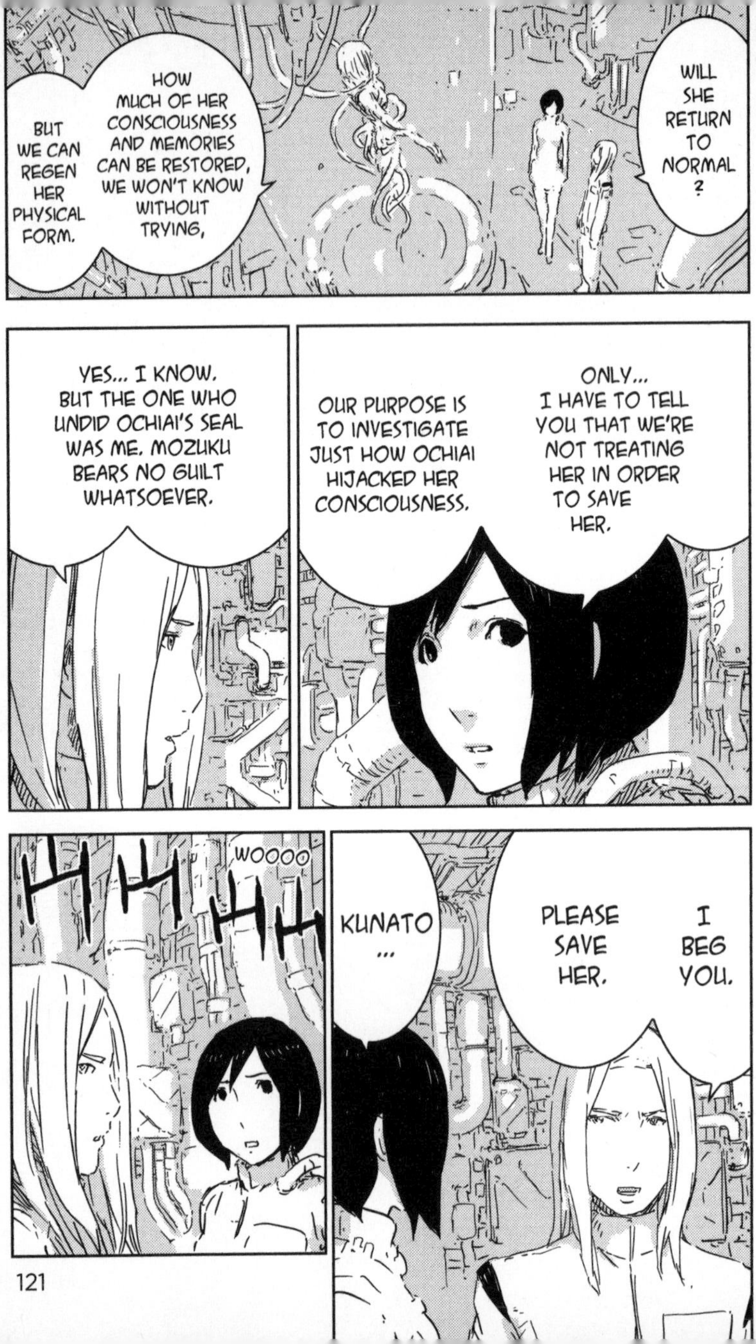
WILL SHE RETURN TO NORMAL?
HOW MUCH OF HER CONSCIOUSNESS AND MEMORIES CAN BE RESTORED, WE WON'T KNOW WITHOUT TRYING,
BUT WE CAN REGEN HER PHYSICAL FORM.
ONLY... I HAVE TO TELL YOU THAT WE'RE NOT TREATING HER IN ORDER TO SAVE HER.
OUR PURPOSE IS TO INVESTIGATE JUST HOW OCHIAI HIJACKED HER CONSCIOUSNESS.
YES... I KNOW. BUT THE ONE WHO UNDID OCHIAI'S SEAL WAS ME. MOZUKU BEARS NO GUILT WHATSOEVER.
I BEG YOU.
PLEASE SAVE HER.
KUNATO...
WOOOO

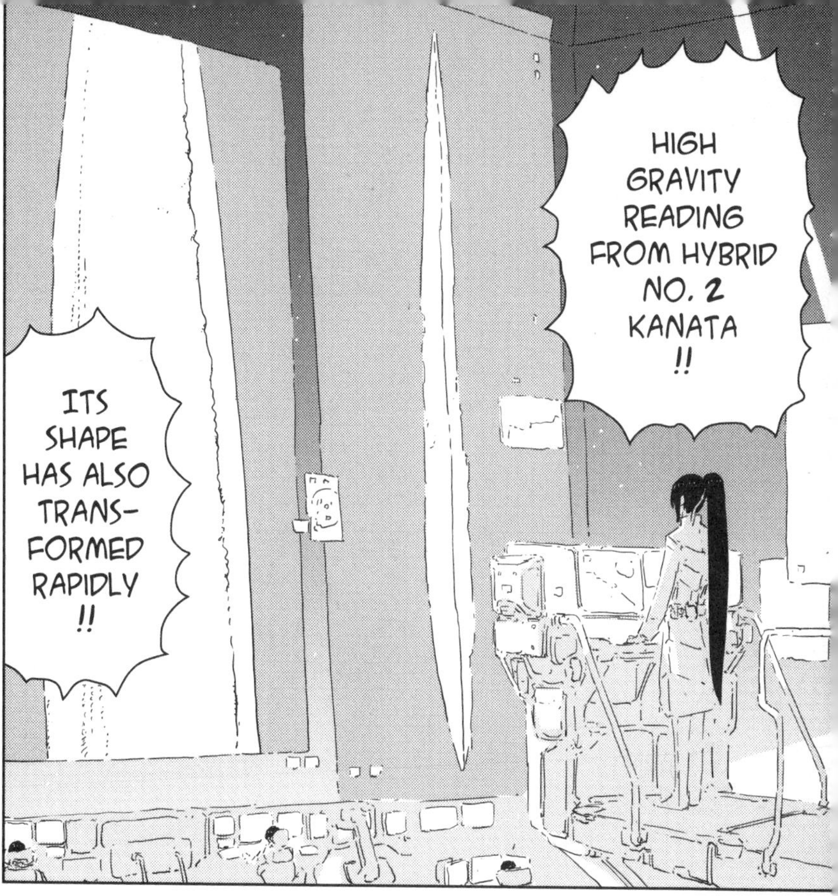
HIGH GRAVITY READING FROM HYBRID NO. 2 KANATA !!
ITS SHAPE HAS ALSO TRANS-FORMED RAPIDLY !!
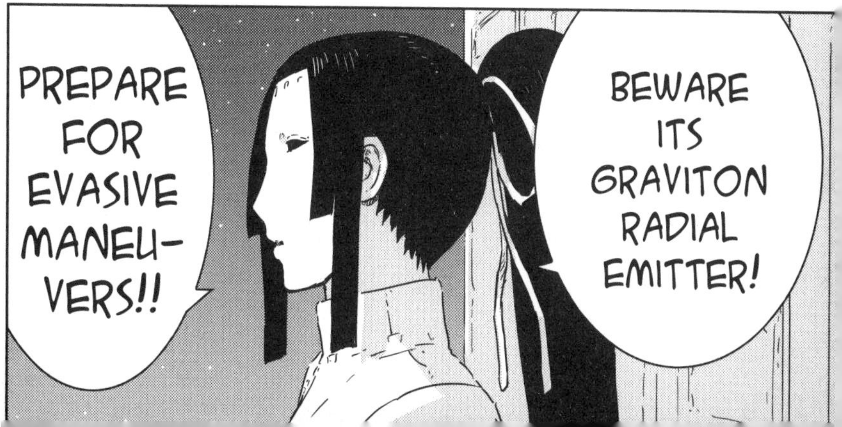
BEWARE ITS GRAVITON RADIAL EMITTER!
PREPARE FOR EVASIVE MANEU-VERS!!

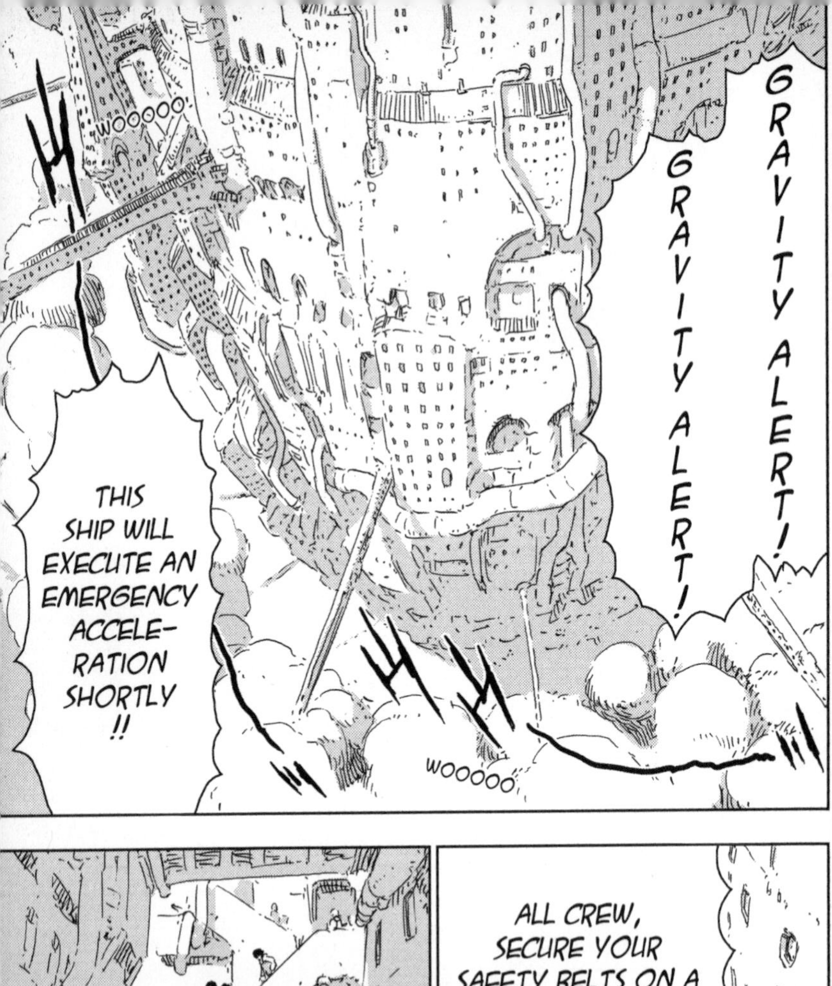
GRAVITY ALERT!
GRAVITY ALERT!
WOOOOO
THIS SHIP WILL EXECUTE AN EMERGENCY ACCELE-RATION SHORTLY !!
WOOOOO
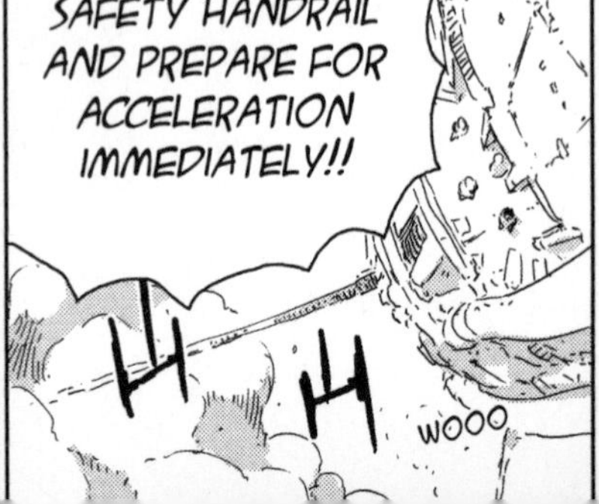
ALL CREW, SECURE YOUR SAFETY BELTS ON A SAFETY HANDRAIL AND PREPARE FOR ACCELERATION IMMEDIATELY!!
WOOO
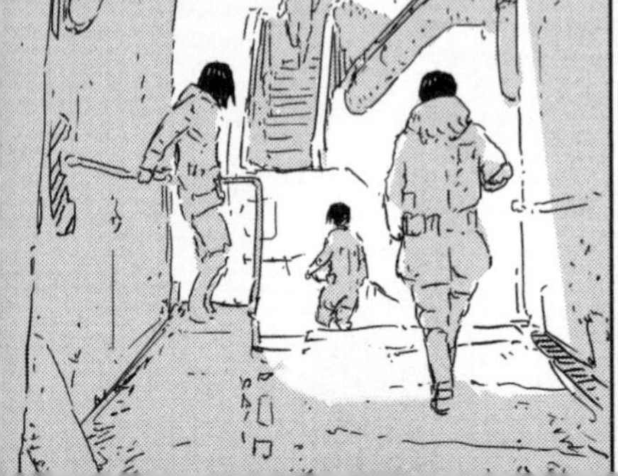

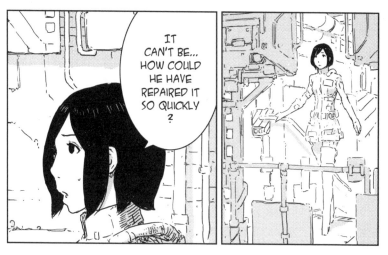

IT CAN'T BE... HOW COULD HE HAVE REPAIRED IT SO QUICKLY?

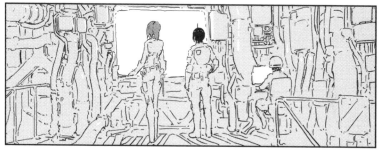

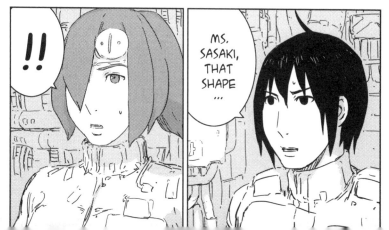

!!

MS. SASAKI, THAT SHAPE ...

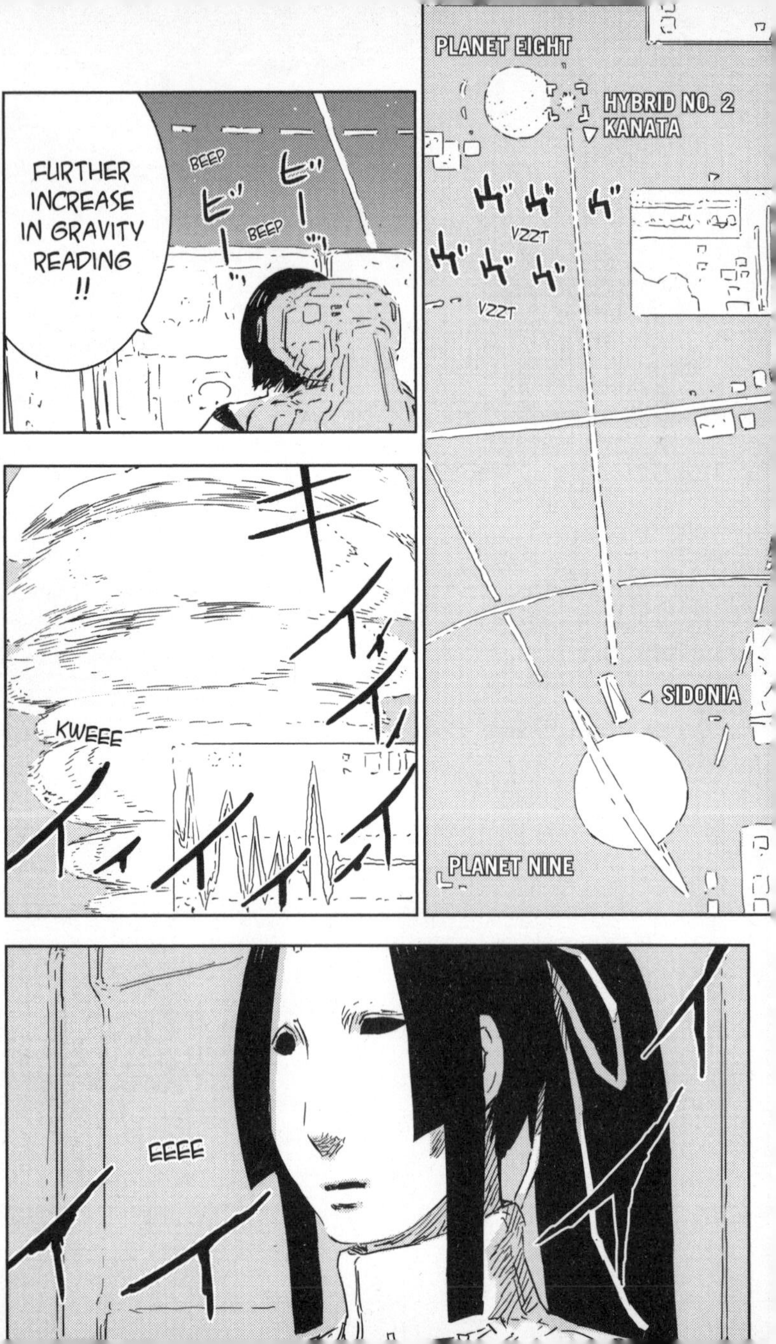
PLANET EIGHT
HYBRID NO. 2 KANATA
VZZT
VZZT
SIDONIA
PLANET NINE
FURTHER INCREASE IN GRAVITY READING !!
BEEP
BEEP
KWEEE
EEEE

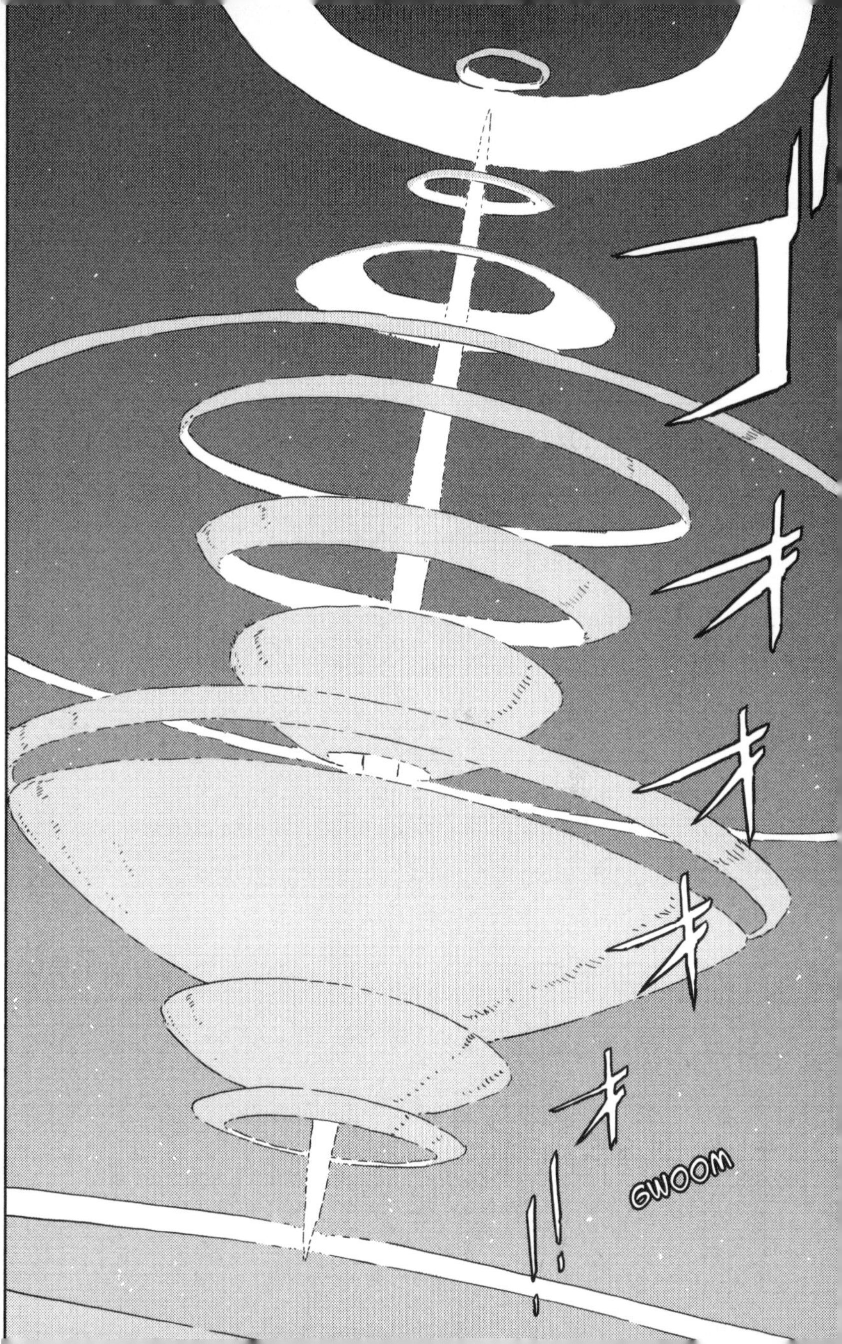
ゴオオオオ!!
GWOOM

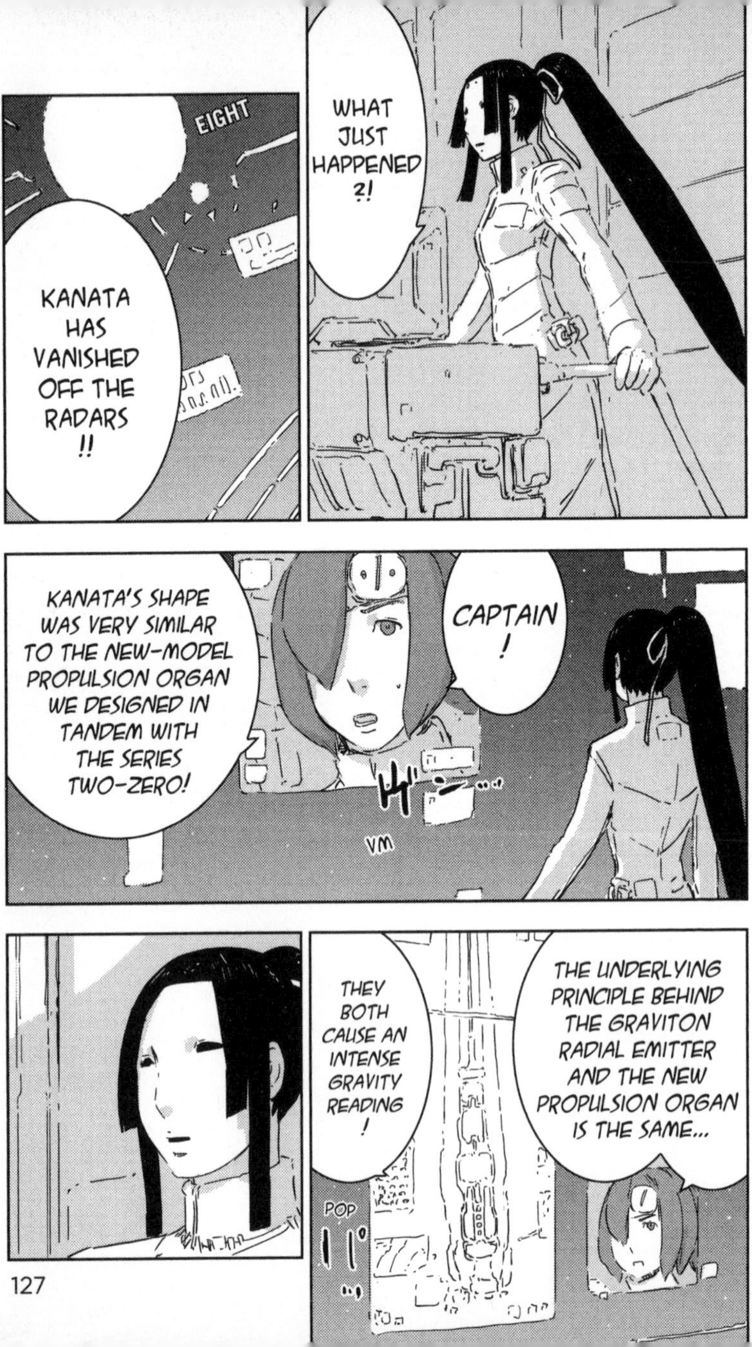
WHAT JUST HAPPENED?!
EIGHT
KANATA HAS VANISHED OFF THE RADARS!!
CAPTAIN!
KANATA'S SHAPE WAS VERY SIMILAR TO THE NEW-MODEL PROPULSION ORGAN WE DESIGNED IN TANDEM WITH THE SERIES TWO-ZERO!
VM
THE UNDERLYING PRINCIPLE BEHIND THE GRAVITON RADIAL EMITTER AND THE NEW PROPULSION ORGAN IS THE SAME...
THEY BOTH CAUSE AN INTENSE GRAVITY READING!
POP

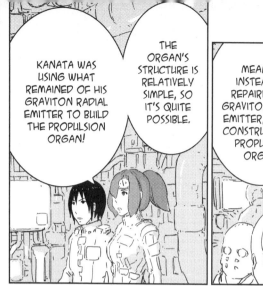

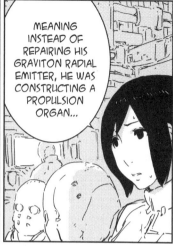

MEANING INSTEAD OF REPAIRING HIS GRAVITON RADIAL EMITTER, HE WAS CONSTRUCTING A PROPULSION ORGAN...
THE ORGAN'S STRUCTURE IS RELATIVELY SIMPLE, SO IT'S QUITE POSSIBLE.
KANATA WAS USING WHAT REMAINED OF HIS GRAVITON RADIAL EMITTER TO BUILD THE PROPULSION ORGAN!
WE HAVE THE LAST IMAGE CAPTURED OF KANATA!
VM
HE'S ON THE MOVE!
BUT WHERE TO?

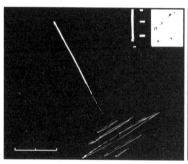

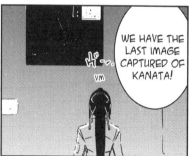

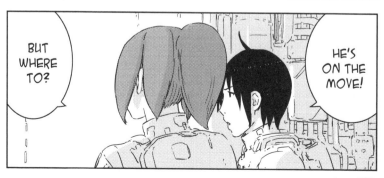

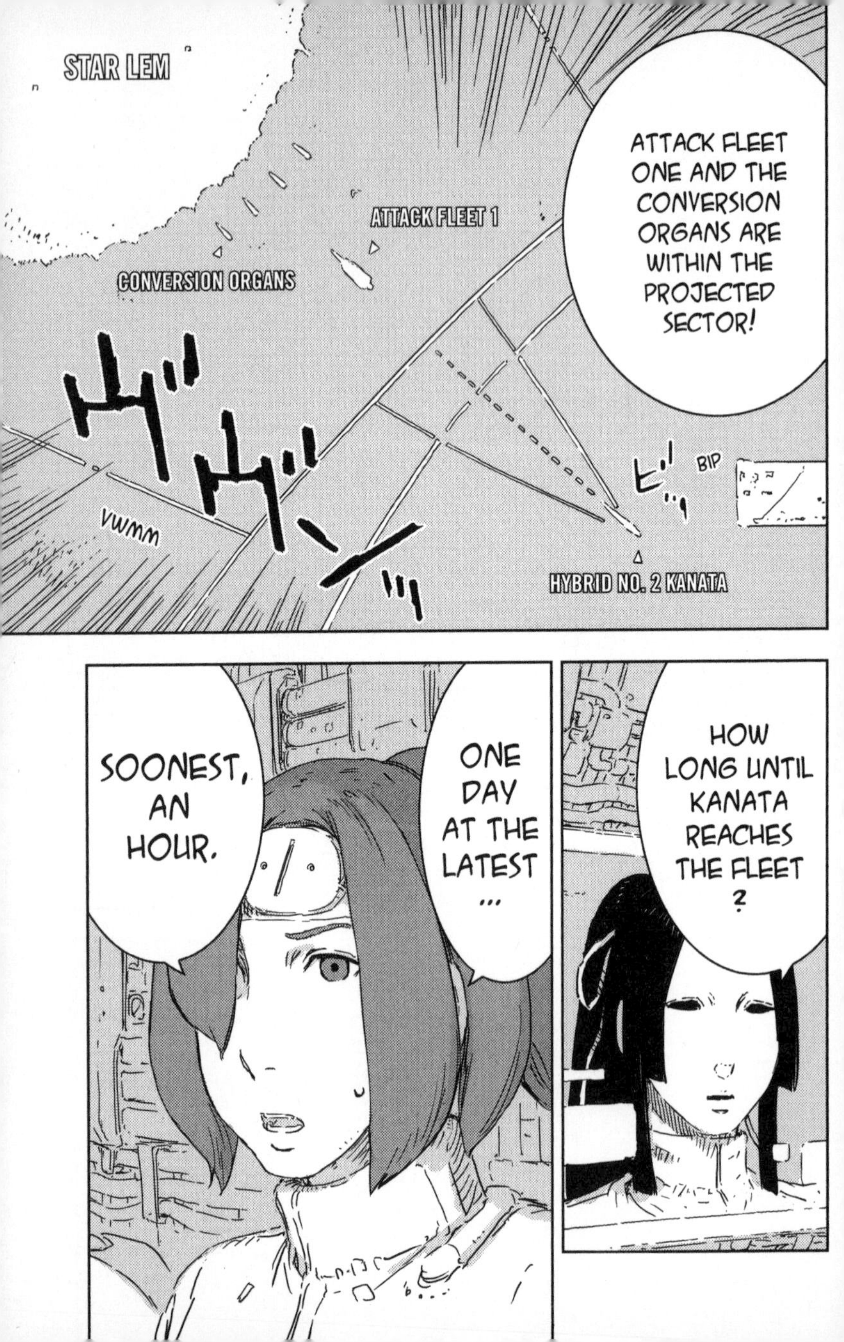
ATTACK FLEET ONE AND THE CONVERSION ORGANS ARE WITHIN THE PROJECTED SECTOR!
STAR LEM
ATTACK FLEET 1
CONVERSION ORGANS
BIP
VWMM
HYBRID NO. 2 KANATA
HOW LONG UNTIL KANATA REACHES THE FLEET?
ONE DAY AT THE LATEST...
SOONEST, AN HOUR.

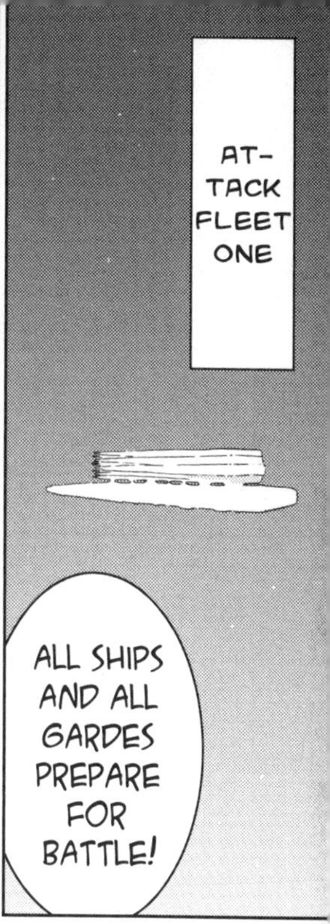
AT-TACK FLEET ONE
ALL SHIPS AND ALL GARDES PREPARE FOR BATTLE!
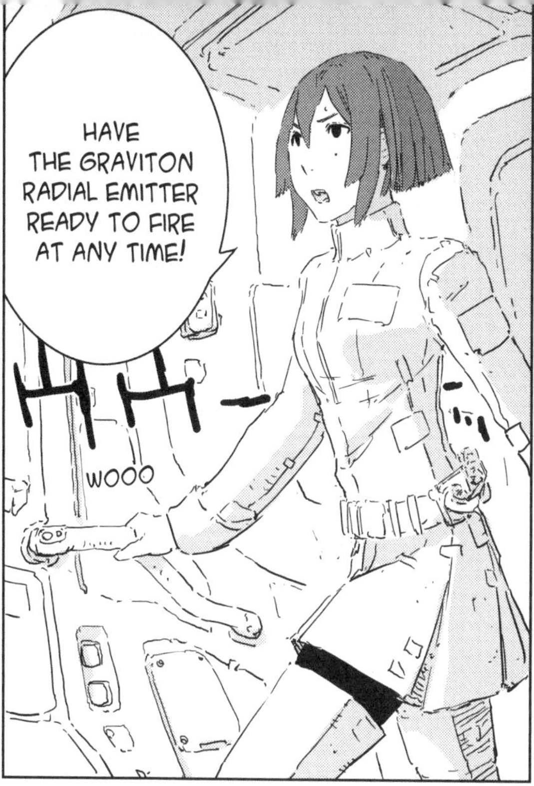
HAVE THE GRAVITON RADIAL EMITTER READY TO FIRE AT ANY TIME!
WOOO
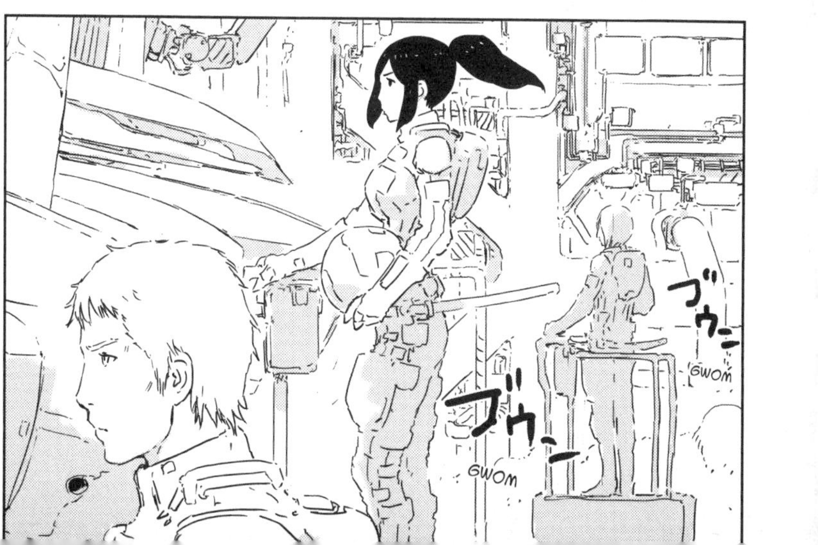
GWOM
GWOM

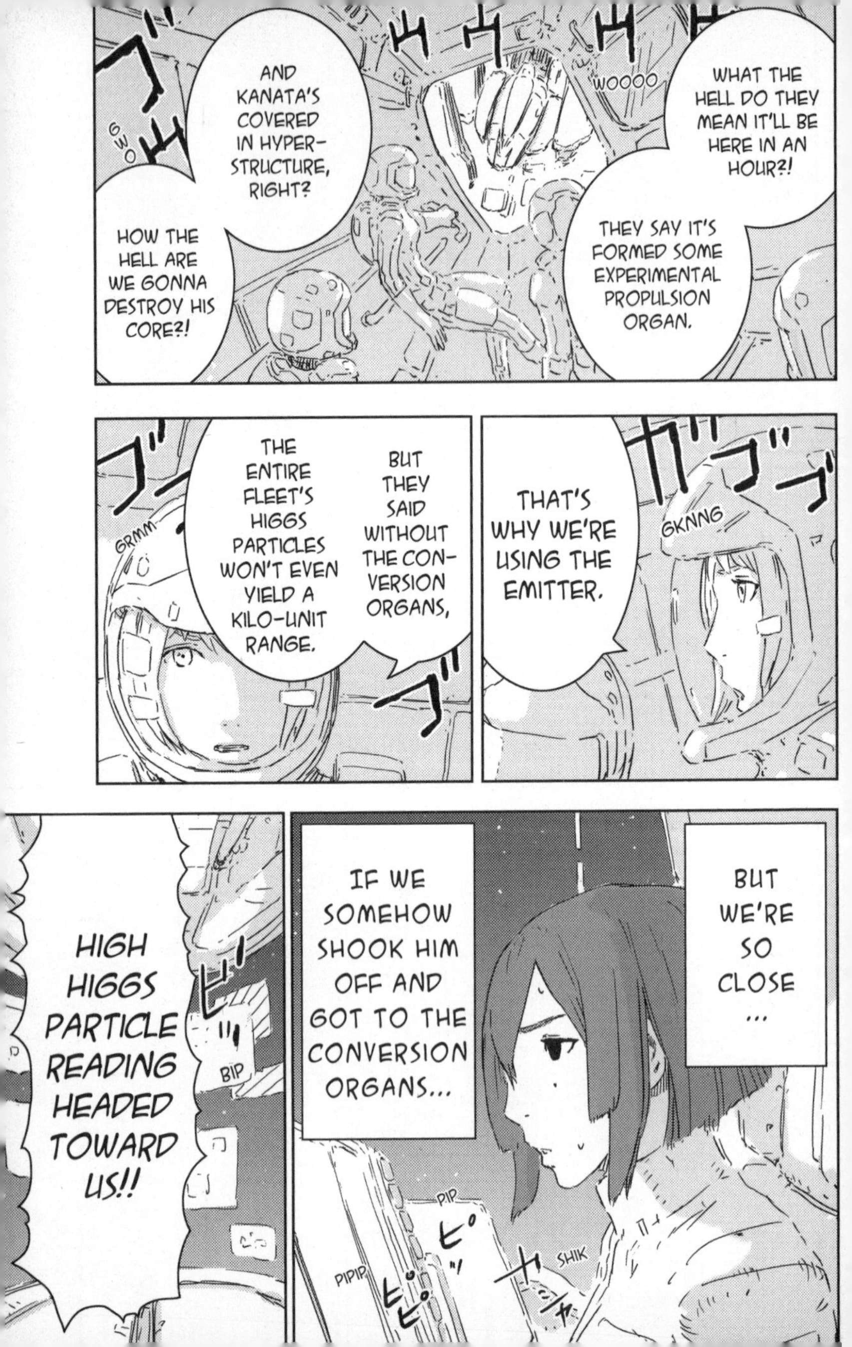
WHAT THE HELL DO THEY MEAN IT'LL BE HERE IN AN HOUR?!
THEY SAY IT'S FORMED SOME EXPERIMENTAL PROPULSION ORGAN.
WOOOO
AND KANATA'S COVERED IN HYPER-STRUCTURE, RIGHT?
HOW THE HELL ARE WE GONNA DESTROY HIS CORE?!
GWO
GKNNG
THAT'S WHY WE'RE USING THE EMITTER.
BUT THEY SAID WITHOUT THE CON-VERSION ORGANS,
THE ENTIRE FLEET'S HIGGS PARTICLES WON'T EVEN YIELD A KILO-UNIT RANGE.
GRMM
BUT WE'RE SO CLOSE ...
IF WE SOMEHOW SHOOK HIM OFF AND GOT TO THE CONVERSION ORGANS...
PIP
PIPIP
SHIK
BIP
HIGH HIGGS PARTICLE READING HEADED TOWARD US!!

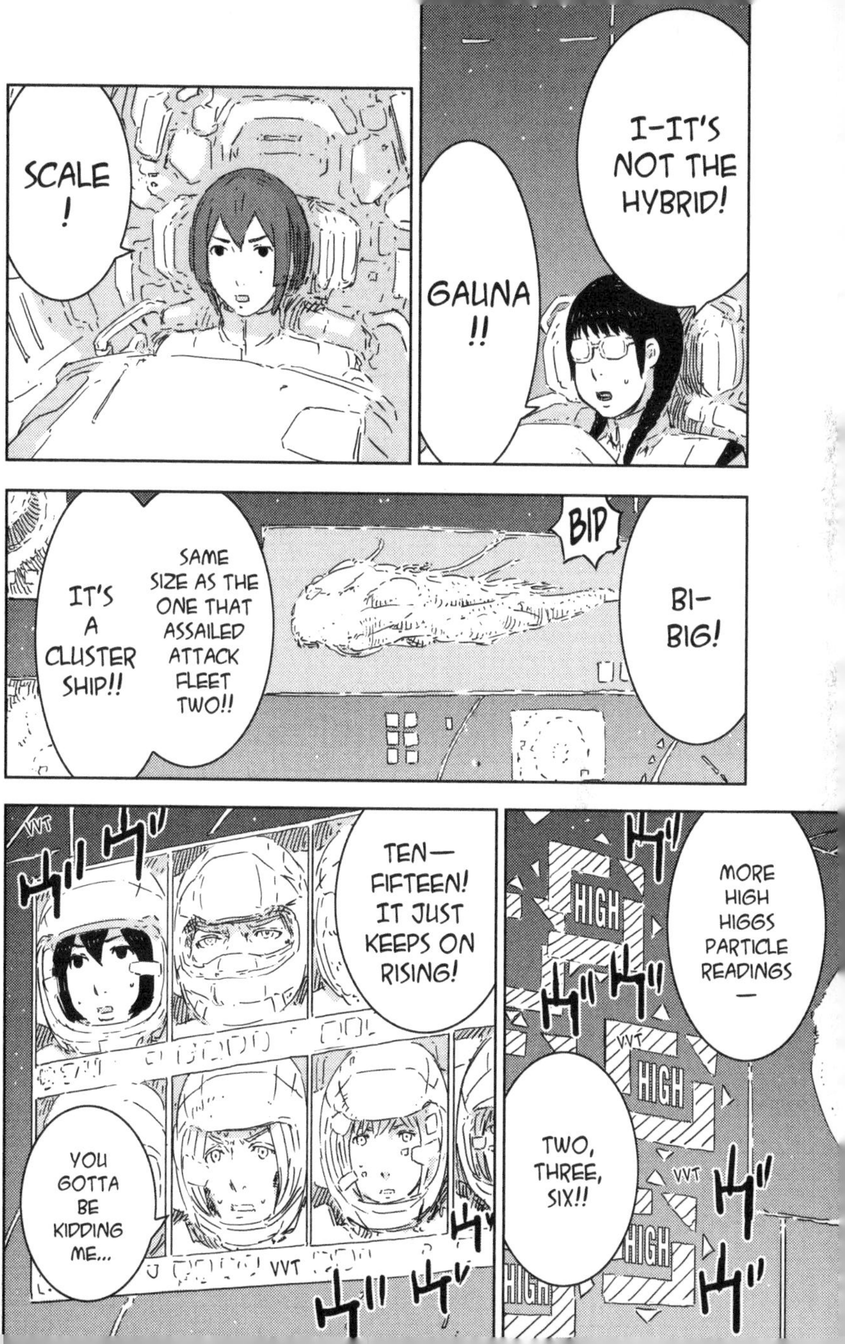
I-IT'S NOT THE HYBRID!
GAUNA !!
SCALE !
BIP
BI- BIG!
SAME SIZE AS THE ONE THAT ASSAILED ATTACK FLEET TWO!!
IT'S A CLUSTER SHIP!!
MORE HIGH HIGGS PARTICLE READINGS —
HIGH
HIGH
TWO, THREE, SIX!!
HIGH
TEN— FIFTEEN! IT JUST KEEPS ON RISING!
YOU GOTTA BE KIDDING ME...

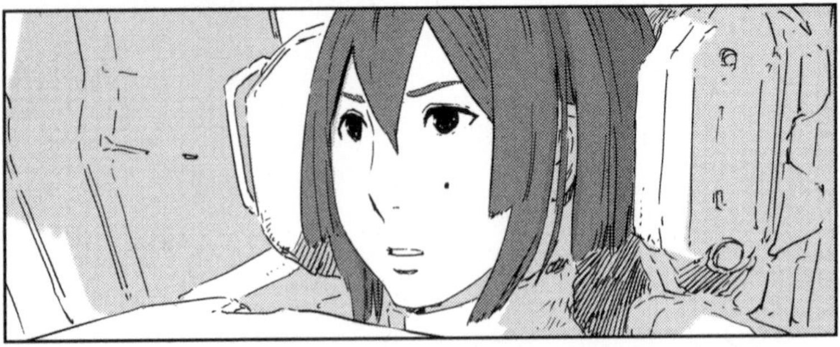

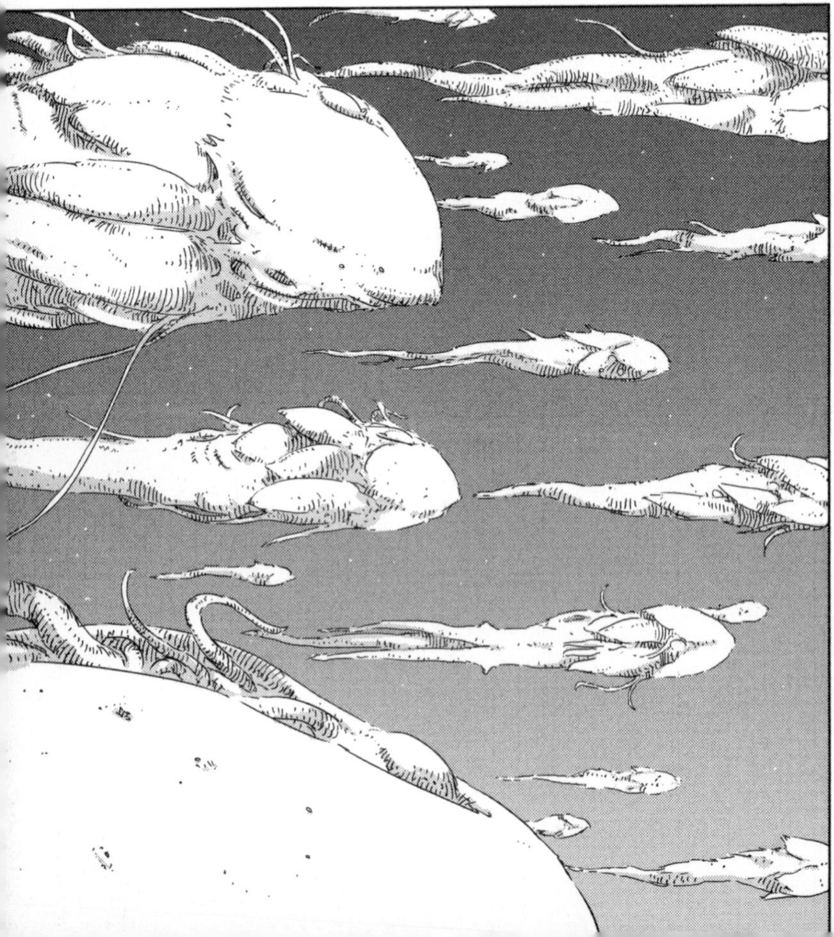

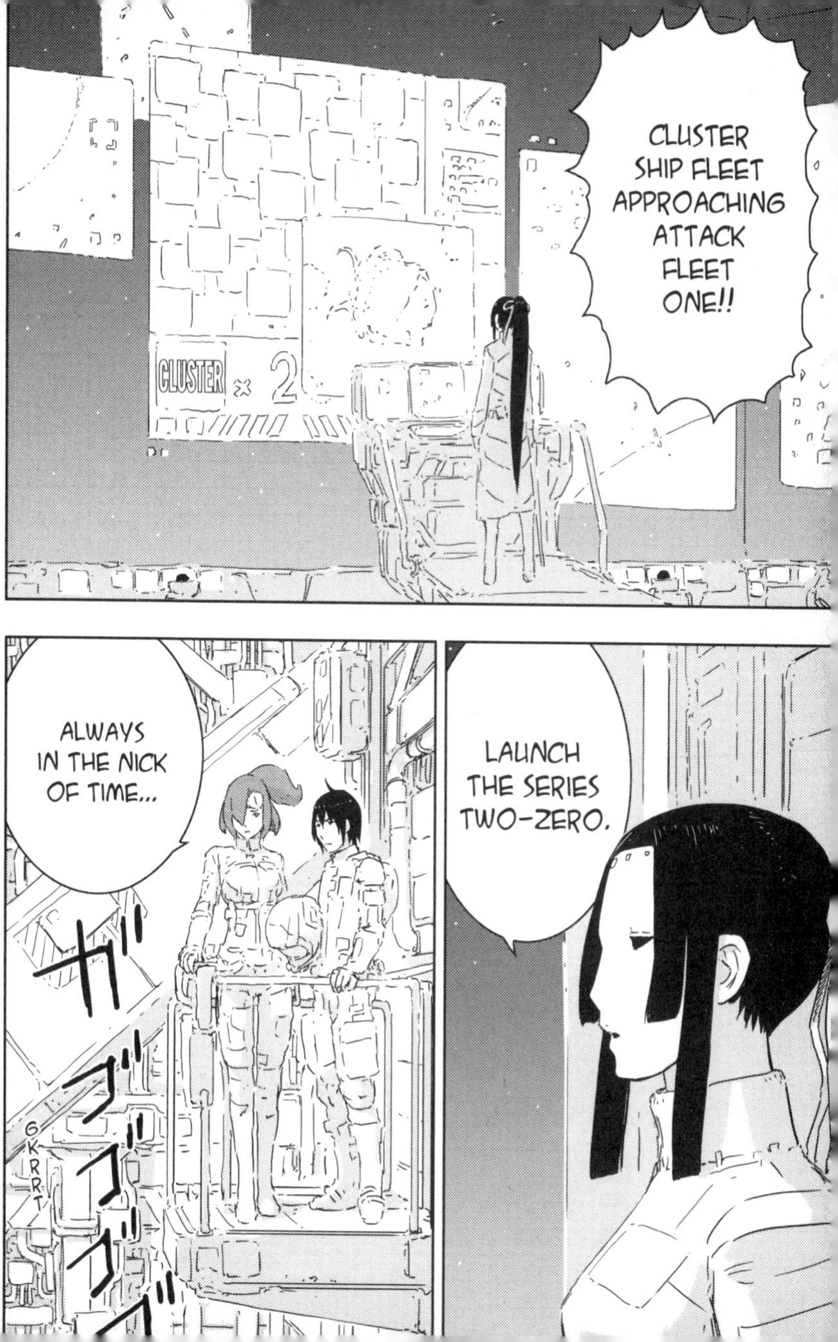
CLUSTER × 2
CLUSTER SHIP FLEET APPROACHING ATTACK FLEET ONE!!
LAUNCH THE SERIES TWO-ZERO.
ALWAYS IN THE NICK OF TIME...
GKRRT

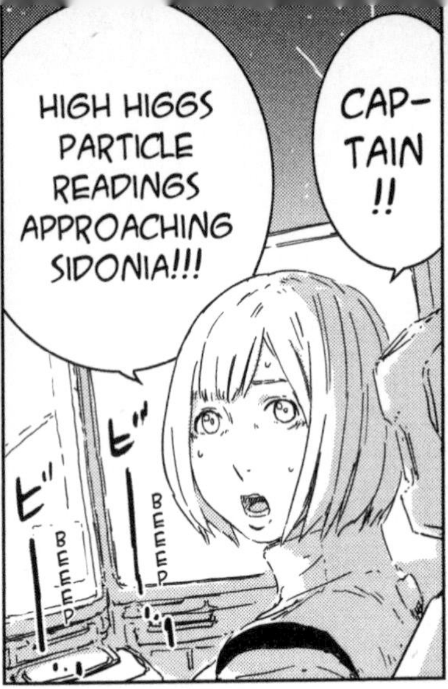
CAP-
TAIN
!!
HIGH HIGGS PARTICLE READINGS APPROACHING SIDONIA!!!
ビ BEEEP
ビ BEEEP
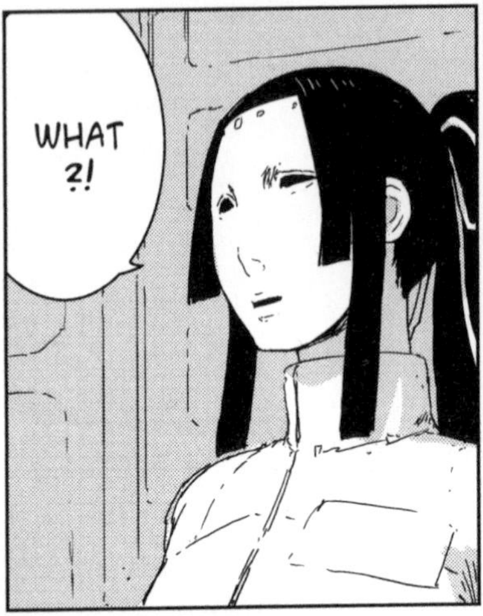
WHAT ?!
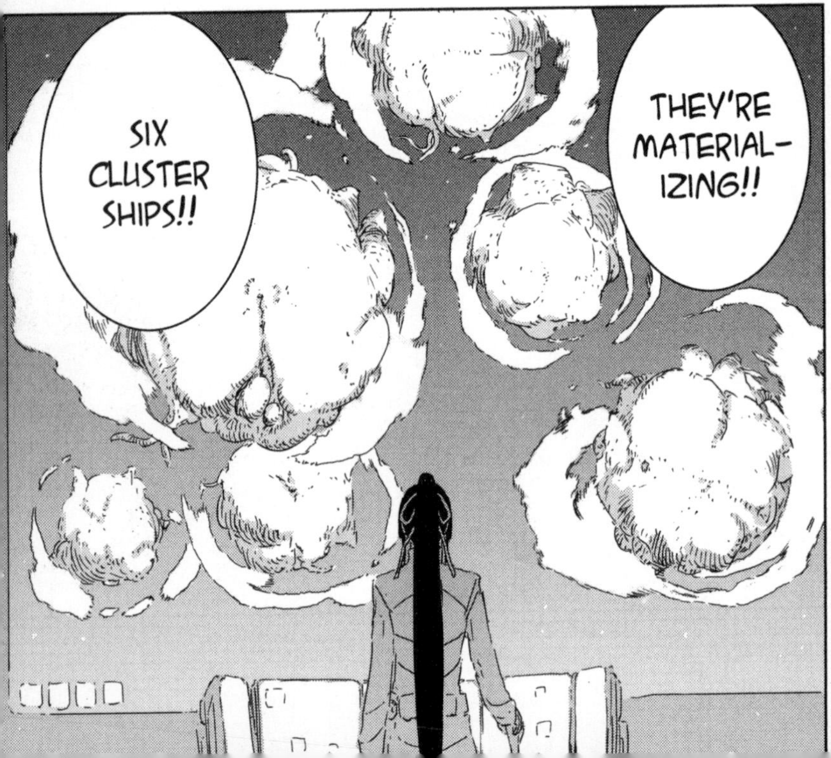
THEY'RE MATERIAL-IZING!!
SIX CLUSTER SHIPS!!

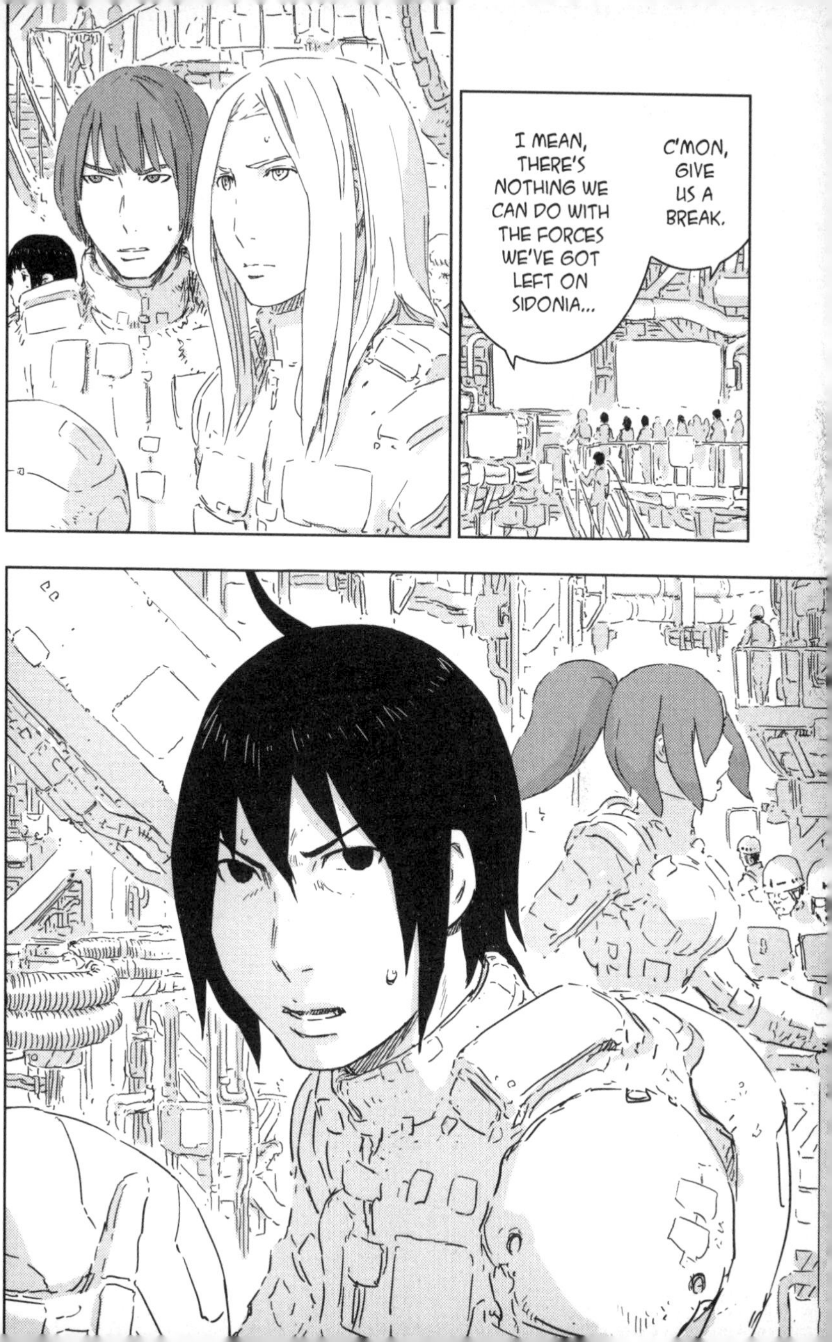
C'MON, GIVE US A BREAK.
I MEAN, THERE'S NOTHING WE CAN DO WITH THE FORCES WE'VE GOT LEFT ON SIDONIA...

シドニアの騎士

KNIGHTS OF SIDONIA

I SHOULD HAVE SHOOK HANDS WITH YOU THAT DAY.

—PLACENTA EIKO YAMANO

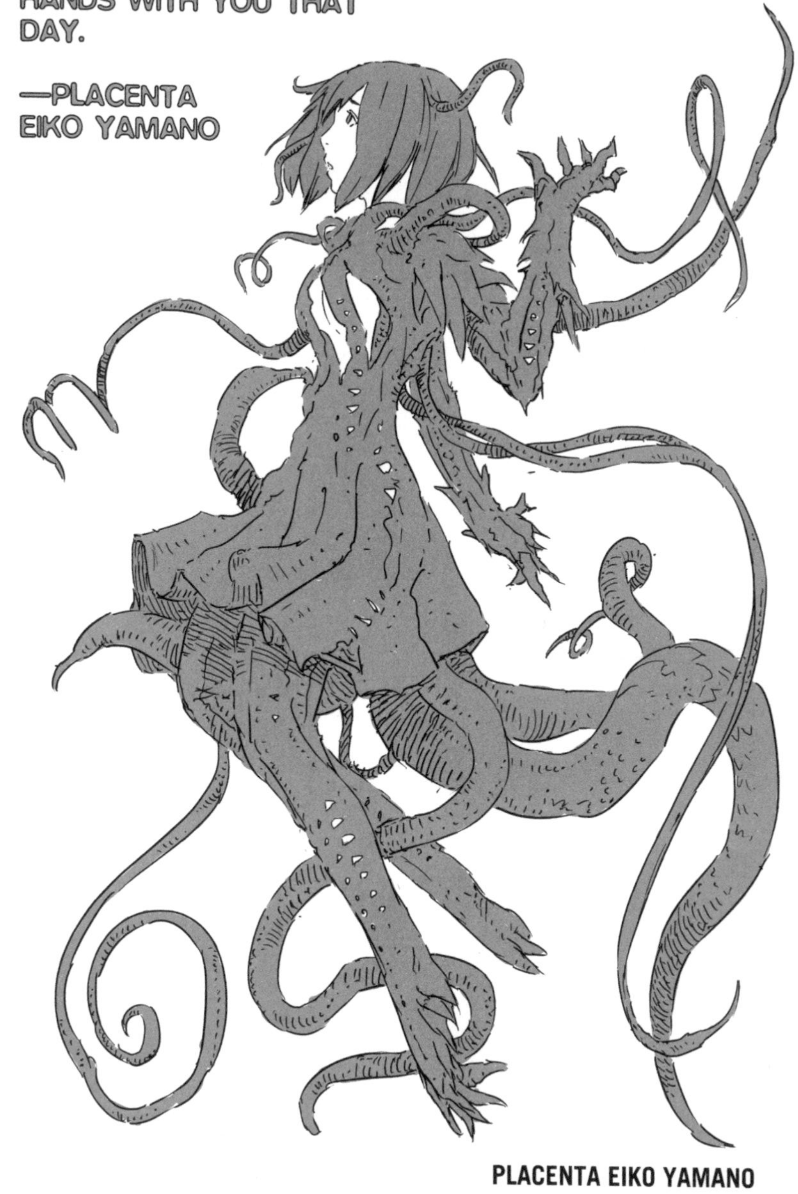

PLACENTA EIKO YAMANO

Chapter 70: The Series Two-Zero's Sortie

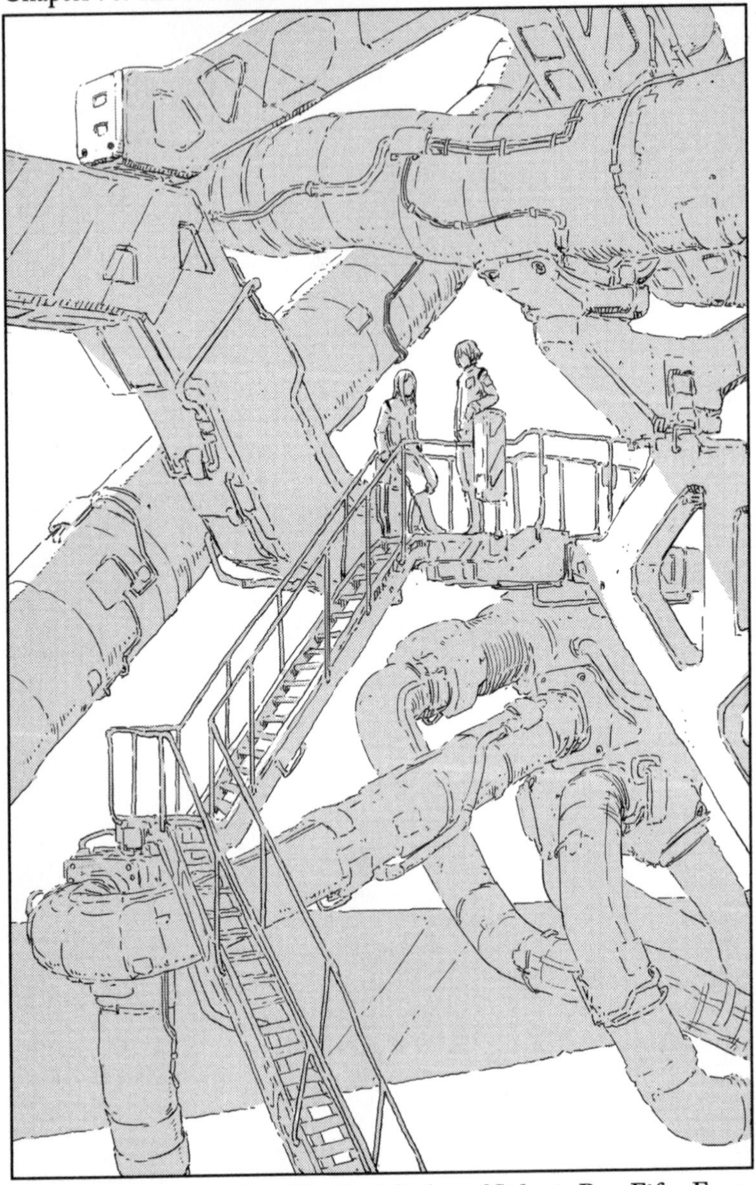

One Hundred Sights of Sidonia Part Fifty-Four:
Garde Hangar No. 3 External Stairwell

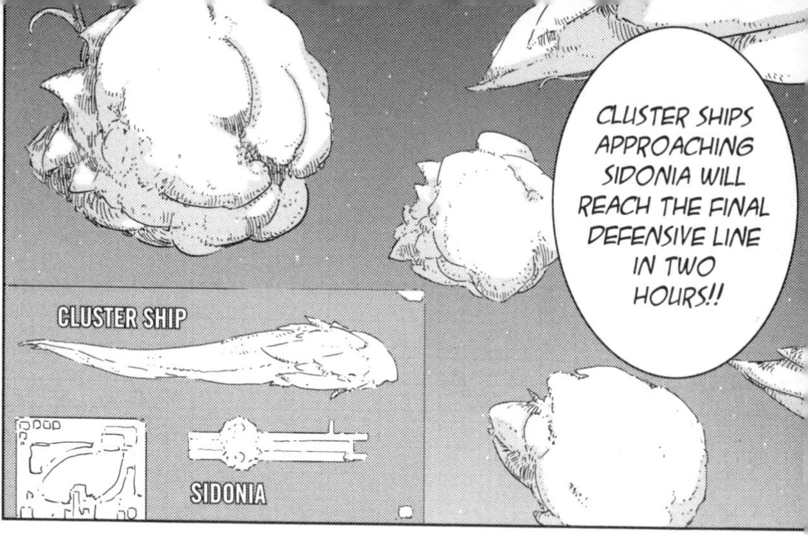
CLUSTER SHIPS APPROACHING SIDONIA WILL REACH THE FINAL DEFENSIVE LINE IN TWO HOURS!!
CLUSTER SHIP
SIDONIA

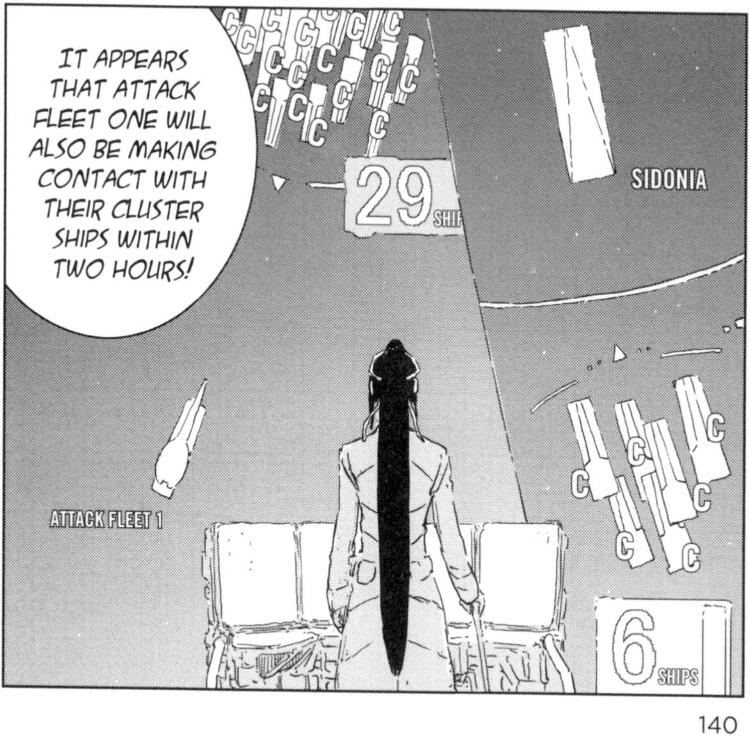
IT APPEARS THAT ATTACK FLEET ONE WILL ALSO BE MAKING CONTACT WITH THEIR CLUSTER SHIPS WITHIN TWO HOURS!
SIDONIA
29 SHIP
ATTACK FLEET 1
6 SHIPS

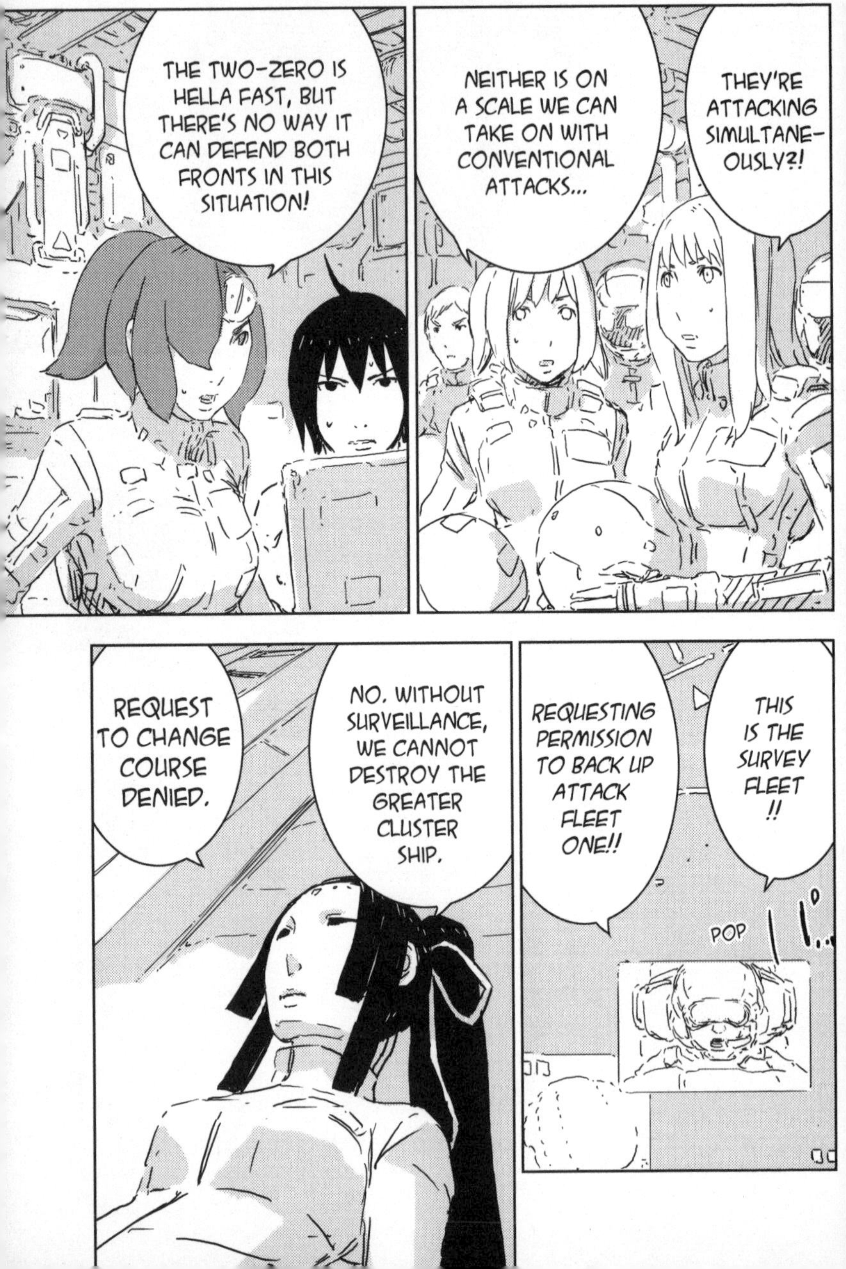
THEY'RE ATTACKING SIMULTANE-OUSLY?!
NEITHER IS ON A SCALE WE CAN TAKE ON WITH CONVENTIONAL ATTACKS...
THE TWO-ZERO IS HELLA FAST, BUT THERE'S NO WAY IT CAN DEFEND BOTH FRONTS IN THIS SITUATION!
THIS IS THE SURVEY FLEET!!
REQUESTING PERMISSION TO BACK UP ATTACK FLEET ONE!!
POP
NO. WITHOUT SURVEILLANCE, WE CANNOT DESTROY THE GREATER CLUSTER SHIP.
REQUEST TO CHANGE COURSE DENIED.

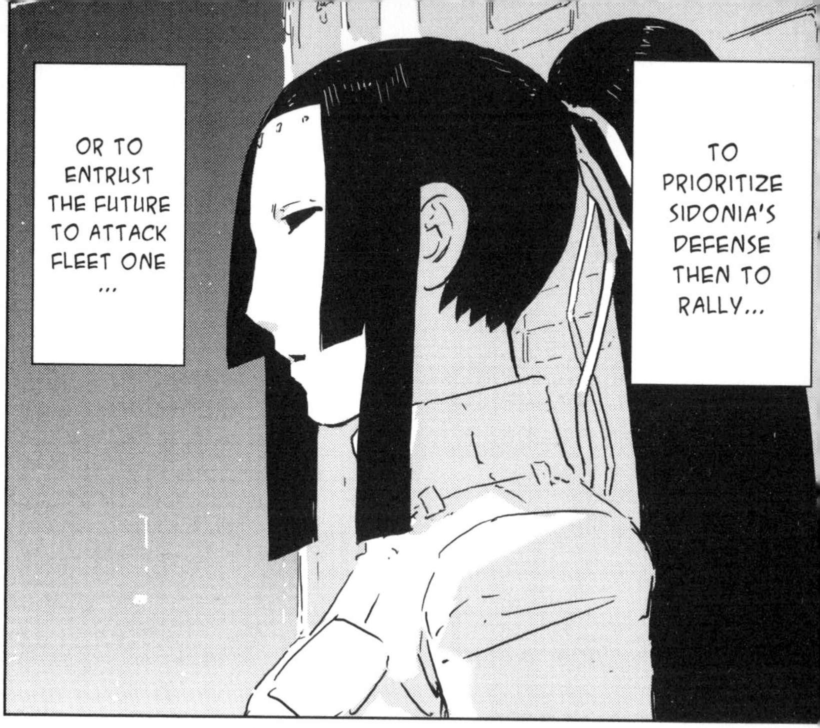
TO PRIORITIZE SIDONIA'S DEFENSE THEN TO RALLY...
OR TO ENTRUST THE FUTURE TO ATTACK FLEET ONE ...

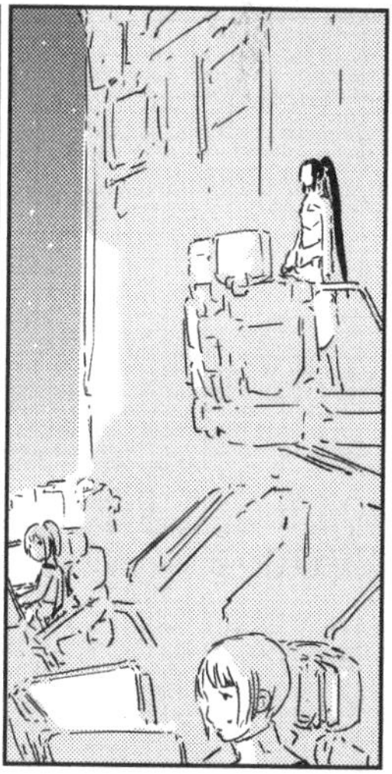

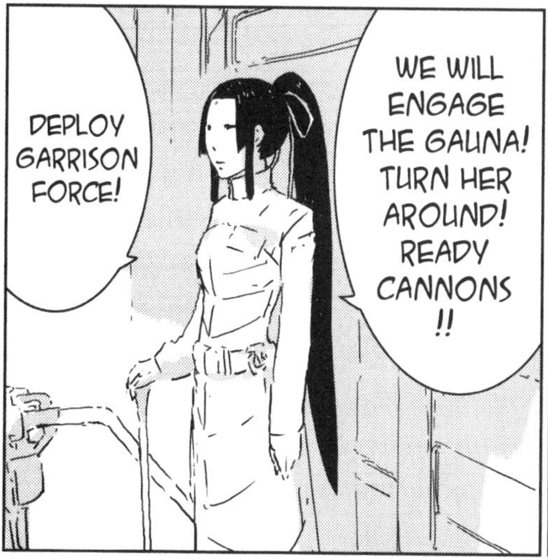
WE WILL ENGAGE THE GAUNA! TURN HER AROUND! READY CANNONS !!
DEPLOY GARRISON FORCE!

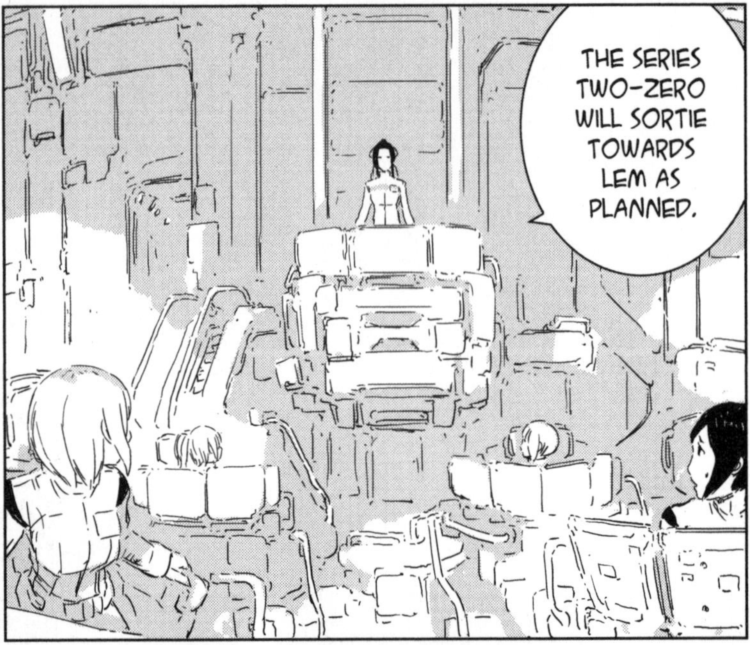
THE SERIES TWO-ZERO WILL SORTIE TOWARDS LEM AS PLANNED.

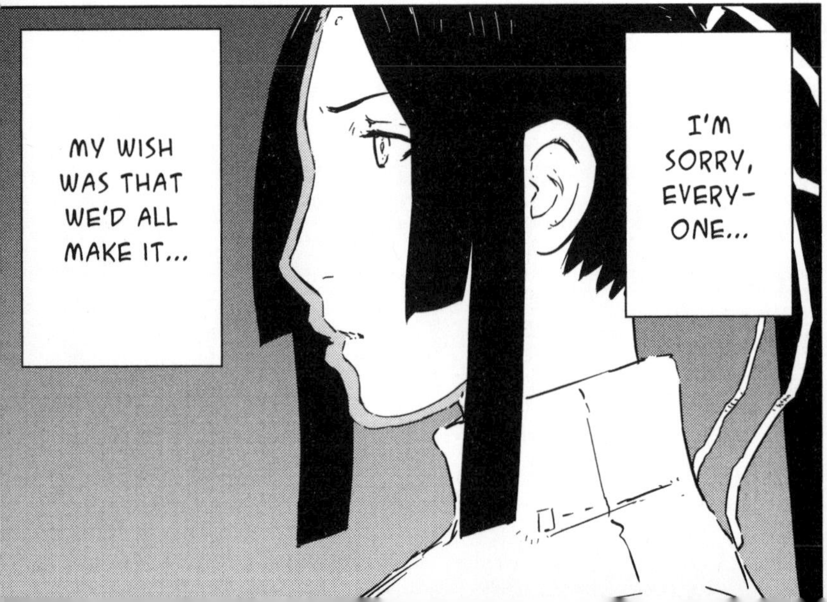
I'M SORRY, EVERY-ONE...
MY WISH WAS THAT WE'D ALL MAKE IT...

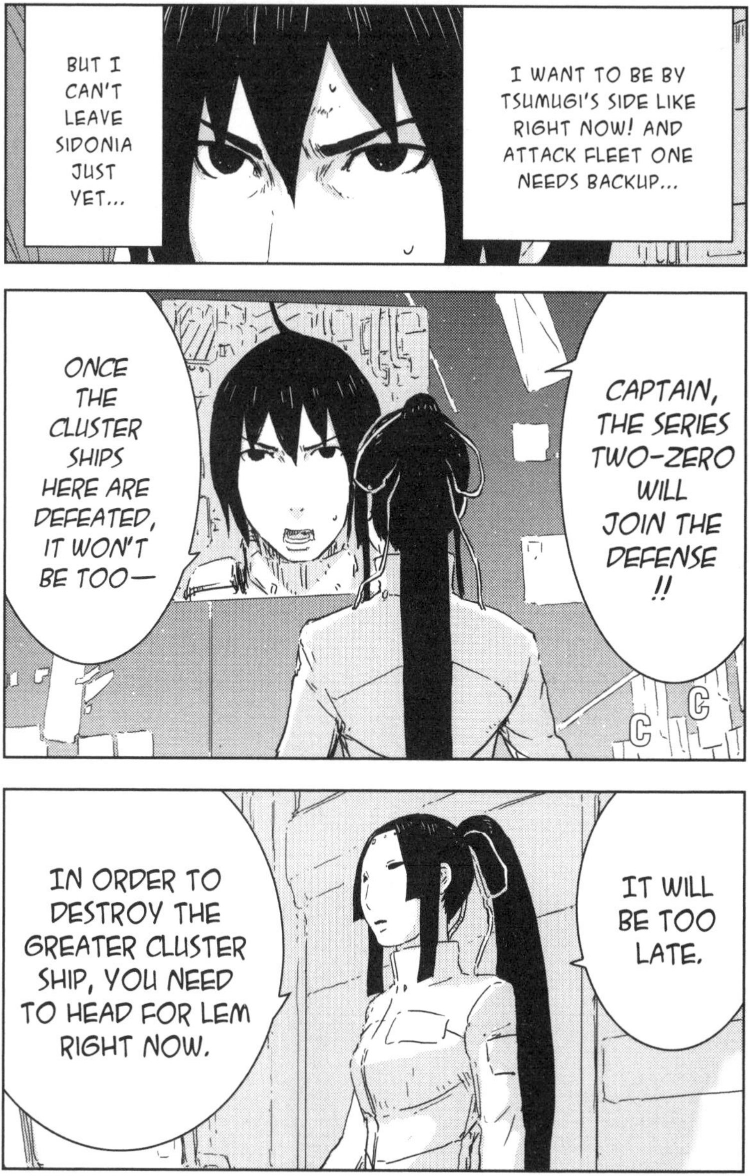
I WANT TO BE BY TSUMUGI'S SIDE LIKE RIGHT NOW! AND ATTACK FLEET ONE NEEDS BACKUP...
BUT I CAN'T LEAVE SIDONIA JUST YET...
CAPTAIN, THE SERIES TWO-ZERO WILL JOIN THE DEFENSE !!
ONCE THE CLUSTER SHIPS HERE ARE DEFEATED, IT WON'T BE TOO—
C C
IT WILL BE TOO LATE.
IN ORDER TO DESTROY THE GREATER CLUSTER SHIP, YOU NEED TO HEAD FOR LEM RIGHT NOW.

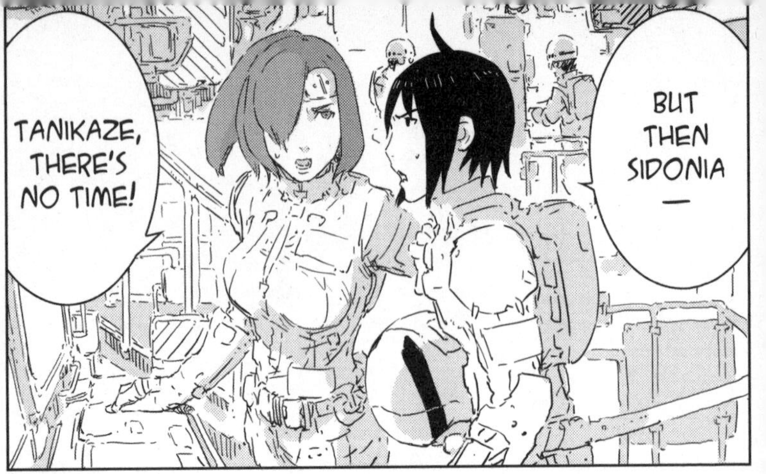
BUT THEN SIDONIA —
TANIKAZE, THERE'S NO TIME!
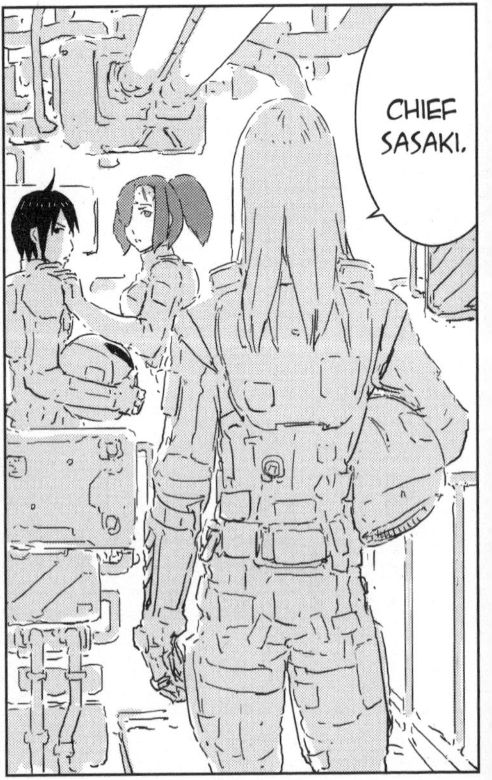
CHIEF SASAKI.
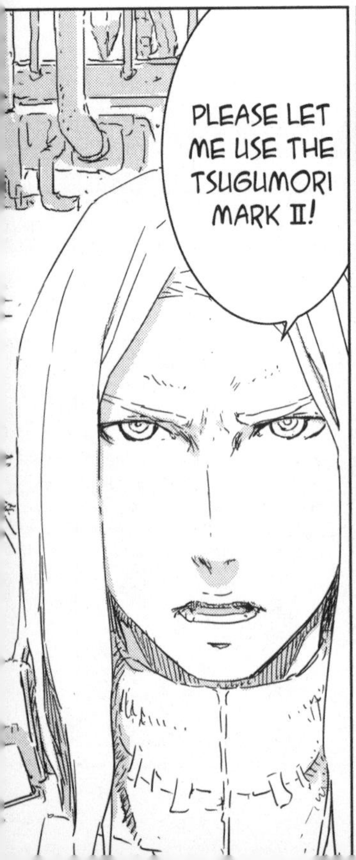
PLEASE LET ME USE THE TSUGUMORI MARK II!

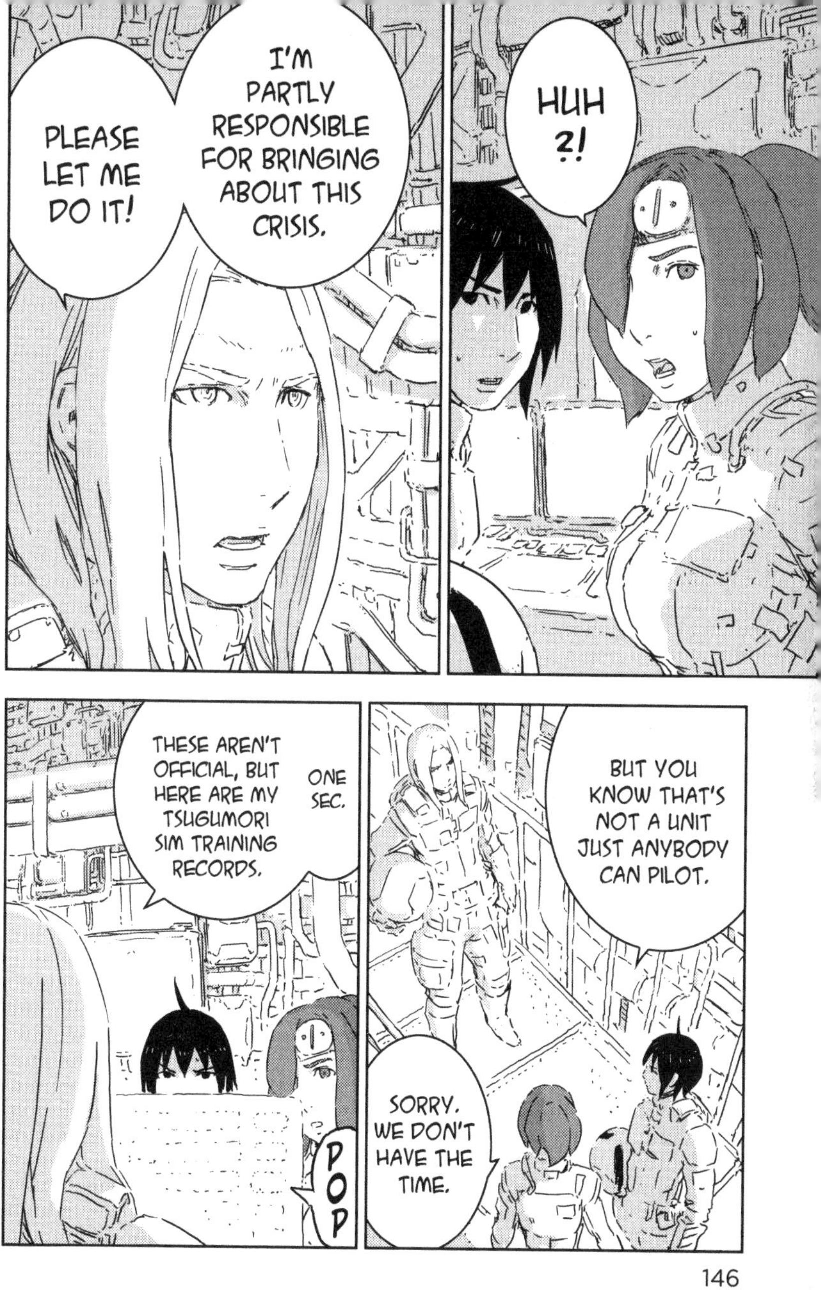
HUH ?!
I'M PARTLY RESPONSIBLE FOR BRINGING ABOUT THIS CRISIS.
PLEASE LET ME DO IT!
BUT YOU KNOW THAT'S NOT A UNIT JUST ANYBODY CAN PILOT.
SORRY. WE DON'T HAVE THE TIME.
ONE SEC.
THESE AREN'T OFFICIAL, BUT HERE ARE MY TSUGUMORI SIM TRAINING RECORDS.
POP

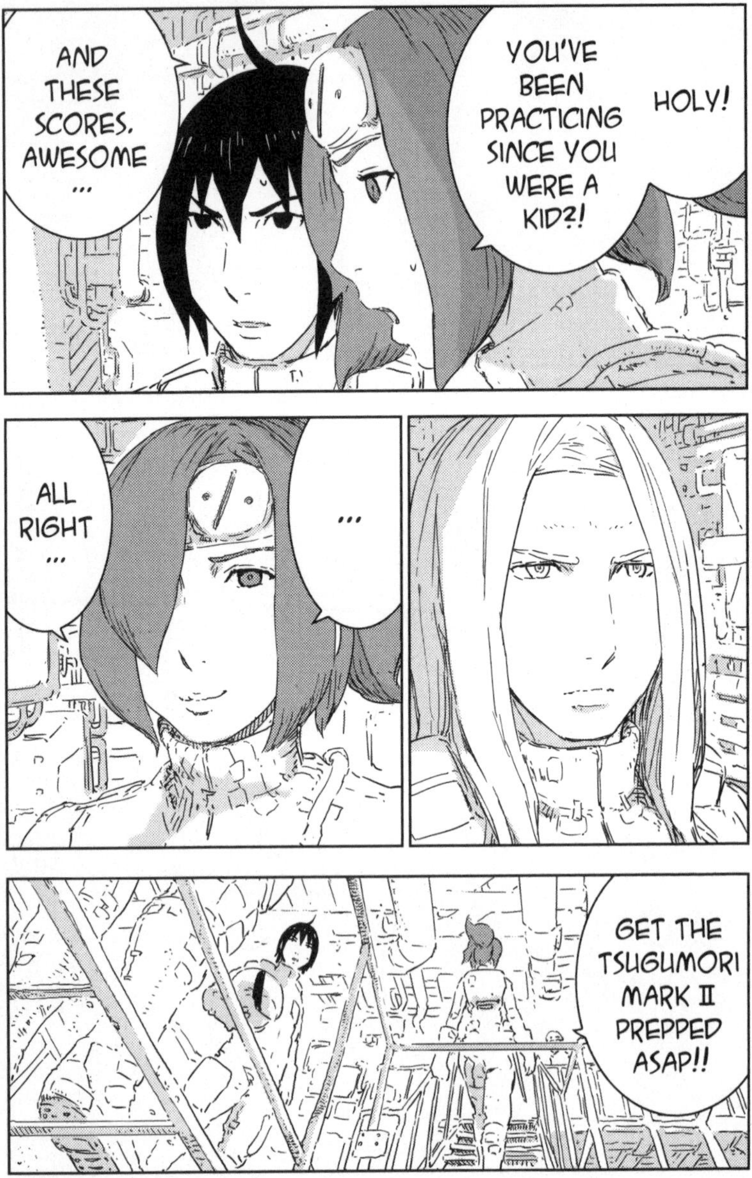
HOLY!
YOU'VE BEEN PRACTICING SINCE YOU WERE A KID?!
AND THESE SCORES. AWESOME ...
...
ALL RIGHT ...
GET THE TSUGUMORI MARK II PREPPED ASAP!!

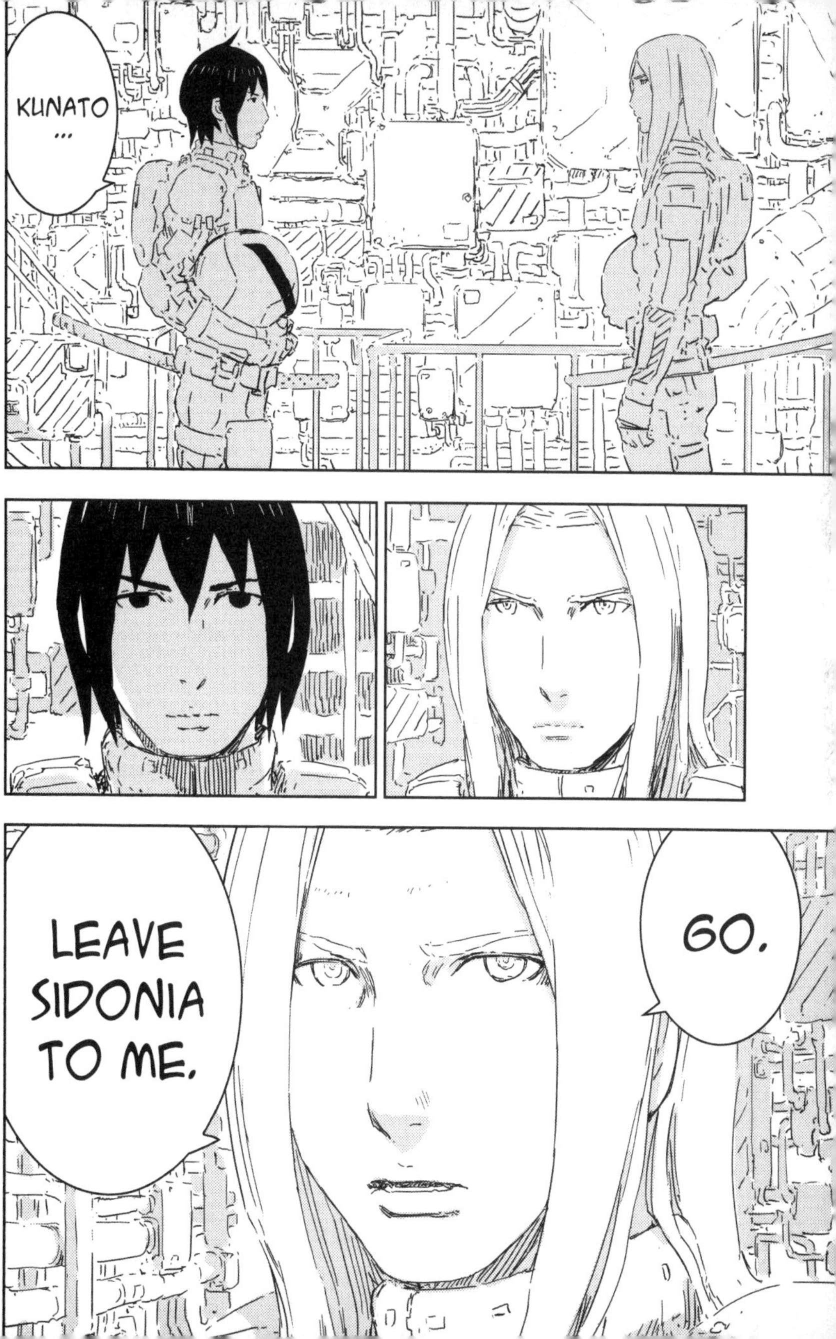
KUNATO ...
GO.
LEAVE SIDONIA TO ME.

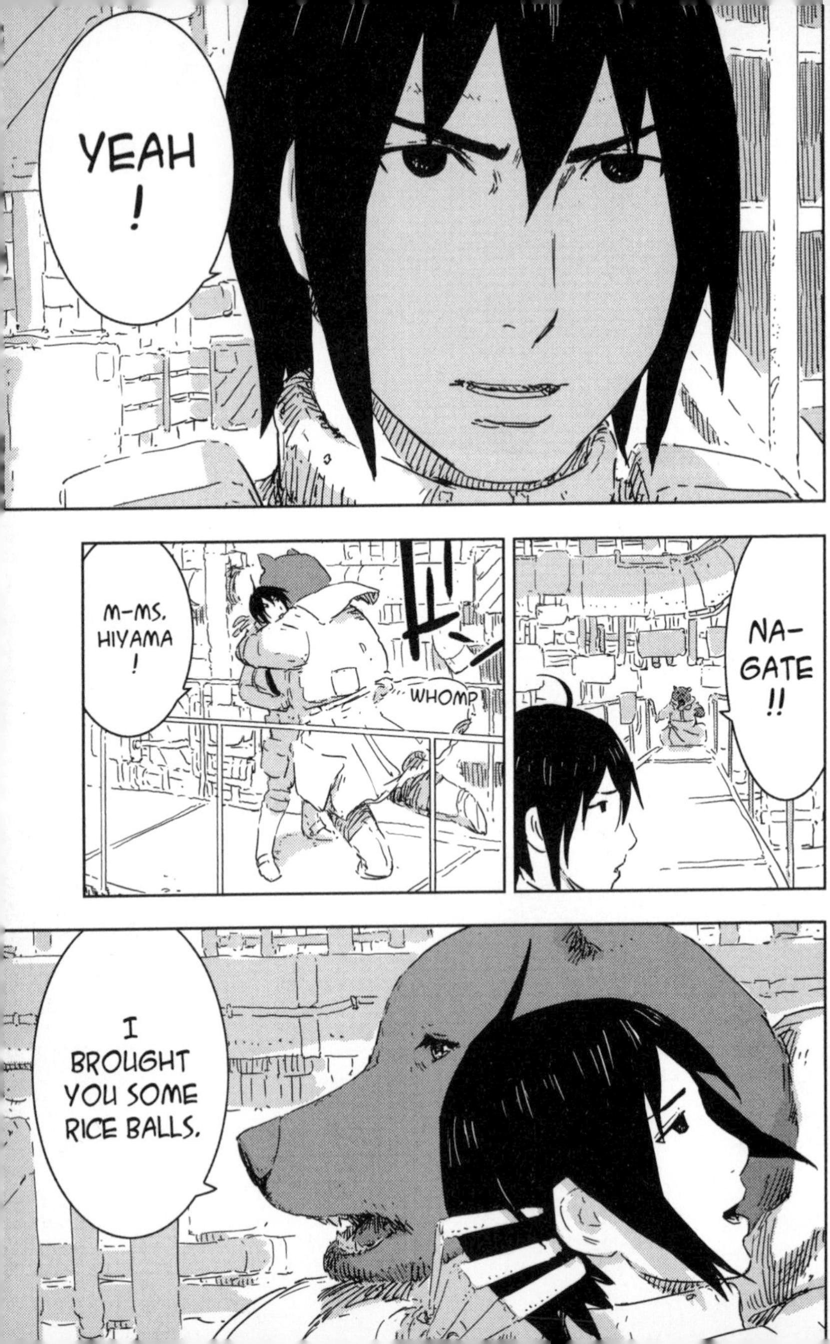
YEAH!
NA-GATE!!
M-MS. HIYAMA!
WHOMP
I BROUGHT YOU SOME RICE BALLS.

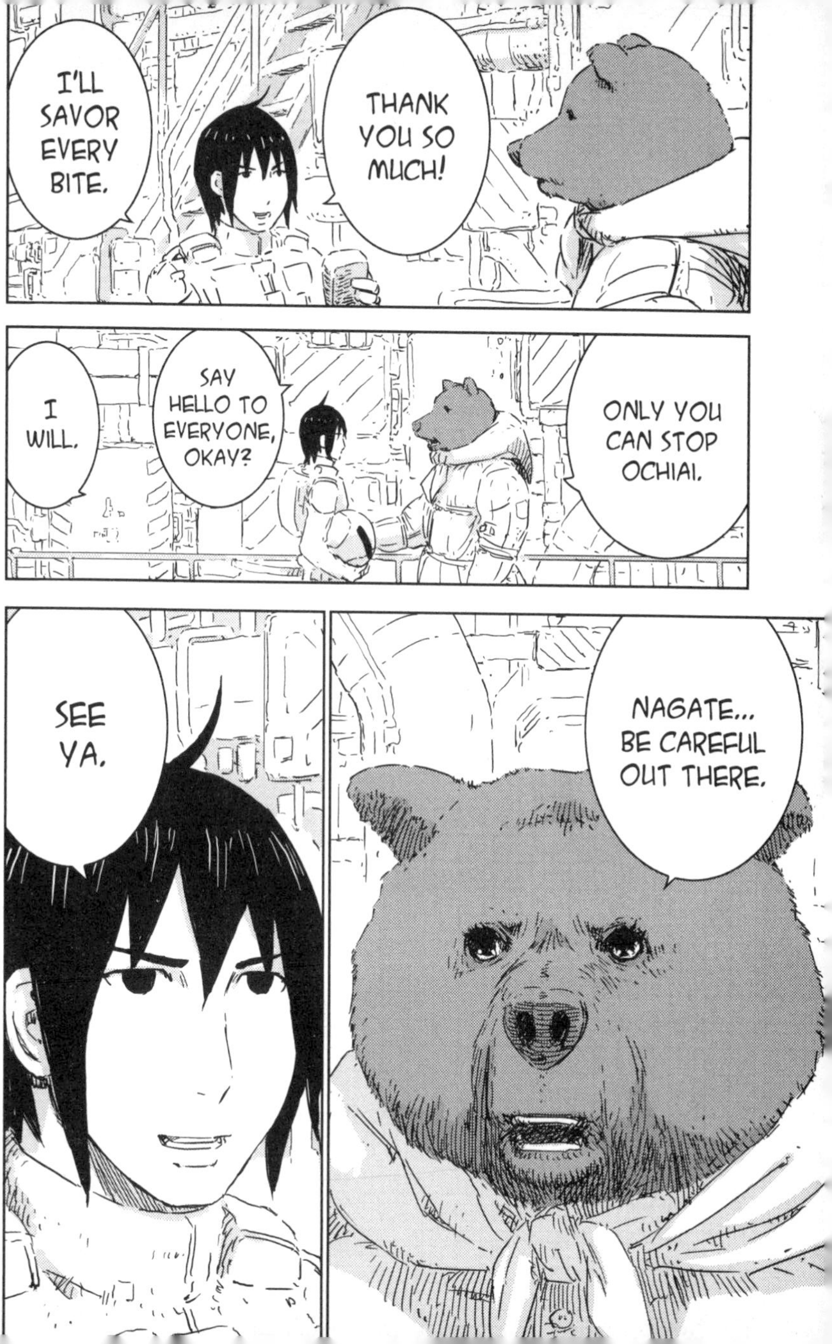
THANK YOU SO MUCH!
I'LL SAVOR EVERY BITE.
ONLY YOU CAN STOP OCHIAI.
SAY HELLO TO EVERYONE, OKAY?
I WILL.
NAGATE... BE CAREFUL OUT THERE.
SEE YA.

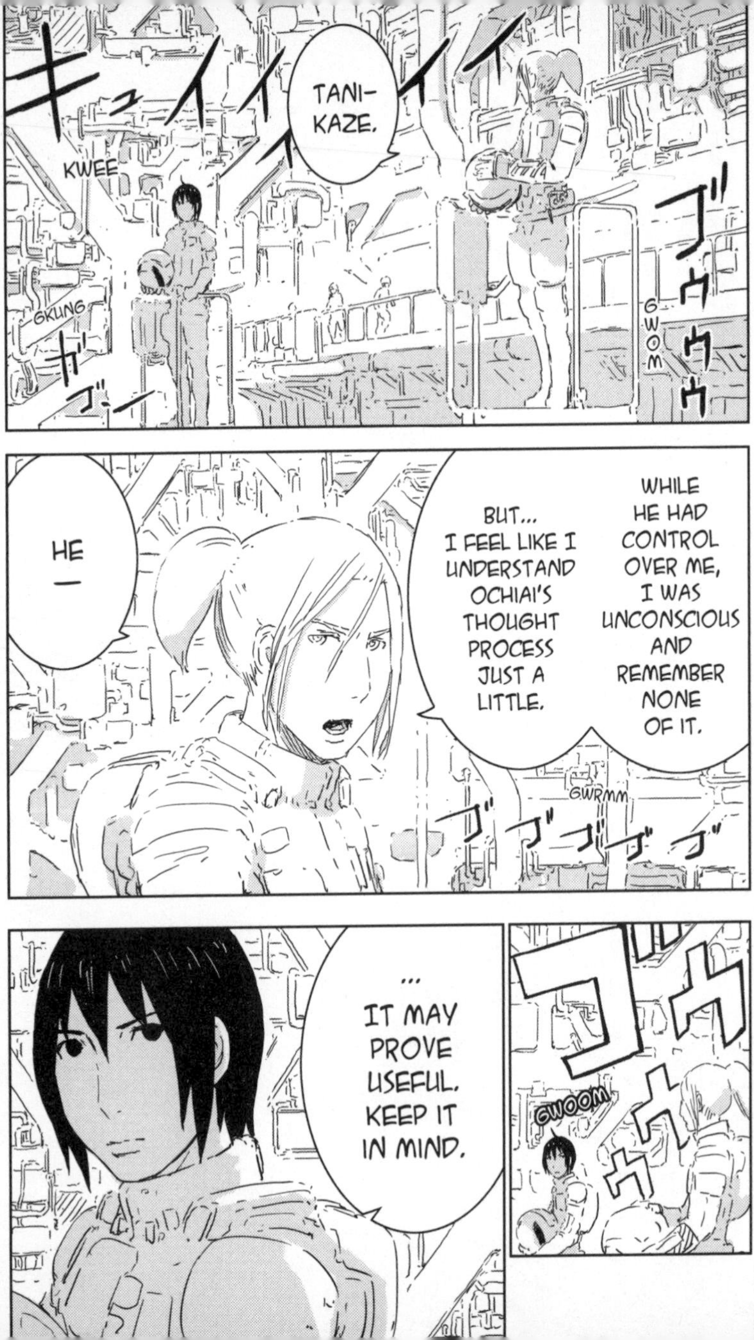
TANI-KAZE.
KWEE
GWOM
GKUNG
WHILE HE HAD CONTROL OVER ME, I WAS UNCONSCIOUS AND REMEMBER NONE OF IT.
BUT... I FEEL LIKE I UNDERSTAND OCHIAI'S THOUGHT PROCESS JUST A LITTLE.
HE —
GWRMM
GWOOM
... IT MAY PROVE USEFUL. KEEP IT IN MIND.

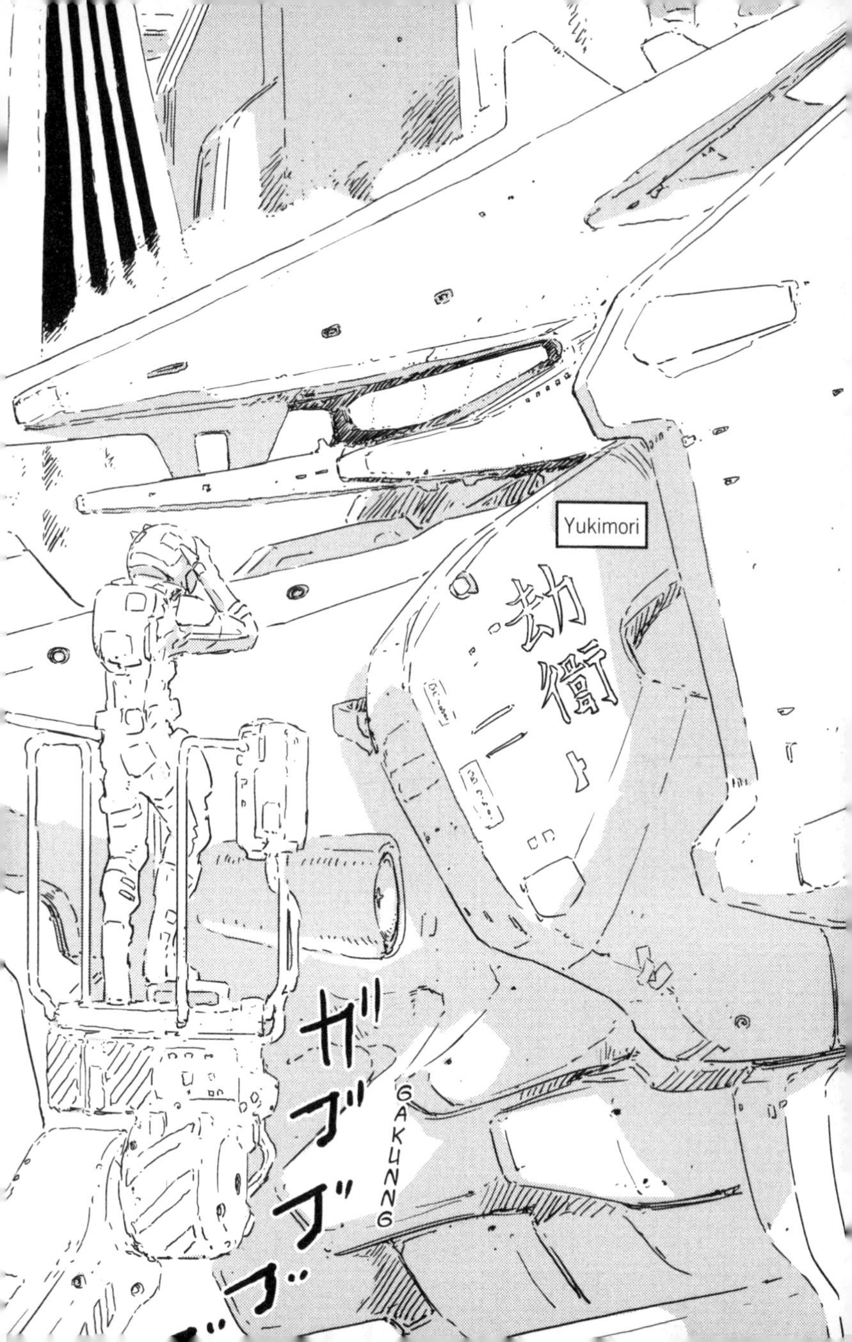
Yukimori
GAKUNNG

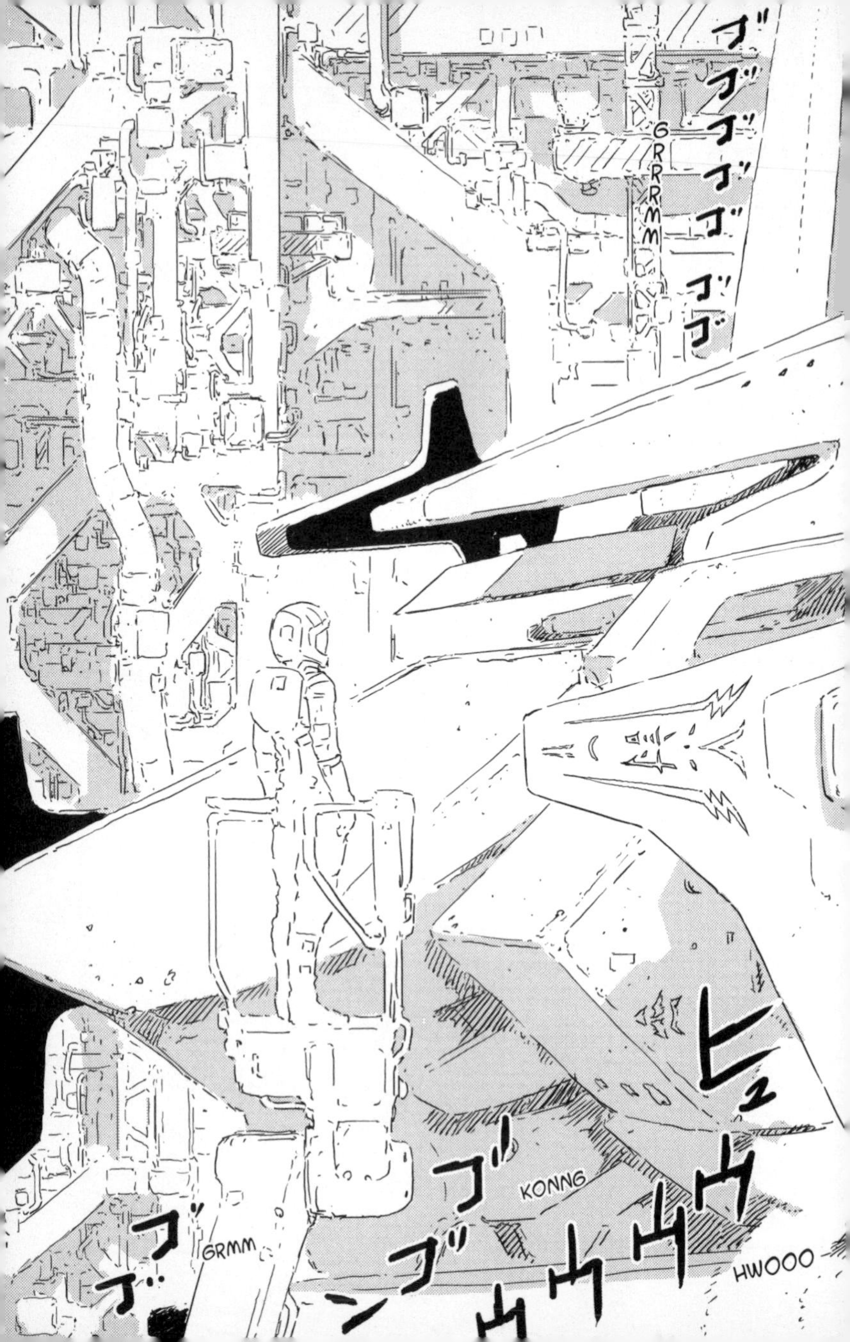
ゴゴッゴッゴッゴゴッゴ
GRRRMM
ヒュウウウウ
HWOOO
ゴゴッン
KONNG
ゴッゴ
GRMM

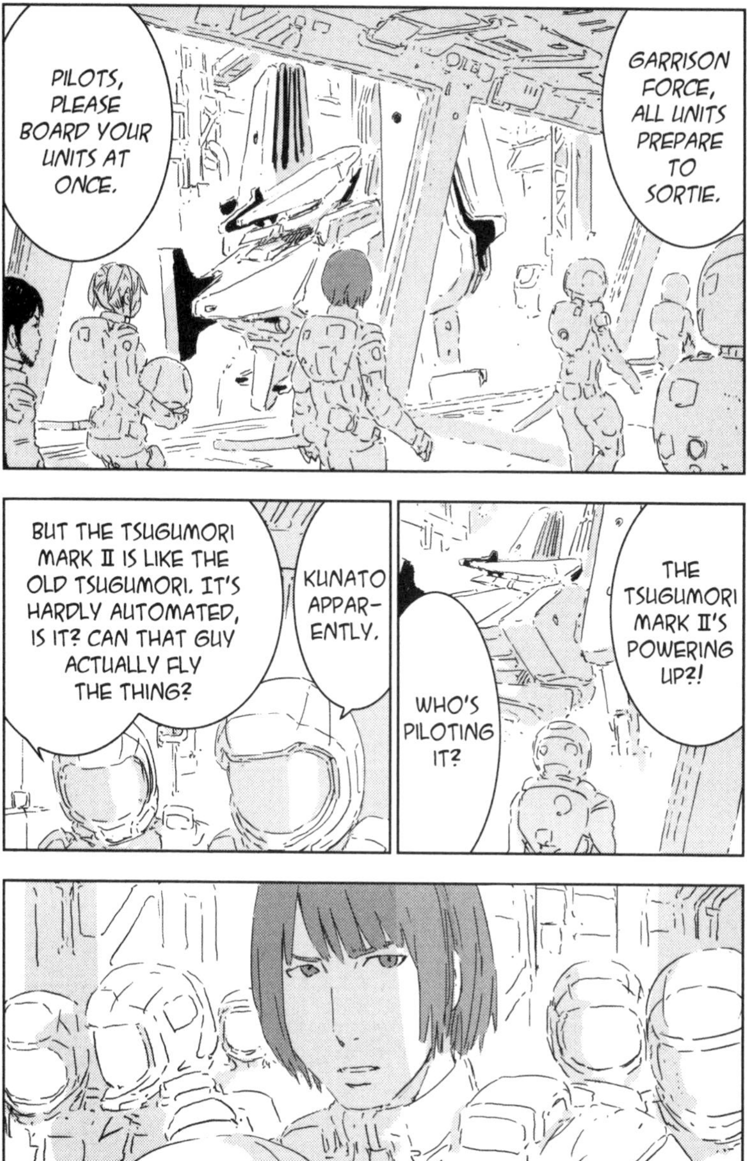
GARRISON FORCE, ALL UNITS PREPARE TO SORTIE.
PILOTS, PLEASE BOARD YOUR UNITS AT ONCE.
THE TSUGUMORI MARK II'S POWERING UP?!
WHO'S PILOTING IT?
KUNATO APPARENTLY.
BUT THE TSUGUMORI MARK II IS LIKE THE OLD TSUGUMORI. IT'S HARDLY AUTOMATED, IS IT? CAN THAT GUY ACTUALLY FLY THE THING?

TSUGUMORI MARK II LOADING INTO LAUNCH LANE!
GAKUNNG
GWOO
GRRM
KUNATO TAKING OFF!
HWOOO
SHINK
GWOOM

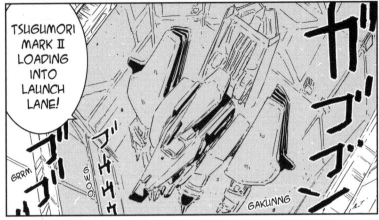

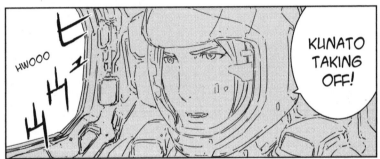

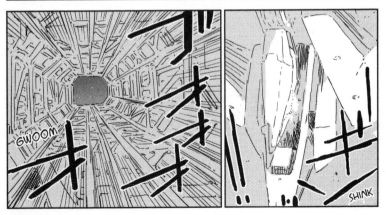

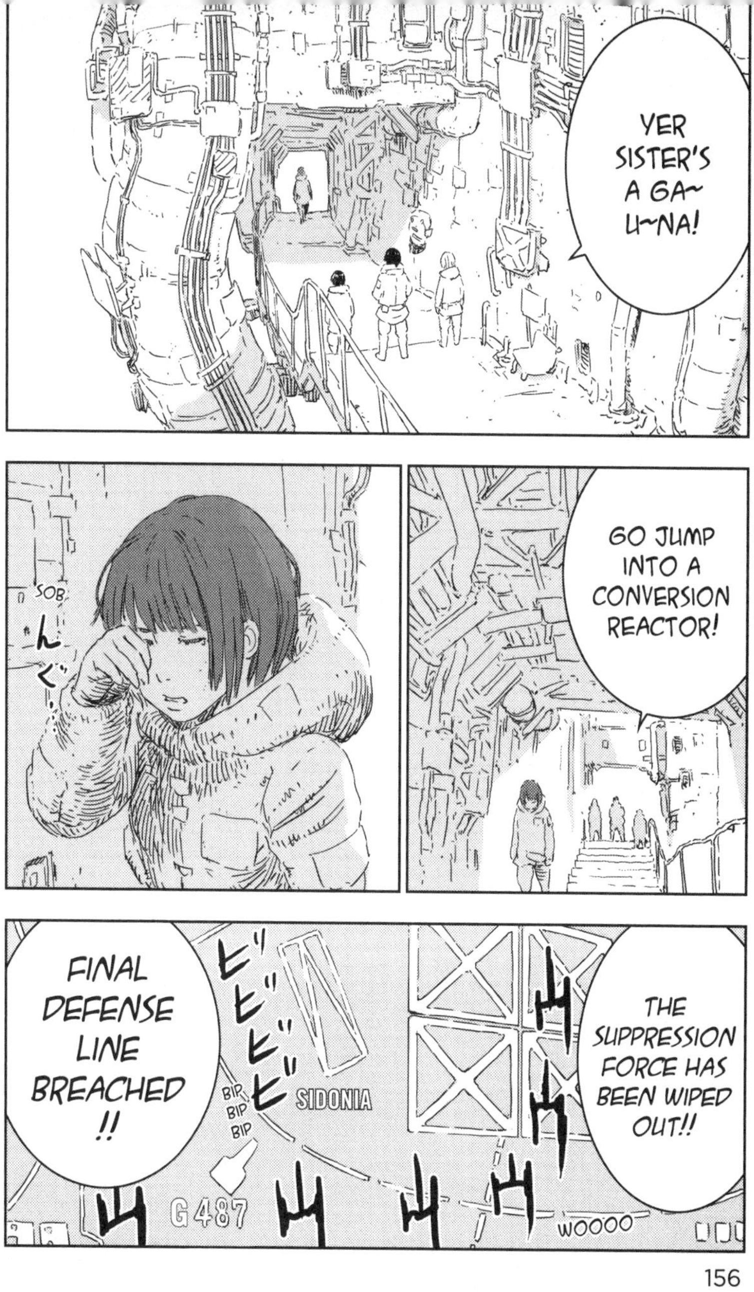
YER SISTER'S A GA~U~NA!
GO JUMP INTO A CONVERSION REACTOR!
SOB
んぐ…
THE SUPPRESSION FORCE HAS BEEN WIPED OUT!!
WOOOO
SIDONIA
G487
BIP BIP BIP
FINAL DEFENSE LINE BREACHED!!

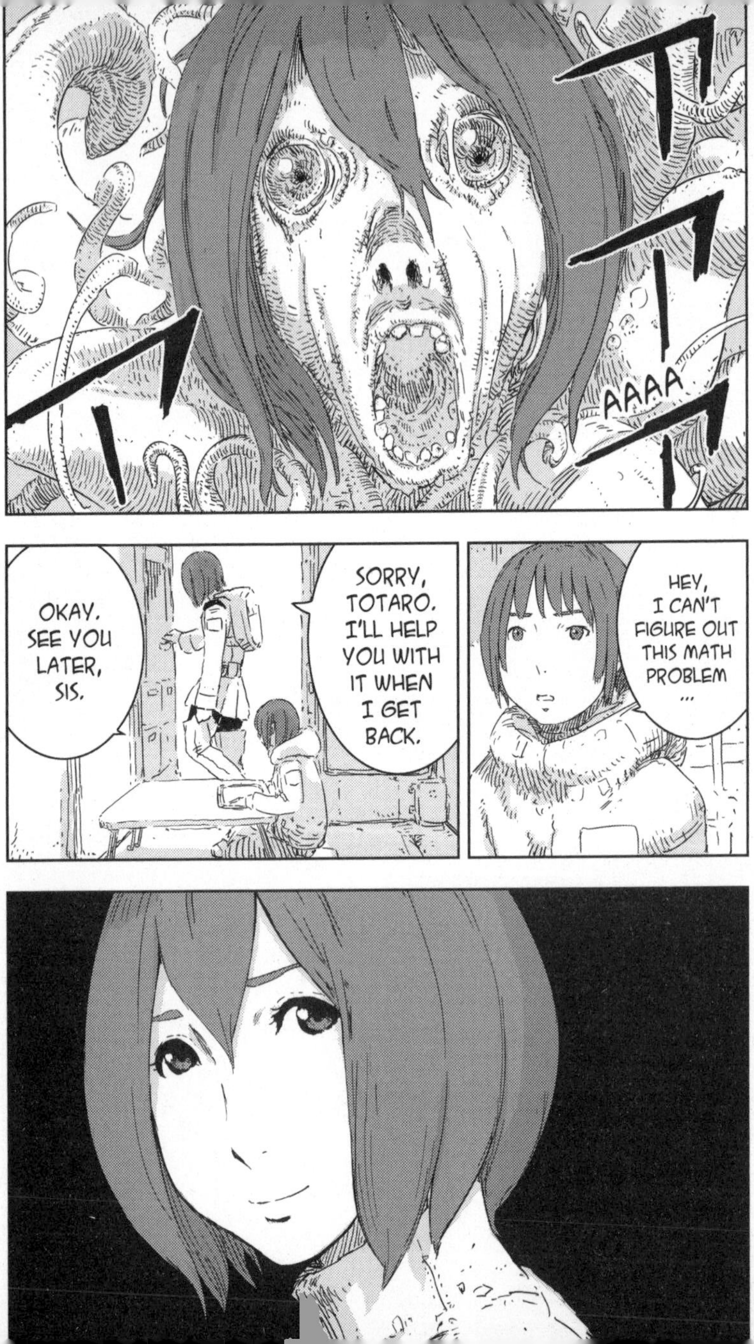
AAAA
HEY, I CAN'T FIGURE OUT THIS MATH PROBLEM ...
SORRY, TOTARO. I'LL HELP YOU WITH IT WHEN I GET BACK.
OKAY. SEE YOU LATER, SIS.

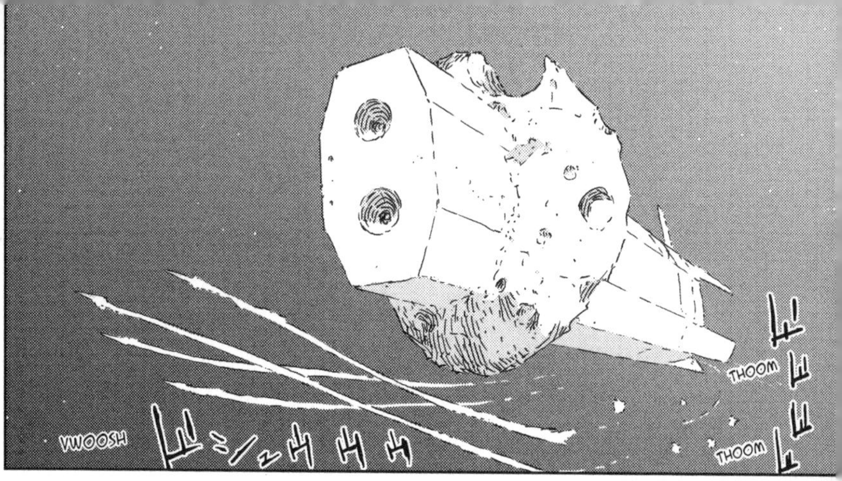
THOOM
THOOM
VWOOSH

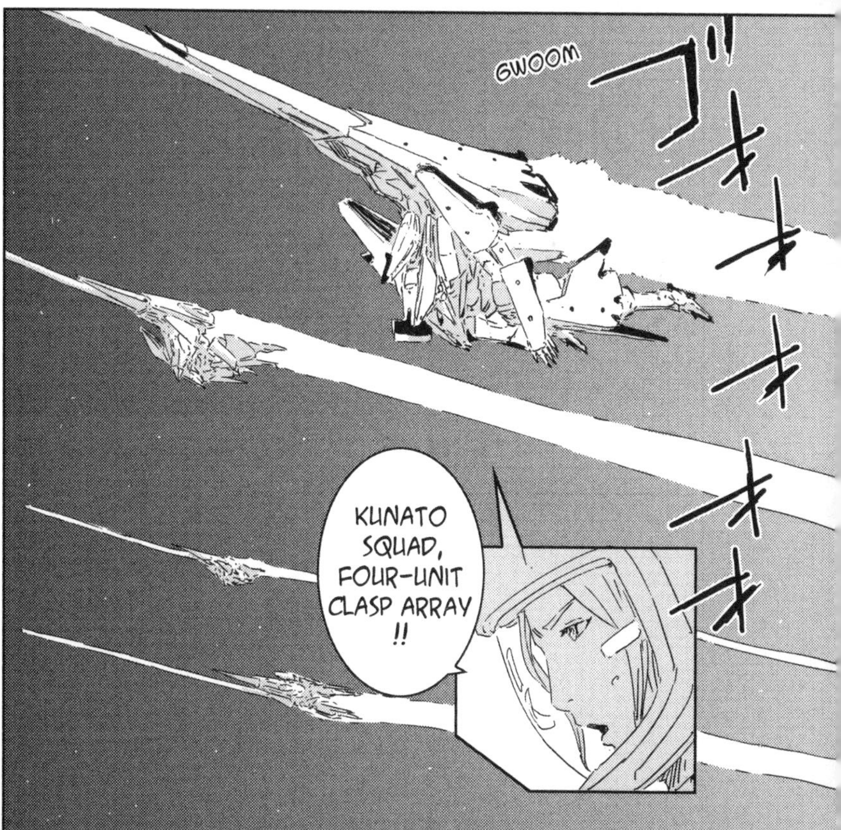
GWOOM
KUNATO SQUAD, FOUR-UNIT CLASP ARRAY !!

ROGER!
I CAN AVENGE YOU AT LAST, SIS.
THOOM
THOOM
DWOM
THOOM

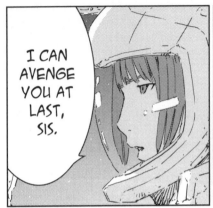

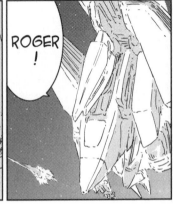

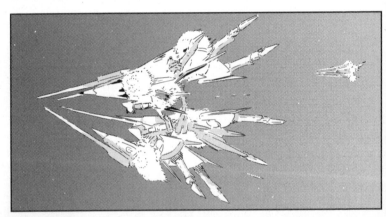

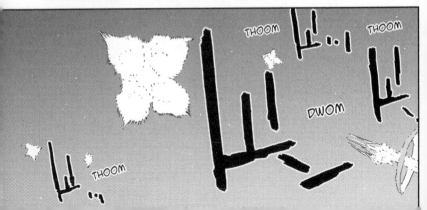

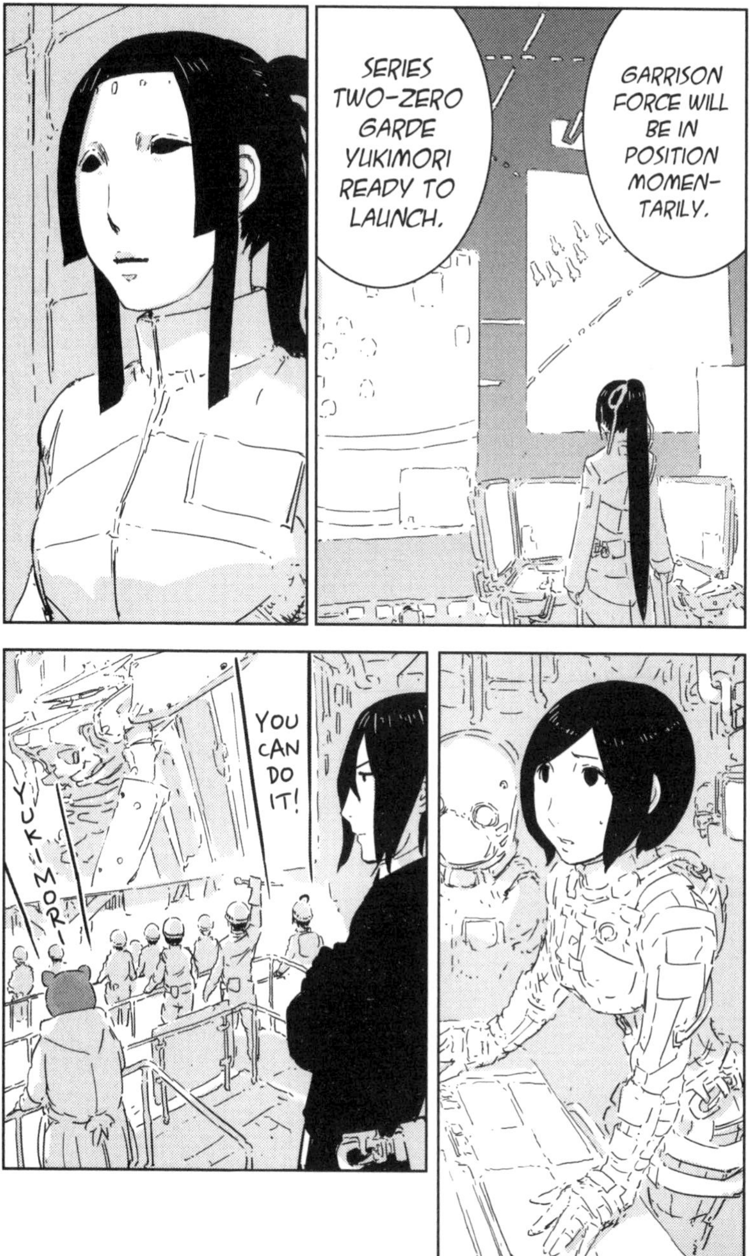
GARRISON FORCE WILL BE IN POSITION MOMEN-TARILY.
SERIES TWO-ZERO GARDE YUKIMORI READY TO LAUNCH.
YOU CAN DO IT!
YUKIMORI

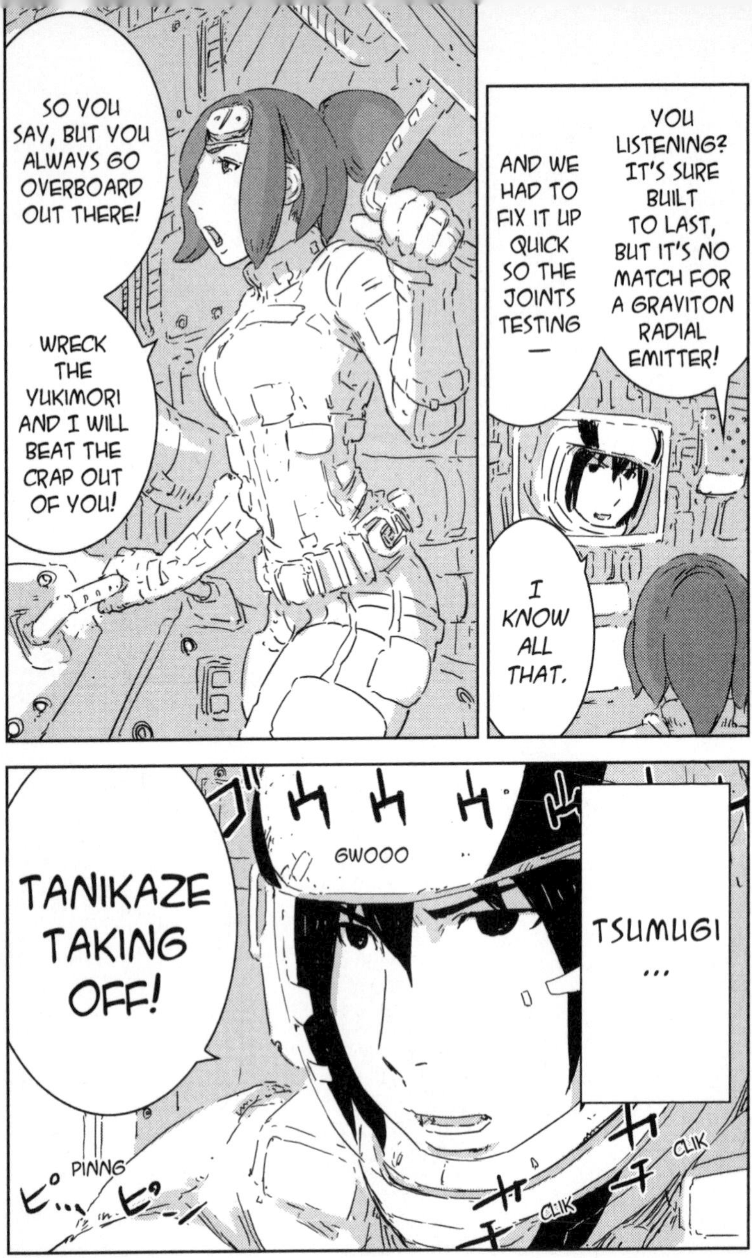
YOU LISTENING? IT'S SURE BUILT TO LAST, BUT IT'S NO MATCH FOR A GRAVITON RADIAL EMITTER!
AND WE HAD TO FIX IT UP QUICK SO THE JOINTS TESTING —
I KNOW ALL THAT.
SO YOU SAY, BUT YOU ALWAYS GO OVERBOARD OUT THERE!
WRECK THE YUKIMORI AND I WILL BEAT THE CRAP OUT OF YOU!
GWOOO
TSUMUGI ...
TANIKAZE TAKING OFF!
CLIK
CLIK
PINNG

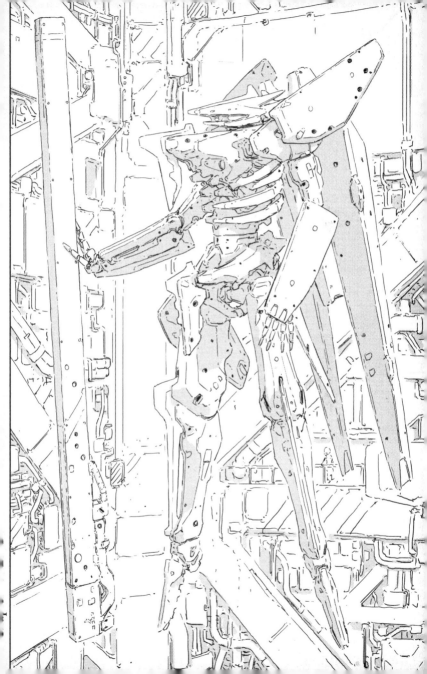

KNIGHTS OF SIDONIA Volume (14): END

Knights of Sidonia, volume 14

Translation: Kumar Sivasubramanian
Production: Grace Lu
Daniela Yamada
Anthony Quintessenza

First published in Japan in 2014 by Kodansha, Ltd., Tokyo
Publication for this English edition arranged through Kodansha, Ltd., Tokyo
English language version produced by Vertical, Inc.

Translation provided by Vertical, Inc., 2015
Published by Vertical, Inc., New York

Originally published in Japanese as *Shidonia no Kishi 14* by Kodansha, Ltd.
Shidonia no Kishi first serialized in *Afternoon*, Kodansha, Ltd., 2009-

ISBN: 978-1-941220-86-3

Manufactured in Canada

First Edition

Vertical, Inc.
451 Park Avenue South
7th Floor
New York, NY 10016
www.vertical-inc.com